T0350607

THE
50 GREATEST PLAYERS
IN
MINNESOTA VIKINGS
HISTORY

ROBERT W. COHEN

LYONS
PRESS

GUILFORD, CONNECTICUT

An imprint of The Rowman & Littlefield Publishing Group, Inc.
4501 Forbes Blvd., Ste. 200
Lanham, MD 20706
www.rowman.com

Distributed by NATIONAL BOOK NETWORK

British Library Cataloguing in Publication Information available

Library of Congress Cataloging-in-Publication Data

Names: Cohen, Robert W., author.
Title: The 50 greatest players in Minnesota Vikings history / Robert W. Cohen.
Other titles: Fifty greatest players in Minnesota Vikings history
Description: Guilford, Connecticut : Lyons Press, 2021. | Includes bibliographical references. | Summary: "Sports historian Robert W. Cohen ranks the top 50 players ever to perform for one of the NFL's most historic franchise. This book includes quotes from the subjects themselves and former teammates, photos, recaps of memorable performances and greatest individual seasons, as well as a statistical summary of each player's career with the Vikings. Also featured are 'honorable mentions,' the next 30 players who have contributed to the Vikings' run as one of America's great sports teams"— Provided by publisher.
Identifiers: LCCN 2021009354 (print) | LCCN 2021009355 (ebook) | ISBN 9781493058204 (hardback) | ISBN 9781493063130 (epub)
Subjects: LCSH: Minnesota Vikings (Football team)—History. | Football players—Minnesota—Biography.
Classification: LCC GV956.M5 C65 2021 (print) | LCC GV956.M5 (ebook) | DDC 796.332/6409776579—dc23
LC record available at https://lccn.loc.gov/2021009354
LC ebook record available at https://lccn.loc.gov/2021009355

CONTENTS

ACKNOWLEDGMENTS

I wish to thank Troy Kinunen of MEARSonlineauctions.com, Kate of RMYAuctions.com, FootballCardGallery.com, SportsMemorabilia.com, George A. Kitrinos, Mike Morbeck, Keith Allison, Jeffrey Beall, Beth Hoole, Joe Bielawa, Matthew Deery, Rick Burtzel, Richard Lippenholz, Michi Moore, and Shawn Ford, each of whom generously contributed to the photographic content of this work.

INTRODUCTION

THE VIKING LEGACY

Professional football arrived in the Minneapolis–Saint Paul area in 1961, almost two years after local businessmen Bill Boyer, H. P. Skoglund, and Max Winter were awarded a franchise in the new American Football League. Reneging on its agreement with the AFL in January 1960, the Minnesota ownership group, which also included *St. Paul Pioneer Press* publisher Bernard H. Ridder and former Duluth Eskimos owner Ole Haugsrud, instead accepted an offer to join the more established NFL as an expansion team, making it the league's 14th member. After appointing former Los Angeles Rams public relations director Bert Rose the team's first general manager, ownership considered several candidates for the head coaching job, before ultimately hiring former Rams and Philadelphia Eagles quarterback Norm Van Brocklin on January 18, 1961. Officially named the Minnesota Vikings on September 27, 1960, as a way of paying tribute to the region's Scandinavian American roots, the Vikings began play in 1961, with Metropolitan Stadium in suburban Bloomington serving as their home venue.

Taking up residence in the NFL's Western Division, which they shared with the Green Bay Packers, Chicago Bears, Detroit Lions, San Francisco 49ers, Los Angeles Rams, and Baltimore Colts, the Vikings experienced very little success their first three seasons under Van Brocklin, compiling an overall record of just 10-30-2 from 1961 to 1963, before posting the first winning mark in franchise history in 1964, when they finished second in the division with a record of 8-5-1. However, two more losing seasons followed, prompting Van Brocklin to hand in his resignation on February 11, 1967. Less than one month later, on March 7, 1967, the Vikings dealt their most tradeable commodity, quarterback Fran Tarkenton, to the New York Giants for two first-round draft picks and a pair of second-round picks to be made over the course of the next three seasons. Meanwhile, the Vikings replaced Van Brocklin with Bud Grant, who had spent the previous 10 years serving as head coach of the Canadian Football League's Winnipeg Blue Bombers, leading them to four Grey Cup championships during that time.

With the NFL undergoing further expansion in 1967, it adopted a new four-division setup that featured four teams in each division. Finding themselves competing with the Packers, Bears, and Lions in the Central Division, the Vikings continued to struggle their first year under Grant, compiling a record of 3-8-3 that gave them an overall mark of just 32-59-7 their first seven years in the league. Nevertheless, several players distinguished themselves during the club's formative years, with Tarkenton, running back Bill Brown, defensive end Jim Marshall, and offensive linemen Mick Tingelhoff and Grady Alderman all excelling at their respective positions.

Things finally began to turn around in Minnesota in 1968, when the Vikings compiled a record of 8-6 that earned them their first division title. Although they subsequently lost to the eventual NFL champion Baltimore Colts in the opening round of the playoffs by a score of 24–14, it appeared to be only a matter of time before the Vikings joined the NFL's elite.

Establishing themselves as one of the league's dominant teams the following year, the Vikings began an exceptional 10-year run during which they won nine division titles and made four Super Bowl appearances. After losing just two games during the 1969 regular season, the Vikings earned a hard-fought 23–20 victory over the Los Angeles Rams in the opening round of the playoffs, before posting a convincing 27–7 win over the Cleveland Browns in the NFL championship game. However, in what turned out to be the final contest played prior to the NFL/AFL merger, the Vikings suffered a humiliating 23–7 defeat at the hands of the Kansas City Chiefs in Super Bowl IV.

Rebounding the following year, the Vikings once again finished 12-2 during the regular season, before losing to the San Francisco 49ers in the opening round of the postseason tournament by a score of 17–14. The 1971 campaign followed a similar script, with the Vikings compiling a regular season mark of 11-3, before being eliminated by the Dallas Cowboys in the opening round of the playoffs by a score of 20–12.

Having leaned heavily the previous few seasons on their smothering "Purple People Eaters" defense that featured standout linemen Alan Page, Carl Eller, Jim Marshall, and Gary Larsen, dependable linebackers Roy Winston, Wally Hilgenberg, and Lonnie Warwick, and exceptional ball-hawks Paul Krause and Bobby Bryant, the Vikings believed that they needed only to add some offensive firepower to reach their ultimate goal of winning a championship. To that end, they reacquired Fran Tarkenton from the Giants and obtained speedy wide receiver John Gilliam from the St. Louis Cardinals prior to the start of the 1972 campaign. However, even though both players performed well, the Vikings ended up posting a disappointing 7-7 record, failing to make the playoffs for the first time in five seasons. But, with the addition of superb rookie running back Chuck Foreman the following year, the Vikings won the division title for the first of six straight times, going 12-2 during the regular season, before laying claim to the NFC championship by defeating Washington (27–20) and Dallas (27–10) in the playoffs. However, they subsequently faltered against the Miami Dolphins in Super Bowl VIII, losing to their AFC counterparts by a score of 24–7. Meanwhile, off the playing field, co-owner Bill Boyer died on February 19, 1973, with his son-in-law Jack Steele replacing him on the team's board of directors.

Remaining one of the NFL's most formidable teams from 1974 to 1976, the Vikings compiled an overall regular season record of 33-8-1, en route to winning three more division titles. Yet they continued to come up short in the postseason, losing to Pittsburgh by a score of 16–6 in Super Bowl IX, suffering a heartbreaking 17–14 defeat at the hands of the Dallas Cowboys in the divisional round of the 1975 playoffs on a controversial last-second "Hail Mary" touchdown pass from Roger Staubach to Drew Pearson, and being thoroughly outplayed during a 32–14 loss to the Oakland Raiders in Super Bowl XI.

The Vikings won the Central Division title again in 1977, a season in which the Tampa Bay Buccaneers became the division's fifth entrant. However, they stumbled once again in the playoffs, this time losing to Dallas in the NFC championship game by a score of 23–6. Although the Vikings gradually revamped their roster during the mid-to-late-1970s, adding talented young players such as quarterback Tommy Kramer, receivers Sammy White and Ahmad Rashad, and linebackers Jeff Siemon, Matt Blair, and Scott Studwell, the core of the team that had experienced so much success for much of the decade had either aged or retired by 1978, resulting in a somewhat disappointing 8-7-1 regular-season record and a 34–10 opening-round playoff loss to the Los Angeles Rams. And, as a new generation of players donned the Purple and Gold, the organization experienced several changes in the front office as well, with team attorney Sheldon Kaplan, general manager Mike Lynn, and John Skoglund replacing Bernard Ridder, Ole Haugsrud, and H. P. Skoglund on the board of directors following the passing of Haugsrud and the elder Skoglund.

With Fran Tarkenton no longer running their offense, and with Alan Page, Carl Eller, and Jim Marshall no longer anchoring their defense, the Vikings subsequently entered into an extended period of mediocrity that lasted nine years. Although the Vikings made three playoff appearances from 1979 to 1987, they compiled an overall record of just 63-73, reaching their nadir in 1984, when they finished just 3-13 under former offensive assistant Les Steckel, who replaced Bud Grant at the helm after the latter stepped down following the conclusion of the previous campaign. Returning to the sidelines for one more year after ownership relieved Steckel of his duties, Grant guided the Vikings to a record of 7-9 in 1985, before retiring for good at season's end. Having led the Vikings to 12 playoff appearances, 11 division titles, four NFC championships, and a regular-season record of 158-96-5 in his 18 years as head coach, Grant retired with the sixth most wins of any coach in NFL history.

Meanwhile, as the links to the franchise's glory days continued to disappear, the Vikings abandoned Metropolitan Stadium for the newly constructed Hubert H. Humphrey Metrodome in 1982. Located in downtown Minneapolis, the Metrodome, which initially seated 62,220 patrons before later being expanded to a seating capacity of 64,121, remained home to the Vikings for the next 32 years.

Following the retirement of Bud Grant, longtime Vikings offensive coordinator Jerry Burns assumed head coaching duties in Minnesota, guiding the team to a pair of second-place finishes in his first two seasons in charge. In fact, after advancing to the playoffs as a wild card in 1987, the Vikings made it all the way to the NFC championship game, before losing to the eventual Super Bowl champion Washington Redskins by a score of 17–10. Continuing to show improvement under Burns, the Vikings made the playoffs in 1988 and 1989 as well, although they ended up losing to the San Francisco 49ers in the divisional round of the postseason tournament both years. But, after the Vikings failed to post a winning record in either of the next two seasons, Burns announced his retirement, ending his six-year stint as head coach with an overall record of 52-43 and one division title and three playoff appearances to his credit. During his tenure in Minnesota, Burns also helped oversee the development of several outstanding young players, including wide receiver Anthony Carter, tight end Steve Jordan, offensive tackle Gary Zimmerman, defensive end Chris Doleman, safety Joey Browner, and defensive tackles Henry Thomas and Keith Millard.

With the departure of Burns, new team president and co-owner Roger Headrick hired former Stanford University head coach Dennis Green, who had spent the previous three seasons turning around a struggling Cardinals program. Making an immediate impact upon his arrival in Minnesota, Green led the Vikings to three straight playoff appearances and two division titles from 1992 to 1994, although they failed to advance beyond the wild card round of the postseason tournament each year. The Vikings subsequently finished just 8-8 in 1995, but they made the playoffs as a wild card in each of the next two seasons by posting identical 9-7 records. However, they exited the tournament quickly both years, suffering a 40–15 defeat at the hands of the Dallas Cowboys in the opening round in 1996, before losing to the San Francisco 49ers by a score of 38–22 in the divisional round the following year, after mounting a memorable fourth-quarter comeback against the Giants one week earlier that resulted in a 23–22 victory.

During the subsequent offseason, ownership of the Vikings passed to billionaire San Antonio, Texas, businessman Red McCombs, who had earlier held stakes in the NBA's San Antonio Spurs and Denver Nuggets. Following McCombs's purchase of the team, the Vikings put together a season to remember in 1998, scoring a then-NFL record 556 points, en route to compiling a franchise-best regular-season mark of 15-1. With an explosive offense led by quarterback Randall Cunningham, who earned NFL Player of the Year honors, running back Robert Smith, and star wide receivers Cris Carter and Randy Moss, the Vikings never scored fewer than 24 points in any single game, tallying more than 40 points on four separate occasions. Continuing their dominance in the divisional round of the playoffs, the Vikings registered a 41–21 victory over the Arizona Cardinals. However, their quest for the league championship ended abruptly in the NFC championship game, when Atlanta kicker Morten Andersen connected on a 38-yard field goal in overtime to give the Falcons a 30–27 victory.

Although the Vikings failed to attain the same level of excellence the following year, they advanced to the playoffs as a wild card after posting a record of 10-6 during the regular season. The Vikings subsequently handled Dallas rather easily in the opening round of the postseason tournament, defeating the Cowboys by a score of 27–10, before losing a 49–37 shootout with Kurt Warner and the Super Bowl bound St. Louis Rams one week later. Led by second-year quarterback Daunte Culpepper, who threw a league-leading 33 touchdown passes, the Vikings captured the division title in 2000 by compiling a regular-season record of 11-5. However, after recording a convincing 34–16 victory over the New Orleans Saints in the divisional round of the playoffs, they lost to the New York Giants by a score of 41-0 in the NFC championship game. Making matters worse, star running back Robert Smith, who finished the season with 1,521 yards rushing, announced his retirement a few weeks later, ending his playing career at only 28 years of age.

Dennis Green remained in Minnesota for one more year, leading the Vikings to a disappointing record of 5-10 in 2001, before being bought out of his contract by team ownership prior to the regular-season finale. Replaced by offensive line coach Mike Tice, Green left the Vikings with an overall record of 97-62 in his 10 seasons as head coach, guiding the team to eight playoff appearances and four division titles in the process. Players who flourished under Green's leadership included offensive lineman Randall McDaniel, defensive tackle John Randle, linebacker Ed McDaniel, and wide receivers Cris Carter, Randy Moss, and Jake Reed.

The hiring of Tice ushered in another period of mediocrity for the Vikings, who posted a composite record of 32-32 under him from 2002 to 2005. Nevertheless, the Vikings managed to make the playoffs as a wild card in 2004, defeating the Green Bay Packers, 31–17, in the opening round of the postseason tournament, before losing to the eventual NFC champion Philadelphia Eagles by a score of 27–14 the following week. And during Tice's tenure as head coach, the Vikings and their traditional division rivals (Packers, Bears, and Lions) became part of the newly formed NFC North in the league's new four-division alignment (both conferences had adopted a three-division setup following the NFL/AFL merger in 1970).

With Red McCombs having sold the Vikings to a new ownership group headed by billionaire real estate developer Zygi Wilf in May of 2005, the front office allowed Tice's contract to expire at the end of the year after the team failed to make the playoffs. Former Philadelphia Eagles offensive coordinator Brad Childress subsequently assumed head coaching duties, leading the Vikings to consecutive division titles in 2008 and 2009 behind the brilliant running of Adrian Peterson, who earned NFL Player of the Year honors in the first of those campaigns. But, after going 10-6 during the 2008 regular season, the Vikings suffered a 26–14 defeat at the hands of the Eagles in the opening round of the playoffs. Faring somewhat better the following year after coaxing longtime foe Brett Favre out of retirement, the Vikings won their second straight division title with a record of 12-4, before advancing to the NFC championship game by recording a convincing 34–3 victory over the Dallas Cowboys in their divisional round playoff matchup. However, the Vikings fell just short of winning the conference championship, losing to the New Orleans Saints in OT by a score of 31–28 on a 40-yard field goal by Garrett Hartley less than five minutes into the overtime session.

After the Vikings got off to a 3-7 start in 2010, Childress received his walking papers, with assistant head coach and defensive coordinator Leslie Frazier replacing him for the season's final six games. Retaining control of the team for the next three years, Frazier led the Vikings to one playoff appearance but an overall record of just 18-29-1, before being replaced by former Cincinnati Bengals defensive coordinator Mike Zimmer in 2014, the same year that the Vikings temporarily moved into TCF Bank Stadium during construction of U.S. Bank Stadium, which opened in 2016. An enclosed stadium built on the former site of the Hubert H. Humphrey Metrodome in downtown Minneapolis, U.S. Bank Stadium, which has a seating capacity of 66,860, has already hosted several notable events in its brief history, including Super Bowl LII (February 4, 2018), the ESPN X Games (July 19–22, 2018), and the NCAA Final Four (April 6–8, 2019).

Since taking over as head coach, Zimmer has improved the fortunes of the Vikings, who have consistently been in contention in the NFC North. After going just 7-9 their first year under Zimmer, the Vikings won the division title for the first time in six years by posting a record of 11-5 in 2015, before losing to Seattle in the wild card round of the playoffs by a score of 10–9. Following a disappointing 8-8 finish in 2016, the Vikings tied Philadelphia for the best record in the NFC in 2017 by going 13-3. They then recorded a miraculous 29–24 victory over New Orleans in the divisional round of the playoffs, winning the contest on a 61-yard touchdown pass from Case Keenum to Stefon Diggs on the game's final play. However, the Vikings subsequently came up flat against Philadelphia in the NFC championship game, losing to the Eagles by a score of 38–7. The Vikings failed to make the playoffs again in 2018, finishing the regular season just 8-7-1. But they advanced to the postseason tournament as a wild card the following year after compiling a regular season mark of 10-6. The Vikings then ended the Saints' season once again by defeating them in the opening round of the playoffs by a score of 26–20, scoring the game-winning touchdown on a 4-yard pass from Kirk Cousins to tight end Kyle Rudolph 4:20 into overtime. Unfortunately, the San Francisco 49ers subsequently eliminated the Vikings from the playoffs the following week by defeating them, 27–10.

Unable to overcome the free agent defection of star defensive end Everson Griffen and serious injuries to defensive stalwarts Anthony Barr and Danielle Hunter, the Vikings surrendered 475 points to the opposition in 2020, resulting in a 7-9 record that failed to earn them a playoff berth. However, a return to full health by Barr and Hunter in 2021 figures to bolster the Minnesota defense, which also includes star safety Harrison

Smith and standout linebacker Eric Kendricks. And, with quarterback Kirk Cousins, explosive running back Dalvin Cook, and receivers Adam Thielen and Justin Jefferson serving as the centerpieces of one of the league's more potent offenses, the Vikings seem poised to re-establish themselves as serious contenders in the NFC North. Their next division title will be their 21st. They have also won three NFC titles and one NFL championship. Featuring a plethora of exceptional performers through the years, the Vikings have inducted 20 players into their Ring of Honor, six of whom have had their numbers retired by the team. Meanwhile, 19 members of the Pro Football Hall of Fame spent at least one full season in Minnesota, with 13 of those men wearing a Vikings uniform during many of their peak seasons.

FACTORS USED TO DETERMINE RANKINGS

It should come as no surprise that selecting the 50 greatest players ever to perform for a team with the rich history of the Minnesota Vikings presented quite a challenge. Even after narrowing the field down to a mere 50 men, I still needed to devise a method of ranking the elite players that remained. Certainly, the names of Adrian Peterson, Fran Tarkenton, Alan Page, Carl Eller, Randall McDaniel, Cris Carter, and Randy Moss would appear at, or near, the top of virtually everyone's list, although the order might vary somewhat from one person to the next. Several other outstanding performers have gained general recognition through the years as being among the greatest players ever to don the Purple and Gold, with Jim Marshall, Chris Doleman, Matt Blair, Chuck Foreman, and John Randle heading the list of other Vikings icons. But how does one compare players who lined up on opposite sides of the ball with any degree of certainty? Furthermore, how does one differentiate between the pass-rushing and run-stopping skills of defensive linemen such as Alan Page and John Randle and the ball-hawking skills of defensive backs such as Paul Krause and Joey Browner? And, on the offensive end, how can a direct correlation be made between the contributions made by Hall of Fame lineman Randall McDaniel and skill position players such as Cris Carter and Chuck Foreman? After initially deciding whom to include on my list, I then needed to determine what criteria I should use to formulate my final rankings.

The first thing I decided to examine was the level of dominance a player attained during his time in Minnesota. How often did he lead the league in a major statistical category? Did he ever capture league MVP honors? How many times did he earn a trip to the Pro Bowl or a spot on the All-Pro Team?

I also chose to assess the level of statistical compilation a player achieved while wearing a Vikings uniform. I reviewed where he ranks among the team's all-time leaders in those statistical categories most pertinent to his position. Of course, even the method of using statistics as a measuring stick has its inherent flaws. Although the level of success a team experiences rushing and passing the ball is affected greatly by the performance of its offensive line, there really is no way to quantifiably measure the level of play reached by each individual offensive lineman. Conversely, the play of the offensive line affects tremendously the statistics compiled by a team's quarterback and running backs. Furthermore, the NFL did not keep an official record of defensive numbers such as tackles and quarterback sacks until the 1980s (although the Vikings kept their own records prior to that). In addition, when examining the statistics compiled by offensive players, the era during which a quarterback, running back, or wide receiver competed must be factored into the equation.

To illustrate my last point, rules changes instituted by the league office have opened up the game considerably over the course of the last two decades. Quarterbacks are accorded far more protection than ever before, and officials have also been instructed to limit the amount of contact defensive backs are allowed to make with wide receivers. As a result, the game has experienced an offensive explosion, with quarterbacks and receivers posting numbers players from prior generations rarely even approached. That being the case, one must place the numbers Daunte Culpepper compiled during his time in Minnesota in their proper context when comparing them to the figures posted by earlier Vikings signal-callers Fran Tarkenton and Tommy Kramer. Similarly, the statistics compiled by Adam Thielen and Stefon Diggs must be viewed in moderation when comparing them to previous Vikings wideouts Ahmad Rashad and Anthony Carter.

Other important factors I needed to consider were the overall contributions a player made to the success of the team, the degree to which he improved the fortunes of the club during his time in the Twin Cities, and the manner in which he impacted the team, both on the field and in the locker room. While the number of championships and division titles the Vikings won during a player's years with the team certainly factored into the equation, I chose not to deny a top performer his rightful place on the list if his years in Minnesota happened to coincide with a lack of overall success by the club. As a result, the names of players such as Keith Millard and Steve Hutchinson will appear in these rankings.

One other thing I should mention is that I only considered a player's performance as a member of the Vikings when formulating my rankings.

That being the case, the names of standout players such as Gary Zimmerman and Jared Allen, both of whom had many of their finest seasons for other teams, may appear lower on this list than one might expect. Meanwhile, the names of exceptional performers such as Herschel Walker and Dave Casper are nowhere to be found.

Having established the guidelines to be used throughout this book, the time has come to reveal the 50 greatest players in Vikings history, starting with number 1 and working our way down to number 50.

1

ADRIAN PETERSON

Adrian Peterson received stiff competition from Alan Page and Fran Tarkenton for the top spot in these rankings, with Page's nine Pro Bowl nominations, eight All-Pro selections, one league MVP trophy, and status as the greatest defensive player in team annals making him a particularly strong contender. In the end, though, Peterson's greater ability to take over a game all by himself proved to be too much for Page to overcome. One of the most dominant running backs in NFL history, Peterson gained more than 1,000 yards on the ground in seven of his eight full seasons in Minnesota, topping the magical 2,000-yard mark once. A three-time league rushing champion, Peterson holds every career and single-season franchise rushing record, with his brilliant play leading the Vikings to four playoff appearances and three division titles. Named NFL Player of the Year twice and league MVP once, Peterson earned the additional distinctions of appearing in seven Pro Bowls and receiving seven All-Pro nominations, before being further honored by being named to the NFL 2010s All-Decade Team.

Born in Palestine, Texas, on March 21, 1985, Adrian Lewis Peterson experienced a considerable amount of adversity as a child, losing his older brother at the age of seven when a drunk driver hit and killed him, after previously watching his parents go their separate ways. Learning to deal with his pain through sports, Peterson grew up rooting for the Dallas Cowboys and his favorite player, Emmitt Smith, while also starring for the Pee Wee football team coached by his father, who helped him develop the aggressive running style for which he later became so well known.

Continuing to develop his athletic skills at Westwood Junior High School after his father received an eight-year prison sentence for laundering money for a crack-cocaine ring, Peterson played football and competed in track and field, winning multiple medals in the 100- and 200-meter dashes, triple jump, and long jump. Excelling in multiple sports at Palestine High School as well, Peterson served as a member of the school's football,

Adrian Peterson earned league MVP honors once and NFL Player of the Year honors twice during his time in Minnesota.
Courtesy of Mike Morbeck

basketball, and track teams. Particularly proficient on the gridiron, Peterson rushed for 2,051 yards and 22 touchdowns as a junior, before breaking his own school records the following year by gaining 2,960 yards on the ground and scoring 32 touchdowns, with his fabulous performance winning him the Hall Trophy, presented annually to the best high school player in the nation.

Subsequently recruited by several major colleges, including Texas, Texas A&M, Arkansas, Miami, UCLA, and USC, Peterson ultimately chose to accept an athletic scholarship to the University of Oklahoma, where he earned First-Team All-America honors and a runner-up finish to USC quarterback Matt Leinart in the Heisman Trophy voting his freshman year by rushing for 1,925 yards, which established a new NCAA freshman rushing record. Plagued by injuries in each of the next two seasons, Peterson failed to perform at the same lofty level. Nevertheless, he still managed to gain 1,108 yards on the ground and score 14 touchdowns as a sophomore, before rushing for 1,112 yards his junior year, with his strong play earning him First-Team All–Big 12 honors for the second and third straight times.

Having rushed for a total of 4,145 yards in his three years at Oklahoma, Peterson decided to leave college early and declare himself eligible for the 2007 NFL Draft. But, just as Peterson prepared to begin a new chapter in his life, tragedy struck again, when he learned the night before the combine that his half-brother had been shot and killed in Houston.

Ultimately selected by the Vikings with the seventh overall pick of the draft, Peterson performed magnificently his first year as a pro, earning Pro Bowl, Second-Team All-Pro, and NFL Offensive Rookie of the Year honors by finishing second in the league with 1,341 yards rushing, 12 rushing touchdowns, and an average of 5.6 yards per carry, while also placing near the top of the league rankings with 1,609 yards from scrimmage and 2,021 all-purpose yards, despite missing two games with an injury he sustained to the lateral collateral ligament in his right knee during a 34–0 loss to the Packers on November 11. Peterson followed that up with six more exceptional seasons, posting the following numbers from 2008 to 2013:

YEAR	YDS RUSHING	RECS	REC YDS	YDS FROM SCRIMMAGE	TDS
2008	**1,760***	21	125	**1,885**	10
2009	1,383	43	436	1,819	**18**
2010	1,298	36	341	1,639	13
2011	970	18	139	1,109	13
2012	**2,097**	40	217	**2,314**	13
2013	1,266	29	171	1,437	11

* Please note that any numbers printed in bold throughout this book indicate that the player led the NFL in that statistical category that year.

Gaining more than 1,000 yards on the ground in all but one of those seasons, Peterson failed to do so only in 2011, when he missed four games due to injury, finishing the year on injured reserve after suffering a torn ACL and MCL during a 33–26 victory over the Washington Redskins in December. In addition to ranking among the league leaders in rushing in each of the other five seasons, Peterson annually placed near the top of the league rankings in yards from scrimmage and rushing touchdowns, with his 18 rushing TDs in 2009 setting a new single-season franchise record. Three years later, Peterson ran for the second-most yards in NFL history, with his 2,097 yards gained on the ground leaving him just 8 yards short of the single-season mark Eric Dickerson established in 1984. It later surfaced that Peterson nearly broke Dickerson's record even though he spent the last few weeks of the season playing with a sports hernia. After being named the winner of the Bert Bell Award as NFL Player of the Year in 2008, Peterson gained recognition as the league's Most Valuable Player and Offensive Player of the Year in 2012. Meanwhile, the Vikings made the playoffs three times, winning the division title in both 2008 and 2009.

Combining size, speed, and strength with tremendous vision, the 6'1", 220-pound Peterson possessed the ability to either run over or away from would-be tacklers. Employing an aggressive style of running, Peterson often used the stiff arm to ward off defenders, who he typically punished before going down. Extremely deceptive as well, Peterson frequently created running room for himself by spinning, wiggling his hips, or cutting back against the grain. And, once he broke into the open field, Peterson had the speed to break away from opposing defenders.

Impressed with Peterson's exceptional all-around ability, legendary Cleveland Browns running back Jim Brown commented, "Adrian Peterson, in my mind, is a special talent."

Deion Sanders expressed his admiration for Peterson's varied skill set when he said, "He has the vision of a Marshall Faulk, the power of a Terrell Davis, and the speed of an Eric Dickerson. Let's pray he has the endurance of an Emmitt Smith."

Former Vikings teammate Darren Sharper also had high praise for Peterson, stating, "You take the best attributes out of all the best backs in the league now—you might even say the best backs in league history—and he has all those things."

Jon Gruden addressed Peterson's aggressive running style when he said, "This guy won't go out of bounds. Every time he carries the ball, he tries to hurt you."

In discussing the attitude that he brought with him to the playing field, Peterson stated, "I run angry. Football allows me to take out some of my pain on the field. . . . I have the mentality that, if you come in playing not to get hurt, that's when you're going to get hurt. So, I play relentless."

Meanwhile, teammate Toby Gerhart spoke of Peterson's dedication to his profession, saying, "It's not just his work ethic, it's his positivity. He's always at 100 miles per hour, pushing himself. But he never complains. You'll never hear him say, 'I'm sore. I'm tired. My legs feel heavy today.'"

Yet, beneath the surface lay a dark side of Peterson that surfaced in September 2014, when a Montgomery County, Texas, grand jury indicted him on charges of reckless or negligent injury to his four-year-old son, who it accused him of beating repeatedly on the back, buttocks, genitals, ankles, and legs with a tree branch. Although Peterson later described the implement he used as a "switch," which he claimed his own father used on him as a form of punishment during his childhood, he made no attempt to deny the allegations, resulting in him being placed on the NFL's Exempt/ Commissioner's Permission list, which required that he "remain away from all team activities." After accepting a plea deal in early November, Peterson was put on probation, fined $4,000, and ordered to undergo 80 hours of community service. Suspended without pay for virtually the entire season, Peterson ended up appearing in just one game in 2014, rushing for only 75 yards and no touchdowns.

Reinstated by the league office on February 26, 2015, after US District Court judge David Doty ruled on his behalf in the NFL Players Association's lawsuit against the NFL, Peterson went on to have an outstanding year, earning Pro Bowl and First-Team All-Pro honors by leading the league with 1,485 yards rushing and amassing 1,707 yards from scrimmage. However, the 2015 campaign proved to be Peterson's last big year for the Vikings. After tearing a meniscus in his right knee during a 17–14 win over the Packers on September 18, 2016, Peterson underwent surgery that kept him out of action for the next three months. Appearing in only three games the entire year, Peterson finished the season with just 72 yards rushing.

Choosing not to exercise the 2017 option on Peterson's contract that would have paid him $18 million, the Vikings allowed the 32-year-old running back to become an unrestricted free agent, with GM Rick Spielman saying at the time, "Adrian is an important part of the Minnesota Vikings organization. We will continue to have conversations with his representatives and leave our future options open while determining what is best for both parties moving forward."

Unhappy with how his tenure in Minnesota ended, Peterson later said, "I'd be lying if I said I wasn't disappointed. After spending 10 years with a team, you would think you would get some type of offer. I talked to Rick Spielman at the exit interviews and he said, 'How do you feel about coming back?' I said, 'I'm open to it.'"

Peterson continued, "The next time I heard from him, he was calling me to say that they signed (Latavius) Murray. . . . They weren't going to pay me $18 million, but from what I'd done over 10 years, maybe I could have been paid something more reasonable. But those conversations never started at any point."

Peterson, who left Minnesota with career totals of 11,747 yards rushing, 241 receptions, 1,945 receiving yards, 13,692 yards from scrimmage, 14,120 all-purpose yards, 97 rushing touchdowns, and 102 total TDs, subsequently signed with the New Orleans Saints, with whom he appeared in just four games before being dealt to the Arizona Cardinals. After gaining a total of only 529 yards on the ground with those two teams in 2017, Peterson experienced something of a resurgence with the Washington Redskins the following year, rushing for 1,042 yards, amassing 1,250 yards from scrimmage, and scoring eight touchdowns. Performing well once again for the Redskins in 2019, Peterson gained 898 yards on the ground, amassed 1,040 yards from scrimmage, and scored five touchdowns, before signing with the Detroit Lions just prior to the start of the 2020 campaign. Appearing in every game for the Lions this past season, Peterson rushed for 604 yards, gained 705 yards from scrimmage, and scored seven touchdowns, giving him career totals of 14,820 yards rushing, 17,286 yards from scrimmage, and 124 touchdowns, with the first figure placing him fifth all-time. Peterson has also caught 301 passes, amassed 2,466 receiving yards and 17,702 all-purpose yards, and rushed for 118 touchdowns, which ranks as the fourth-highest total in NFL history. As of this writing, the 36-year-old Peterson has not yet indicated if he plans to continue playing in 2021. Therefore, he may yet add to those lofty totals.

VIKINGS CAREER HIGHLIGHTS

Best Season

Peterson had several exceptional seasons for the Vikings, with the 2008 and 2009 campaigns ranking among the finest of his career. En route to earning First-Team All-Pro honors for the first of four times in 2008,

Peterson scored 10 touchdowns, amassed 1,901 all-purpose yards, and led the league with 1,760 yards rushing and 1,885 yards from scrimmage, with his fabulous performance gaining him recognition as the NFL Player of the Year. Peterson followed that up in 2009 by rushing for 1,383 yards, accumulating 1,819 yards from scrimmage, and setting a single-season franchise record by scoring a league-leading 18 touchdowns on the ground. However, Peterson reached the apex of his career in 2012, when he earned NFL MVP and NFL Player of the Year honors by establishing single-season franchise marks with 2,097 yards rushing, 2,314 yards from scrimmage, and 2,314 all-purpose yards, while also scoring 13 touchdowns and averaging a career-best 6 yards per carry.

Memorable Moments/Greatest Performances

Peterson excelled in his first game as a pro, leading the Vikings to a 24–3 win over the Atlanta Falcons in the opening game of the 2007 regular season by rushing for 103 yards and scoring the first touchdown of his career when he took a short swing pass from Tarvaris Jackson and ran 60 yards to paydirt.

Peterson earned NFC Offensive Player of the Week honors for the first time by rushing for 224 yards, accumulating 361 all-purpose yards, and scoring three touchdowns during a 34–31 win over the Bears on October 14, 2007, with his TDs coming on runs of 67, 73, and 35 yards.

Peterson earned that distinction again by rushing for an NFL-record 296 yards, amassing 315 yards from scrimmage, and scoring three touchdowns during a 35–17 win over the San Diego Chargers on November 4, 2007, with the longest of his TD runs covering 64 yards.

Peterson led the Vikings to a 28–27 victory over the Packers on November 9, 2008, by gaining 192 yards on the ground and scoring one touchdown, which came on a game-winning 29-yard run late in the fourth quarter.

Peterson contributed to a 35–14 win over the Arizona Cardinals on December 14, 2008, by carrying the ball 28 times for 165 yards.

Peterson starred in the 2009 regular-season opener, rushing for 180 yards and three touchdowns during a 34–20 win over the Browns, with his longest TD run of the day covering 64 yards.

Peterson led the Vikings to a 27–10 win over the Lions on November 15, 2009, by gaining 133 yards on only 18 carries and scoring two touchdowns.

Although the Vikings lost the 2009 NFC championship game to the Saints by a score of 31–28 in overtime, Peterson starred in defeat, rushing for 122 yards and three touchdowns, the longest of which came on a 19-yard run.

Peterson earned NFC Offensive Player of the Week honors by rushing for 160 yards and two touchdowns during a 24–10 win over the Lions on September 26, 2010, with his 80-yard TD run late in the third quarter representing the longest in the NFL all year.

Peterson rushed for 122 yards and three touchdowns during a 34–10 victory over Arizona on October 9, 2011, earning in the process NFC Offensive Player of the Week honors once again.

Although the Vikings suffered a 33–27 defeat at the hands of the Packers on October 23, 2011, Peterson rushed for a season-high 175 yards and one touchdown.

Peterson proved to be the difference in a 21–14 win over the Cardinals on October 21, 2012, earning NFC Offensive Player of the Week honors by rushing for 153 yards and one touchdown.

Peterson led the Vikings to a 34–24 victory over the Lions on November 11, 2012, by gaining 171 yards on the ground and scoring one touchdown, which came on a 61-yard run.

Peterson starred in defeat against the Packers on December 2, 2012, rushing for 210 yards and one touchdown during a 23–14 Vikings loss, with his TD coming on a career-long 82-yard run.

Peterson earned NFC Offensive Player of the Week honors by rushing for 154 yards and two touchdowns during a 21–14 win over the Bears on December 9, 2012.

Peterson rushed for 212 yards and equaled his career-long run by scoring on an 82-yard scamper during a 36–22 win over the St. Louis Rams on December 16, 2012.

Peterson helped the Vikings clinch a playoff berth in the final game of the 2012 regular season by rushing for 199 yards and scoring two touchdowns during a 37–34 win over the Packers.

Peterson rushed for 140 yards and two touchdowns, in leading the Vikings to a 34–27 victory over the Steelers on September 29, 2013, with one of his TD runs covering 60 yards.

Peterson helped the Vikings forge a 26–26 tie with the Packers on November 24, 2013, by rushing for 146 yards and one touchdown.

Peterson followed that up by carrying the ball 35 times for a season-high 211 yards during a 23–20 overtime win over the Bears on December 1, 2013.

Peterson amassed 192 yards from scrimmage during a 26–16 win over the Lions on September 20, 2015, gaining 134 yards on the ground and another 58 on two pass receptions.

Peterson led the Vikings to a 30–14 victory over the Oakland Raiders on November 15, 2015, by rushing for 203 yards and one TD, which came on an 80-yard run late in the fourth quarter.

Peterson provided much of the offensive firepower during a 20–10 win over the Atlanta Falcons on November 29, 2015, rushing for 158 yards and both Vikings touchdowns, the longest of which came on a 35-yard run.

Notable Achievements

- Rushed for more than 1,000 yards seven times, topping 1,500 yards twice and 2,000 yards once.
- Amassed more than 1,500 yards from scrimmage six times, topping 2,000 yards once.
- Amassed more than 2,000 all-purpose yards twice.
- Scored at least 10 touchdowns eight times.
- Scored more than 100 points once.
- Averaged more than 5 yards per carry twice.
- Led NFL in rushing attempts once, rushing yards three times, yards from scrimmage twice, rushing touchdowns twice, and touchdowns once.
- Finished second in NFL in rushing attempts twice, rushing yards once, all-purpose yards once, rushing touchdowns once, and rushing average twice.
- Finished third in NFL in yards from scrimmage twice, rushing touchdowns twice, and touchdowns twice.
- Led Vikings in rushing eight times.
- Holds NFL single-game record for most rushing yards (296 vs. San Diego on November 4, 2007).
- Holds Vikings single-season records for most rushing yards (2,097 in 2012), yards from scrimmage (2,314 in 2012), all-purpose yards (2,314 in 2012), and rushing touchdowns (18 in 2009).
- Holds Vikings career records for most rushing attempts (2,418), rushing yards (11,747), rushing touchdowns (97), yards from scrimmage (13,692), and all-purpose yards (14,120).
- Ranks among Vikings career leaders with 102 touchdowns (2nd) and 614 points scored (4th).

- Ranks among NFL career leaders with 14,820 rushing yards (5th) and 118 rushing touchdowns (4th).
- Three-time division champion (2008, 2009, and 2015).
- Seven-time NFC Offensive Player of the Week.
- Two-time NFC Offensive Player of the Month.
- Member of 2007 NFL All-Rookie Team.
- 2007 NFL Offensive Rookie of the Year.
- Two-time Bert Bell Award winner as NFL Player of the Year (2008 and 2012).
- 2012 NFL MVP.
- 2012 NFL Offensive Player of the Year.
- Seven-time Pro Bowl selection (2007, 2008, 2009, 2010, 2012, 2013, and 2015).
- Four-time First-Team All-Pro selection (2008, 2009, 2012, and 2015).
- Three-time Second-Team All-Pro selection (2007, 2010, and 2013).
- NFL 2010s All-Decade Team.

2
ALAN PAGE

aving fallen just short of earning the top spot on this list, Alan Page lays claim to the number two position, edging out Fran Tarkenton for that distinction. One of the greatest defensive tackles in NFL history, Page spent 11½ seasons starring on the right side of the Vikings' defensive line, never missing a game as a member of the team. Blessed with extraordinary quickness and tremendous anticipation, Page did an exceptional job of applying pressure to opposing quarterbacks, recording the fourth-most sacks in franchise history. Outstanding against the run as well, Page also ranks extremely high in team annals in tackles and fumble recoveries, with his brilliant all-around play earning him nine Pro Bowl selections, eight All-Pro nominations, and one NFL MVP trophy. A huge contributor to Vikings teams that won nine division titles and made four Super Bowl appearances, Page also gained recognition as the NFC Defensive Player of the Year on three separate occasions, before being further honored following the conclusion of his playing career by having his #88 retired, being included on both the NFL Network's and the *Sporting News'* respective lists of the 100 Greatest Players in NFL History, being named to the NFL 100 All-Time Team, and being elected to the Pro Football Hall of Fame.

Born in Canton, Ohio, on August 7, 1945, Alan Cedric Page learned the importance of education from his parents, revealing that his mother and father insisted that he and his three older siblings always put learning ahead of sports when he said, "Our parents, my mother in particular, were very strong on making sure we got educated. She realized early on that was the key to the only way out to a better life."

Following in the footsteps of his brother and two sisters, Page enrolled at Canton Central Catholic High School, recalling, "My mother had the perceptions that the education at Central Catholic was better than the public schools. She thought it was important even in the face of paying tuition."

Developing into an outstanding all-around athlete at Central Catholic, Page starred in multiple sports, proving to be particularly proficient in

In 1971, Alan Page became the first defensive player in NFL history to be named league MVP.

football, although he never seriously considered pursuing a career on the gridiron. Looking back at his motivation for joining the school's team, Page said, "My brother did it. Being in Canton, a lot of people played, but it never occurred to me until my brother, a year ahead of me, started playing as a freshman. He did it, so I thought, 'Why don't I give it a try?'"

The younger Page ended up performing so well that he earned an athletic scholarship to the University of Notre Dame, where he arrived in 1963 feeling a bit uncomfortable. Finding a virtually all-white campus at

South Bend, Page took some time to adjust to his new surroundings, which, coupled with his focus on football, prevented him from reaching his full potential in the classroom. Remembering his college days, Page said, "Notre Dame gave me a solid academic foundation, but I was too distracted at the time to discover a love of learning for its own sake, which would only come later." However, Page experienced no such distractions on the football field, where he excelled at defensive end for three seasons, earning All-America honors as a senior in 1966, when he led the Fighting Irish to a 9-0-1 record and the National Championship.

Selected by the Vikings with the 15th overall pick of the 1967 NFL Draft, Page became a starter four games into his rookie campaign, manning the left defensive tackle position, before being moved to the right side of Minnesota's defense the following year. Performing well his first year in the league, Page recovered three fumbles and displayed an ability to defend against the run and pressure opposing quarterbacks. Nevertheless, many of Page's new teammates did not accept him immediately, with Jim Marshall recalling, "When he first came to the Minnesota Vikings, we thought he was a little strange. He had his own ways, and he seemed stubborn. We knew he had a lot of talent, but he didn't seem like he was gonna' fit with the group. Alan was sort of a loner type as I recall."

Paul Krause added, "Alan was a tough person to get to know, and, I don't know why, but Alan and I got along very well. Some other people didn't get along with him very well."

Page, though, soon ingratiated himself to his teammates with his strong work ethic, marvelous instincts, and exceptional athletic ability, with Mick Tingelhoff stating, "It seemed like he caught on to all the plays, and it looked like he had played a few years before. He just stepped right in and took over."

Establishing himself as one of the NFL's best defensive tackles in 1968, Page earned the first of his nine consecutive Pro Bowl selections. He followed that up by gaining All-Pro recognition in each of the next eight seasons, being named to the first team six times and the second team twice. Along the way, Page recorded double-digit sacks on six separate occasions, with his dominant performance in 1971 earning him NFL MVP honors, making him the first defensive player in league history to earn that distinction. Looking back on Page's MVP campaign, Paul Krause commented, "The 1971 season for Alan, it was very unlikely for him to be the most valuable player, but so many good things were happening to him. I mean, he just dominated football."

Serving as the centerpiece of the Purple People Eaters, the 6'4" Page, who spent his first several seasons in Minnesota playing at close to 250 pounds, employed an unusual three-point stance in which he placed his left, rather than his right hand on the ground. Extremely aggressive, Page preferred to seek out the ball-carrier, rather than wait for him to come to him, saying, "A defensive player should think of himself more as an aggressor, not as a defender. . . . My view of the world was, from the snap of the ball, the goal was to shut the play off, and, the sooner you get there, the better. And it didn't have to be particularly spectacular."

Combining tremendous quickness with good strength and superior intelligence, Page proved to be virtually impossible for one man to block, with longtime NFL announcer Pat Summerall saying, "He was almost unblockable. He was a target that the offensive linemen would look at and, by the time they got to where they had to hit him, he was no longer there."

Giving credence to Summerall's assessment, Dallas Cowboys guard John Wilbur stated, "You could never pinpoint the guy. It was like trying to block a ball bearing because he was so slippery and so hard to read. He was so quick. His feet were so quick that he was like a ballet dancer down there on the field. You'd be flat on your stomach and he'd be tackling the ballplayer, and you'd be as embarrassed as heck."

Also blessed with long arms and great instincts, Page drew praise from Vikings head coach Bud Grant, who claimed, "He had instinct that was beyond the average football player. Alan is a very bright guy and was always interested in why we did things. Not many players ask why, you just say do this. . . . But Alan was more interested in why and how, and it made him a better player."

Grant added, "His instincts were always good. You'd say, 'Well, players guess.' Well, I don't think that Alan guessed as much as his instincts told him this is where to be."

Page's rare combination of physical talent and football smarts enabled him to establish himself as the preeminent player at his position, with former Vikings assistant coach Neill Armstrong saying, "He created havoc. He just exploded off the ball. Often as not, we'd let him call his own stunt, because he had such a great feel for what was happening. For a defensive tackle to make the plays he made was unheard of. He was unique, an exception to every rule."

Yet even though Minnesota's coaching staff greatly appreciated everything Page contributed to the team on the playing field, Bud Grant eventually grew weary of his stubborn, nonconformist nature. Page, who missed parts of training camp to attend law school at the University of Minnesota from 1975 to 1978, often butted heads with his conservative head coach, who he further antagonized by serving as a member of the NFLPA Executive Committee. While serving in that capacity, Page proved to be instrumental in the 1974 labor dispute that canceled the College All-Star Game and led to a brief strike by veteran players during the preseason.

Everything finally came to a head in 1978, when, while training to be a marathon runner, Page trimmed down to 225 pounds, making him less effective at defending against the run. After substituting for Page in short-yardage situations the first six weeks of the season, Grant chose to release him in early October, saying at the time, "Alan can no longer meet the standard he set for himself. He just can't make the plays anymore. Here is a man we had to take out in short-yardage situations, who was not strong enough to rush the passer. . . . He was not doing his job."

Page left the Vikings having recorded an unofficial total of 108½ sacks. He also registered 1,120 tackles, recovered 19 fumbles, scored two touchdowns on defense, and appeared in 160 straight games, starting all but three of those.

Signed by the Bears just hours after the Vikings released him, Page spent the next 3½ years in Chicago performing well for one of Minnesota's fiercest rivals. After recording 11½ sacks in the final 10 games of 1978, Page registered another 28½ sacks over the course of the next three seasons, before announcing his retirement following the conclusion of the 1981 campaign. Ending his career with 148½ sacks, 23 fumble recoveries, 28 blocked kicks, three touchdowns, and three safeties, Page never missed a game in his 15 years in the league, appearing in 218 consecutive contests.

After retiring as an active player, Page briefly dabbled in the media, spending parts of two seasons doing commentary on college football radio broadcasts. However, he soon transitioned into a career in law that led to him eventually becoming a Minnesota Supreme Court justice. Page, who earned a BA in political science from Notre Dame and a JD from the University of Minnesota Law School in 1978, first began practicing law in 1979 at Lindquist and Vennum, a Minneapolis law firm that specialized in labor issues. He also worked in the office of the Attorney General of the State of Minnesota, where he enjoyed great success as a courtroom attorney. But Page assumed a far more prominent role in 1993, when he was elected to the Minnesota Supreme Court as an associate judge, becoming in the process the first African American to serve on that court. Reelected in 1998, 2004, and 2010, Page continued to serve as a Minnesota Supreme Court justice until 2015, when he reached the court's mandatory retirement age of 70. Now 76 years of age, Page remains active in the Twin Cities community through the Page Education Foundation, which provides financial and mentoring assistance to students of color.

Looking back on his playing career from a rather unique perspective, Page, who entered the Pro Football Hall of Fame in 1988 and the Vikings Ring of Honor in 1998, says, "From the day I showed up at football practice, all of a sudden, I was somebody different. I got put on the pedestal right away. I liked the attention—who doesn't? But, at the same time, I didn't understand it. I struggled with trying to figure out why is this so important to people?"

VIKINGS CAREER HIGHLIGHTS

Best Season

Page stated during an interview with *Pro Football Journal* many years ago that he likely performed just as well in 1970 and 1976 as he did during his MVP campaign of 1971. Gaining First-Team All-Pro recognition for the second straight time in 1970, Page recorded 10½ sacks, a league-leading seven fumble recoveries and 77 fumble-return yards, and his only interception as a member of the Vikings. Meanwhile, Page registered a career-high 18 sacks in 1976. Nevertheless, 1971 is generally considered to be Page's signature season. En route to earning league MVP honors, Page recorded 10 sacks, 42 quarterback hurries, and 109 solo tackles, assisted on 35 other stops, and led the NFL with two safeties.

Memorable Moments/Greatest Performances

Page helped anchor a Vikings' defense that allowed just 41 yards rushing and 133 yards of total offense during a 27–14 win over the Washington Redskins on November 3, 1968.

Page led the defensive charge when the Vikings surrendered just 54 yards on the ground and 119 total yards to the Bears during a 31–0 man-handling of their division rivals on October 12, 1969.

Page combined with teammate Jim Marshall to score a memorable touchdown during a 27–0 win over the Detroit Lions on Thanksgiving Day 1969. After tipping a pass that fell into the hands of Marshall, Page followed his line-mate downfield as he began running toward the Detroit end zone. Then, as Marshall was being tackled, he lateraled the ball to Page, who jaunted the rest of the way for the first touchdown of his career.

Page proved to be a huge factor when the Vikings defeated the Los Angeles Rams by a score of 23–20 in the divisional round of the 1969 playoffs. After leading a goal-line stand at the end of the first half that prevented the Rams from increasing their lead from 17–7 to 24–7, Page intercepted a Roman Gabriel pass in the fourth quarter, which he subsequently returned 29 yards deep into Los Angeles territory, to help set up what proved to be the game-winning touchdown.

Page followed that up by recording a sack of quarterback Bill Nelsen during the Vikings' convincing 27–7 victory over the Cleveland Browns in the 1969 NFL championship game.

Page scored the second touchdown of his career when he ran 65 yards to paydirt after recovering a fumble during a 24–0 win over the Bears on October 11, 1970.

Page recorded his only interception as a member of the Vikings during a 54–13 rout of the Cowboys on October 18, 1970, subsequently returning the ball 27 yards into Dallas territory.

In addition to anchoring a defense that allowed just 56 yards rushing and 64 yards of total offense during a 19–0 victory over Buffalo on October 3, 1971, Page recorded a safety when he sacked Bills quarterback Dennis Shaw in the end zone.

Page turned in arguably the most memorable performance of his career during a 29–10 victory over the Detroit Lions on December 11, 1971, earning in the process NFL Defensive Player of the Week honors for one of three times. Taking over the game all by himself in the second quarter, Page, angered by being called for offsides penalties on consecutive plays, first sacked quarterback Greg Landry, then stopped two running plays for losses, forcing the Lions to punt. Page later punctuated his brilliant performance in the fourth quarter by blocking a punt out of the end zone for a safety. In describing Page's extraordinary effort, longtime *Minneapolis Star Tribune* columnist Jim Klobuchar wrote, "He was all over the field. He was uncontainable. I think the best performance I've ever seen by a defensive lineman."

Notable Achievements

- Never missed a game in parts of 12 seasons, appearing in 160 consecutive contests.
- Scored two defensive touchdowns.
- Finished in double digits in sacks six times.
- Recorded 109 solo tackles in 1971.

- Led NFL with seven fumble recoveries and 77 fumble-return yards in 1970.
- Led NFL with two safeties in 1971.
- Ranks among Vikings career leaders with 108½ sacks (4th), 1,120 tackles (5th), and 19 fumble recoveries (4th).
- Nine-time division champion (1968, 1969, 1970, 1971, 1973, 1974, 1975, 1976, and 1977).
- 1969 NFL champion.
- Three-time NFC champion (1973, 1974, and 1976).
- Three-time NFL Defensive Player of the Week.
- 1971 NFL MVP.
- 1971 NFL Defensive Player of the Year.
- 1973 Newspaper Enterprise Association (NEA) NFL Defensive Player of the Year.
- Three-time Kansas City Committee of 101 NFC Defensive Player of the Year (1970, 1971, and 1974).
- Nine-time Pro Bowl selection (1968, 1969, 1970, 1971, 1972, 1973, 1974, 1975, and 1976).
- Six-time First-Team All-Pro selection (1969, 1970, 1971, 1973, 1974, and 1975).
- Two-time Second-Team All-Pro selection (1972 and 1976).
- Seven-time First-Team All-NFC selection (1970, 1971, 1972, 1973, 1974, 1975, and 1976).
- Pro Football Reference All-1970s First Team.
- NFL 1970s All-Decade Second Team.
- Named to NFL 100 All-Time Team in 2019.
- Number 34 on the *Sporting News'* 1999 list of the 100 Greatest Players in NFL History.
- Number 43 on the NFL Network's 2010 list of the NFL's 100 Greatest Players.
- #88 retired by Vikings.
- Inducted into Minnesota Vikings Ring of Honor in 1998.
- Elected to Pro Football Hall of Fame in 1988.

3

FRAN TARKENTON

A man truly ahead of his time, Fran Tarkenton served as a precursor to the more mobile quarterbacks that began entering the NFL some two decades after he first arrived in Minnesota in 1961. Often referred to as "The Scrambler" and "Frantic Fran" during his playing days, Tarkenton proved to be extraordinarily difficult for opposing teams to defend against due to the unpredictable nature of his game. A true innovator who longtime Vikings head coach Bud Grant called "the greatest quarterback who's ever played," Tarkenton drove defenders crazy with his ability to avoid would-be tacklers, while also frequently causing players on his own team to experience a considerable amount of anxiety. Yet, by the time Tarkenton retired following the conclusion of the 1978 campaign, he held NFL records for most pass completions, passing yards, touchdown passes, and wins by a starting quarterback. And, during his two tours of duty with the Vikings that covered a total of 13 seasons, Tarkenton completed more passes for more yards and touchdowns than any other signal-caller in franchise history, earning in the process five trips to the Pro Bowl, five All-NFC selections, two All-Pro nominations, and one league MVP trophy. A member of Vikings teams that won six division titles and three NFC championships, Tarkenton also earned spots on the NFL Network's and the *Sporting News'* respective lists of the 100 Greatest Players in NFL History and a place in the Pro Football Hall of Fame.

Born in Richmond, Virginia, on February 3, 1940, Francis Asbury Tarkenton grew up in Washington, DC, where he began playing football at an early age, recalling, "We played touch football every day, and you had to be elusive because the alleys were narrow, and you didn't have much room to dodge." The son of a Methodist minister, Tarkenton moved with his family to Athens, Georgia, at the age of 12, where he went on to star on the gridiron while attending Athens High School. Offered an athletic scholarship to the University of Georgia, Tarkenton continued to excel at

Fran Tarkenton retired as the NFL's all-time leader in pass completions, passing yards, and touchdown passes.
Courtesy of RMYAuctions.com

quarterback in college, leading the Bulldogs to the Southeastern Conference title in 1959, and earning All-SEC honors in both 1959 and 1960.

Subsequently selected by the expansion Minnesota Vikings in the third round of the 1961 NFL Draft, with the 29th overall pick, and the Boston Patriots in the fifth round of that year's AFL Draft, with the 35th overall pick, Tarkenton chose to sign with the Vikings, who he joined at the tender age of 21. Making an immediate impact upon his arrival in Minnesota,

Tarkenton led the Vikings to a 37–13 upset win over the Chicago Bears in their very first game by coming off the bench to throw four touchdown passes and run for another score. Unfortunately, the Vikings won just two more games in their inaugural season, with Tarkenton experiencing the usual growing pains of any rookie quarterback after taking over as the team's starter early in the year. Still, Tarkenton posted decent numbers in his first pro season, throwing for 1,997 yards, finishing third in the league with 18 touchdown passes, completing 56.1 percent of his passes, and running for 308 yards and five touchdowns.

Although Tarkenton performed relatively well over the course of the next two seasons, throwing for a total of 4,906 yards and tossing 37 touchdown passes, the Vikings posted a composite record of just 6-19-2, prompting most people around the league to view him as something of an oddity, with Tarkenton noting years later, "When I began my NFL career in 1961, I was a freak. The reason was simple: I played quarterback and I ran. There were no designed runs in our playbook, but I would scramble out of the pocket when a play broke down—nowadays, that likely would be called 'extending the play.' When I ran forward for yardage, it was never the design of the play, but just something that happened when nothing else worked. . . . It was not a skill set that was embraced. Plenty of people mocked it, and the rest wrote it off."

Tarkenton continued, "I was always distressed when I saw quarterbacks, when their protection broke down, just give up, fold themselves in the pocket, accept a seven or eight-yard loss, and go to the next play. And, if you didn't get protection, they would lose. And I just made up my mind when I got up to pro football that I was not gonna give up on a play—ever. And, if the pocket broke down, if the protection broke down, I was gonna run, scramble, whatever I had to do to make something out of the play."

Commenting on his quarterback's scrambling tendencies, Vikings offensive lineman Grady Alderman said, "He was not afraid to run. Everything he did was aimed at making the play positive rather than negative. He ran more because we allowed him to get in trouble rather than provide him with great protection. After a while, you learned that, if you lost your man, he was probably the guy making Fran run, and, if you stayed on your feet and held your ground and waited, Fran would come back, and you would get a chance to block your guy."

Longtime Vikings offensive line coach John Michels added, "When Fran took off, he was on his own, and he knew that. It was part of the deal. If I had my guys take off with him, it would be pure anarchy, and then we'd all be in trouble. . . . He'd cause us trouble every game with that scrambling of his. He'd drive us a little crazy, but he drove the opposition even crazier. So, we loved the scrambler."

Los Angeles Rams Hall of Fame defensive end Deacon Jones admitted that he dreaded going up against the 6-foot, 190-pound Tarkenton, saying, "He was the one guy I did not want to see on the other side of the line of scrimmage. He was fast, elusive, quick, and all of that. I got him a few times, but you were just exhausted after playing against him. . . . Fran was exceptionally quick, he had that ability to scramble, and we always thought he had eyes in the back of his head because he would reverse his field just when you were getting ready to tackle him. It was the best timing I had ever seen."

Chicago Bears linebacker Doug Buffone expressed similar sentiments when he said, "You were never so tired after a game as when you were playing against Tarkenton. He was so quick you couldn't catch him. Normally with a pocket passer, you have to cover a back or tight end two or three seconds before he gets rid of the ball. But with Tarkenton, you had to cover a guy, I don't know, five seconds or more. That's because he was running around, and you could never catch him."

Buffone continued, "He would be running around back there, and you didn't know whether to stay with your guy or go after Tarkenton. Enough time goes by and you go after him. He sees an open running back and he shot puts the ball over your head, and he's got another completion. It was so frustrating . . . I remember I intercepted him once. It was just a straight drop back, and he got rid of the ball quickly from the pocket. I was there, and I made the play. But, if he was running around, it was impossible to intercept those passes."

Tarkenton, who once defended his scrambling by saying, "I scramble because I'm good at it, because I can twist and dodge those big pass rushers better than most guys, and we get a lot of touchdowns that way," infuriated defenders with his ability to evade them, with Merlin Olsen stating, "I always hated Tarkenton. I really did. I mean that little wimp would run around out there for hours and hours and hours, and we had to chase him. Wherever he went. Sometimes he'd run 40 yards back and forth and up and down the field. And, at the end of a game against Tarkenton, your tongue was right on the ground."

Olsen's Rams teammate Deacon Jones put it more bluntly when he said, "Tarkenton was a pain in the ass. He'd gamble. He'd run anywhere. I mean, he'd be up into the stands if he had to. He's the one man that we tried desperately to end his career. We tried, and I must say that, in this day and age, we tried desperately to get rid of him. Because on a hot day in the Coliseum, chasing Fran Tarkenton was not what you wanted to do."

Tarkenton, though, proved to be much more than just an elusive runner. Developing into one of the NFL's top passers by 1964, Tarkenton earned Pro Bowl honors for the first of nine times by ranking among the league leaders with 2,506 passing yards, 22 touchdown passes, a passer rating of 91.8, and a pass completion percentage of 55.9, with his strong performance helping the Vikings compile a regular-season record of 8-5-1 that represented their first winning mark. Choosing to address concerns over his purported lack of arm strength, Tarkenton stated on one occasion, "The name of the game is passing, and I think the whole thing with the arm is overrated. I mean, I can throw the ball far enough. I can throw it hard enough. I can throw it with touch."

Tarkenton continued his solid play in each of the next two seasons, earning one more Pro Bowl selection, while totaling 5,170 passing yards, 36 TD passes, and 27 interceptions. But, with the Vikings going a combined 11-14-1 during that time, head coach Norm Van Brocklin grew increasingly disenchanted with his starting signal-caller. Van Brocklin, who earlier starred at quarterback for the Rams and Eagles during a Hall of Fame career, made his distaste for running quarterbacks well known to Tarkenton, who often found himself clashing with his dictatorial head coach. Having finally reached his boiling point, Tarkenton asked to be traded to another team—a request Vikings management granted by dealing him to the struggling New York Giants on March 7, 1967, for their first- and second-round picks in each of the next two drafts.

Joining a team in New York that compiled the league's worst record the previous year, Tarkenton performed wonders, leading the Giants to a record of 7-7 in each of his first two seasons with them. Despite being physically overmatched by their opponents on many occasions, the Giants remained competitive, due primarily to Tarkenton's ingenuity and sense of originality. Particularly proud of the contributions he made to the 1967 Giants team that scored 106 more points than the previous year's squad, Tarkenton stated years later:

That team in New York, that first year that I was there, we finished 7-7. That was the finest accomplishment of any of my 18 years in professional football. It was a rag-a-muffin team that played hard and played together, had heart and had soul. Allie [Sherman] did a great job with that team and, for us to be 7-7, was like being 14-0 for any other team. It was the best year any team I ever played on ever had. We spread the field, we put men in motion, we had nobody in the backfield, and the reason we had to do this is that we didn't have a big offensive line. So, we had to use the short passing game to be our running game. The "West Coast Offense" as we know it today was absolutely started in New York, and they let me be a part of that architecture, and we had more fun with it.

Tarkenton ended up spending five years in New York, earning four Pro Bowl selections and one All-Pro nomination, although he led the Giants to a winning record just once during that time. But, even Tarkenton found himself unable to improve the Giants' situation in 1971, when the team finished a disappointing 4-10. Believing that he had no chance of winning in New York, Tarkenton expressed to management his desire to go elsewhere, prompting the team to send him back to Minnesota for three players (quarterback Norm Snead, wide receiver Bob Grim, and running back Vince Clements) and two high draft picks.

Performing well upon his return to Minnesota, Tarkenton ranked among the NFL leaders with 2,651 yards passing, 18 touchdown passes, a 56.9 completion percentage, and a passer rating of 80.2 in 1972. Nevertheless, the Vikings struggled as a team, finishing just 7-7 and failing to make the playoffs for the first time in five years. However, with Tarkenton leading the way, they captured the next six division titles. Playing some of the best ball of his career, Tarkenton posted the following numbers over the course of those six seasons, with the 1977 campaign being excluded from this graphic since he suffered a season-ending injury during a 42–10 win over Cincinnati in Week 9:

YEAR	YDS PASSING	TD PASSES	INTS	COMP %	QBR
1973	2,113	15	7	61.7	93.2
1974	2,598	17	12	56.7	82.1
1975	2,994	25	13	64.2	91.8
1976	2,961	17	8	61.9	89.3
1978	3,468	25	32	60.3	68.9

In addition to leading the NFL with a career-high 3,468 passing yards in 1978, Tarkenton finished second in the league in that category two other times. He also topped the circuit in pass completions three times and TD passes once, while finishing second in the league in passer rating and pass completion percentage twice each. Tarkenton's exceptional play in 1975, coupled with the Vikings' 12-2 regular-season record, earned him First-Team All-Pro, NFL MVP, and NFL Offensive Player of the Year honors. Tarkenton also gained Pro Bowl recognition in three of those seasons.

However, the Vikings ultimately came up short in the playoffs each year, losing in the divisional round of the postseason tournament twice, the NFC championship game once, and the Super Bowl three times. And Tarkenton failed to distinguish himself in any of his three Super Bowl appearances, struggling against Miami, Pittsburgh, and Oakland in Super Bowls VIII, IX, and XI, respectively.

Choosing to announce his retirement following the conclusion of the 1978 campaign, Tarkenton ended his career as the NFL's all-time leader in pass completions (3,686), passing yards (47,003), and touchdown passes (342). He also rushed for 3,674 yards and 32 touchdowns, with the first figure placing him fourth all-time among NFL quarterbacks, behind only Randall Cunningham, Steve Young, and Michael Vick. Tarkenton completed 57 percent of his passes and posted a career QBR of 80.4. Tarkenton's numbers with the Vikings include 2,635 pass completions, 33,098 passing yards, 239 touchdown passes, 194 interceptions, a pass-completion percentage of 57.7, a QBR of 80.1, 2,548 rushing yards, and 22 rushing touchdowns.

Following his retirement, Tarkenton appeared on the television show *That's Incredible!* and worked part-time on *Monday Night Football*. He later established himself as a pioneer in the computer software industry, founding a program generator company he called Tarkenton Software. After touring the country promoting CASE (computer-aided software engineering) with Albert F. Case Jr. of Nastec Corporation, Tarkenton eventually merged his software firm with James Martin's KnowledgeWare. He served as president there until he sold the company to Sterling Software in 1994. Since then, Tarkenton has been promoting various products and services including Tony Robbins and 1-800-BAR-NONE.

Despite Tarkenton's many on-field accomplishments, his inability to win a championship and poor performance in the three Super Bowls in which he appeared prevent many people from viewing him as one of the greatest quarterbacks in NFL history. The Pro Football Hall of Fame didn't necessarily agree, though, inducting Tarkenton into its ranks in 1986, in just his third year of eligibility. Tarkenton can also include among his supporters several of his former teammates and coaches, with Carl Eller calling him "a football genius."

Former Vikings center Mick Tingelhoff said, "He is 'Fran the Man,' no doubt about that. Fran is one of a kind. He was a great quarterback for us, very smart and really knew defenses. He truly understood the game."

Vikings wide receiver Ahmad Rashad suggested, "People always talked about his weak arm. But Fran Tarkenton was the master quarterback of all because he got you to do the things that he wanted you to do. He never played against his weaknesses. He always played against yours. If he couldn't throw the long ball, he'd throw the short ball to death until you got all the way up close and tried to stop the short ball, and then he used to throw the medium-long ball, which, in the end, would get you nonetheless."

Bud Grant expressed his admiration for his team's longtime signal-caller when he said, "Fran Tarkenton was the best quarterback that's ever played professional football because you never achieve greatness without durability. Fran Tarkenton, in addition to all the physical abilities, all the records he had, he had durability—he played every week. In my mind, there's nobody who's played football at that position that was better than Fran Tarkenton—ever."

Looking back on his playing career, Tarkenton said, "People didn't want to believe that I could succeed being the type of quarterback that I was, and it took them a longer time to accept me as something more than a freak quarterback. . . . I was a strategist. I knew where to throw the football. I wasn't blessed with all the physical skills in the world, but those things—understanding the game, knowing defenses, knowing offenses, being able to call plays, being able to read defenses—I felt that I could do that as well as anybody. I took great pride in that."

VIKINGS CAREER HIGHLIGHTS

Best Season

Although Tarkenton passed for more yards in 1978 (3,468), posted a higher QBR in 1973 (93.2), and threw fewer interceptions in five other campaigns, he had easily his finest all-around season as a member of the Vikings in 1975, when he earned NFL MVP honors and his lone First-Team All-Pro selection by leading the league with 25 touchdown passes and finishing second in the circuit with 2,994 passing yards, a passer rating of 91.8, and a pass completion percentage of 64.2, with the last figure representing a career-high mark.

Memorable Moments/Greatest Performances

Tarkenton began his pro career in fine fashion, coming off the bench during the early stages of the 1961 regular-season opener to lead the Vikings to a 37–13 win over the Bears in their inaugural NFL game by running for one score and throwing for 250 yards and four touchdowns, the longest of which went 29 yards to Jerry Reichow.

Although the Vikings lost to the Los Angeles Rams by a score of 31–17 on November 5, 1961, Tarkenton ran for a career-high 99 yards during the contest, with 52 of those coming on a long TD run.

Tarkenton helped the Vikings gain a measure of revenge against the Rams in the second meeting between the two teams on December 3, 1961, throwing for 252 yards and four touchdowns during a 42–21 Minnesota victory, with his longest TD pass of the day going 51 yards to Jerry Reichow.

Tarkenton starred in defeat on September 20, 1964, throwing for 311 yards and four touchdowns during a 34–28 loss to the Bears.

Tarkenton led the Vikings to a 42–41 win over the San Francisco 49ers on October 24, 1965, by passing for 407 yards and three touchdowns, the longest of which went 58 yards to Paul Flatley.

Tarkenton had a big game against the Rams on October 16, 1966, earning NFL Offensive Player of the Week honors by running for one score and throwing for 327 yards and three touchdowns during a 35–7 Vikings win, with his longest TD pass going 68 yards to Red Phillips.

Tarkenton accounted for all four touchdowns the Vikings scored during a 28–3 win over the 49ers on October 30, 1966, running for two scores and passing for two others, the longest of which came on a 40-yard connection with Preston Carpenter. Tarkenton finished the game with 71 yards rushing and 278 yards passing.

Tarkenton gave the Vikings a 23–20 victory over the Denver Broncos on October 15, 1972, by throwing a 31-yard touchdown pass to Gene Washington late in the fourth quarter.

Tarkenton torched the Los Angeles defensive secondary for 319 yards and four touchdowns during a 45–41 win over the Rams on November 19, 1972, collaborating with Bill Brown, John Henderson, and John Gilliam on long scoring plays that covered 76, 70, and 66 yards, respectively.

Tarkenton performed exceptionally well during a 51–10 rout of the Houston Oilers on October 13, 1974, completing 18 of 24 pass attempts for 274 yards and three touchdowns, the longest of which came on an 80-yard connection with John Gilliam on the game's opening possession.

Tarkenton had another big day against the New Orleans Saints on December 1, 1974, leading the Vikings to a 29–9 win by throwing for 317 yards and three touchdowns, with his two fourth-quarter TD passes to John Gilliam putting the game out of reach.

Tarkenton helped the Vikings improve their record to 7-0 by throwing for 285 yards and three touchdowns during a 28–17 win over the Packers on November 2, 1975, putting the game away in the final period with TD passes to John Gilliam and Chuck Foreman.

Although the Vikings suffered a 31–30 defeat at the hands of the Washington Redskins four weeks later that ended their hopes of an undefeated season, Tarkenton excelled behind center, running for one touchdown, throwing for another, and completing 27 of 37 pass attempts for 357 yards.

Tarkenton led the Vikings to a 31–23 victory over the Lions on November 7, 1976, by passing for 347 yards and two touchdowns, both of which went to Sammy White.

Tarkenton followed that up by completing 26 of 31 pass attempts for 274 yards and two touchdowns during a 27–21 win over the Seattle Seahawks on November 14, 1976.

Notable Achievements

- Passed for more than 2,500 yards nine times, topping 3,000 yards once.
- Threw more than 20 touchdown passes four times.
- Completed more than 60 percent of passes five times.
- Posted touchdown-to-interception ratio of better than 2–1 three times.
- Posted passer rating above 90.0 three times.
- Led NFL in pass completions three times, passing yards once, touchdown passes once, and pass completion percentage once.
- Finished second in NFL in pass completions once, passing yards twice, touchdown passes once, pass completion percentage twice, and passer rating twice.
- Finished third in NFL in pass completions once, passing yards three times, touchdown passes four times, pass completion percentage five times, and passer rating once.
- Holds Vikings career records for most pass attempts (4,569), pass completions (2,635), passing yards (33,098), and touchdown passes (239).
- Six-time division champion (1973, 1974, 1975, 1976, 1977, and 1978).
- Three-time NFC champion (1973, 1974, and 1976).
- 1966 Week 6 NFL Offensive Player of the Week.

- 1975 NFL MVP.
- 1975 Bert Bell Award winner as NFL Player of the Year.
- 1975 NFL Offensive Player of the Year.
- Five-time Pro Bowl selection (1964, 1965, 1974, 1975, and 1976).
- 1975 First-Team All-Pro selection.
- 1973 Second-Team All-Pro selection.
- Three-time First-Team All-NFC selection (1972, 1975, and 1976).
- Two-time Second-Team All-NFC selection (1973 and 1974).
- Pro Football Reference All-1960s First Team.
- Pro Football Reference All-1970s Second Team.
- Number 59 on the *Sporting News'* 1999 list of the 100 Greatest Players in NFL History.
- Number 91 on the NFL Network's 2010 list of the NFL's 100 Greatest Players.
- #10 retired by Vikings.
- Inducted into Minnesota Vikings Ring of Honor in 1998.
- Elected to Pro Football Hall of Fame in 1986.

4

CARL ELLER

One of the premier pass-rushers of his era, Carl Eller spent 15 seasons in Minnesota, recording more sacks during that time than any other player in franchise history. Excelling at left defensive end for the Vikings from 1964 to 1978, Eller brought down opposing quarterbacks behind the line of scrimmage a total of 130 times, recording at least 10 sacks in a season on seven separate occasions. A solid run-defender as well, Eller proved to be a dominant figure up front for the Vikings, with his outstanding all-around play earning him six trips to the Pro Bowl, six All-Pro nominations, and a spot on the NFL 1970s All-Decade Team. And, following the conclusion of his playing career, Eller received the additional honor of being elected to the Pro Football Hall of Fame.

Born in Winston-Salem, North Carolina, on January 25, 1942, Carl Lee Eller grew up in the segregated South, spending his teenage years living with his mother and grandparents after losing his father at the age of 13. After starring in football at Akins High school, Eller accepted an athletic scholarship to the University of Minnesota, where he spent three seasons excelling at defensive tackle for the Gophers, gaining All-America recognition twice, and nearly winning the Outland Trophy as a senior in 1963, when he finished second in the voting for the award presented annually to the nation's best interior lineman.

Reflecting back on how his college days prepared him for life in the NFL, Eller said, "At Minnesota and in the Big Ten Conference, I was playing against the best, and it helped me greatly. When I got drafted by the Vikings, I was really pleased because there was never a doubt where I wanted to play professionally. I wanted to stay in Minnesota. I loved the area and everything about the Twin Cities."

Although the Buffalo Bills made Eller their first-round pick in the 1964 AFL Draft, the two-time All-American wasted little time in signing with the Vikings after they selected him with the sixth overall pick of that year's NFL Draft. Earning a starting job immediately upon his arrival in Minnesota,

Carl Eller recorded more sacks than any other player in franchise history.

Eller had a solid rookie season, doing an excellent job of applying pressure to opposing quarterbacks, while also recovering four fumbles, one of which he returned for a touchdown. In addressing Eller's development at one point during the campaign, Vikings head coach Norm Van Brocklin stated, "He's coming along faster than we had anticipated."

Giving credence to Van Brocklin's assessment years later, Packers Hall of Fame offensive tackle Forrest Gregg recalled, "I remember playing him that first time and thinking, 'I don't know how much longer I want to hang around.' There was a play in which I moved to left guard, and my job was to pull and kick out the left end. I didn't get past the center. I took my first step and hit a wall. I looked up and it was No. 81, Carl Eller."

With the Vikings struggling as a team during the early stages of Eller's career, he failed to garner any individual postseason honors. Nevertheless, Eller soon emerged as one of the NFL's top defensive ends, with Fran Tarkenton later writing in his autobiography, *Every Day Is Game Day*, "In my first tour with the Vikings, Carl was still young and did some things during games that were hard to fathom. I saw him literally throw people aside as if they were mannequins. He was magnificent in every respect."

Minnesota's vast improvement on defense, which Purple People Eaters Eller, Page, Marshall, and Larsen spearheaded, enabled the Vikings to establish themselves as contenders by 1968, allowing Eller to begin a string of four consecutive seasons in which he gained Pro Bowl and First-Team All-Pro recognition. And, during that time, Eller established himself as one of the league's most dominant defensive linemen, with the NFLPA identifying him as its NFL Defensive Lineman of the Year in 1969, and the Newspaper Enterprise Association (NEA) according him NFL Defensive Player of the Year honors in 1971.

Blessed with tremendous speed and agility, the 6'6", 247-pound Eller also possessed great strength, with former Vikings teammate Jim Lindsey once saying, "He was the greatest physical specimen I have ever seen. It was as if he had been chiseled out of stone."

St. Louis Cardinals Hall of Fame offensive tackle Dan Dierdorf said of his longtime adversary, "If you took some clay and tried to sculpt the perfect defensive end, I don't know if you'd do any better than what God did with Carl Eller. He was perfect."

Impressed with Eller's unique skill set, Kansas City Chiefs defensive lineman Aaron Brown stated prior to Super Bowl IV, "I think he's the best defensive end in pro football."

Meanwhile, Ron Yary, who joined the Vikings in 1968, said, "I have more problems in practice than against any defensive end I've faced in a game. . . . You know, he's going to make me into a good offensive tackle."

Yet, even with all his physical talent, Eller possessed several intangible qualities that helped him attain elite status among NFL defensive ends, with longtime teammate Paul Krause stating, "Carl was a great athlete and football player. He was a very determined player that was never satisfied with just playing the game. You had to respect him because he wasn't out there to play. He was out there to win."

Motivated by his desire to be considered one of the greatest players ever at his position, Eller once stated, "I'd like to be remembered as a great defensive end. I'd like to go down alongside all the other great defensive linemen that have ever played the game. I'd like to stand out in all the things—tackling the quarterback, defending against the run—all the things that make a great defensive end. I'd like the simple statement: 'He was a great defensive end.'"

Speaking of Eller in 1972, Vikings general manager Jim Finks said, "He has the physical requirements. Beyond that, intelligence. And he still has the young man's approach to the game. He likes it, enjoys it, and wants to be the best."

Vikings head coach Bud Grant suggested, "One way you achieve greatness in this game is through super ability. Carl has that, and he also has super durability. He plays with pain, with hurts, and he plays just as well. Some players play with pain, but they cannot play as well when they are hurting."

Eller's mental and physical toughness enabled him to appear in 209 out of a possible 210 games during his 15 seasons in Minnesota, starting all but eight of those contests at his familiar position of left defensive end. Remaining a force at that post the entire time, Eller recorded an unofficial total of 44 sacks from 1975 to 1977, playing the last of those seasons at 35 years of age.

Eller spent one more year in Minnesota, sharing playing time with Mark Mullaney in 1978, before being dealt to the Seattle Seahawks following the conclusion of the campaign. After one season in Seattle, Eller announced his retirement, ending his career with an unofficial total of 133 sacks, 130 of which came as a member of the Vikings. In addition to recording more sacks than any other player in team annals, Eller ranks among the franchise's all-time leaders with 23 fumble recoveries (2nd), 15 seasons played (tied for 3rd), and 209 games played (4th).

Eller continued to draw words of praise from those he competed with and against following his retirement, with Hall of Fame offensive tackle Bob Brown, when asked to rank the best defensive ends he played against, saying, "Well, I'd rank the top five defensive ends I played against as Carl Eller, Claude Humphrey, L.C. Greenwood, Deacon Jones, and everybody else."

Unfortunately, an unsavory side of Eller has surfaced since he retired as an active player. After admitting several years earlier that he had played under the influence of drugs, Eller told the House of Representatives Select Committee on Narcotics Abuse and Control during a July 1985 hearing on cocaine abuse, "I was then one of the highest-paid defensive ends in the league, earning about $100,000. I figure I must have spent about $2,000 a week on drugs because almost my total income went into chemicals. . . . Cocaine certainly ended my career prematurely and caused me tremendous financial and personal loss. I'm a very lucky person not to have gone to prison. I was always paranoid that I would be arrested."

In an effort to get his life together, Eller became a licensed drug and alcohol counselor, founding a group of substance-abuse clinics in the Twin Cities called Triumph Life Centers in 1986. Eight years later, he obtained a degree in human services from Metropolitan State University and went to work for the Minnesota Department of Human Services, addressing issues of health disparities between white people and people of color. However, since that time, Eller has strayed from the straight-and-narrow on multiple occasions, pleading guilty to DUI charges in 2006, and serving 60 days in the county workhouse in 2008 after being arrested for fourth-degree assault of a police officer and second-degree refusal to submit to chemical testing.

VIKINGS CAREER HIGHLIGHTS

Best Season

Eller played his best ball for the Vikings from 1968 to 1971, earning four consecutive First-Team All-Pro nominations during that time. The NEA also named Eller its NFL Defensive Player of the Year in 1971. But Eller had his finest all-around season in 1969, when he established career-high marks with 15 sacks and 10 tackles for loss, earning in the process NFLPA NFL Defensive Lineman of the Year honors and a runner-up finish to Chicago's Dick Butkus in the NEA NFL Defensive Player of the Year voting.

Memorable Moments/Greatest Performances

Eller scored the only touchdown of his career during a 27–22 victory over San Francisco on October 25, 1964, when, after teammate Jim Marshall separated 49ers quarterback John Brodie from the football, he picked up the loose pigskin and rumbled 45 yards into the opponent's end zone.

Eller lit the scoreboard again during a 31–29 loss to Detroit on September 26, 1965, when he sacked Lions QB Milt Plum in the end zone for a safety.

Eller led the defensive charge when the Vikings sacked Bart Starr eight times during a 19–7 win over the Packers on October 5, 1969.

Eller starred during the Vikings' 23–20 win over the Los Angeles Rams in the divisional round of the 1969 playoffs, recording two sacks of Roman

Gabriel, the second of which resulted in a safety that increased Minnesota's lead to three points late in the fourth quarter.

Eller led an assault on Randy Johnson in the final game of the 1970 regular season that resulted in the Atlanta quarterback being sacked a total of nine times during a lopsided 37–7 Vikings victory.

Eller recorded the only interception of his career during a 38–0 man-handling of the Falcons on November 9, 1975.

Although the Vikings ended up losing the 1975 NFC championship game to the Cowboys by a score of 17–14 on Roger Staubach's controversial last-minute 50-yard "Hail Mary" touchdown pass to Drew Pearson, Eller starred in defeat, sacking the Dallas signal-caller three times.

Eller also came up big for the Vikings in the 1976 NFC championship game, sacking Pat Haden twice during a 24–13 victory over the Los Angeles Rams.

Eller scored the first two points that the Vikings registered during a 9–3 win over Tampa Bay on September 24, 1977, when he sacked Buccaneers quarterback Randy Hedberg in the end zone for a safety.

Notable Achievements

- Missed just one game in 15 seasons, appearing in 209 out of 210 contests.
- Scored one defensive touchdown.
- Recorded 15 sacks twice.
- Finished third in NFL with four fumble recoveries in 1966.
- Holds Vikings career record for most sacks (130).
- Ranks among Vikings career leaders with 23 fumble recoveries (2nd), 15 seasons played (tied for 3rd), and 209 games played (4th).
- Nine-time division champion (1968, 1969, 1970, 1971, 1973, 1974, 1975, 1976, and 1977).
- 1969 NFL champion.
- Three-time NFC champion (1973, 1974, and 1976).
- 1969 NFLPA NFL Defensive Lineman of the Year.
- 1971 NEA NFL Defensive Player of the Year.
- Six-time Pro Bowl selection (1968, 1969, 1970, 1971, 1973, and 1974).
- Five-time First-Team All-Pro selection (1968, 1969, 1970, 1971, and 1973).
- 1972 Second-Team All-Pro selection.

- Four-time First-Team All-NFC selection (1970, 1971, 1973, and 1975).
- Two-time Second-Team All-NFC selection (1972 and 1974).
- Pro Football Reference All-1970s First Team.
- NFL 1970s All-Decade First Team.
- Inducted into Minnesota Vikings Ring of Honor in 2002.
- Elected to Pro Football Hall of Fame in 2004.

5

RANDALL MCDANIEL

tremendous force on the left side of the Vikings' offensive line for 12 seasons, Randall McDaniel established himself as one of the greatest guards in NFL history during his time in Minnesota. Perhaps the most versatile player ever to man his position, McDaniel combined speed, strength, and tenacity to dominate his opponent at the line of scrimmage, earning him the respect and admiration of his peers, who accorded him NFC Offensive Lineman of the Year honors once and Pro Bowl honors 11 straight times. A member of Vikings teams that won four division titles and advanced to the playoffs nine times, McDaniel also gained All-Pro recognition on nine occasions, before being further honored following the conclusion of his playing career by being named to the NFL 100 All-Time Team and elected to the Pro Football Hall of Fame.

Born in Phoenix, Arizona, on December 19, 1964, Randall Cornell McDaniel grew up in nearby Avondale, where his size prevented him from competing in sports with children his own age. Recalling his earliest days as an athlete, McDaniel said, "My parents never pushed sports on us, but I did spend a lot of time in the streets participating, mostly with older kids. . . . Most of my friends got involved with Pop Warner football, but I was too big. I had to pass on it until high school, when I started as a sophomore playing tight end and linebacker. Early on in my youth, I had played most sports except football. Later, I was into just about everything, playing football, basketball, and baseball. I also ran track at Agua Fria High School."

Excelling in multiple sports at Agua Fria, McDaniel not only starred on the gridiron, but also averaged 24.2 points per game on the hardwood one year, threw the shotput 55 feet and the discus more than 160 feet, and posted a personal-best time of 10.64 seconds in the 100-meter dash. Particularly proud of his accomplishments as a sprinter, McDaniel, who weighed 220 pounds at the time, remembered, "I'm sure opponents were thinking, 'No way this guy can run.' I'd just smile at them. The gun would go off,

Randall McDaniel's brilliant play at left guard earned him a spot on the NFL 100 All-Time Team.
Courtesy of MearsOnlineAuctions.com

the race would be over, and I'd look across at the guys and say, 'Surprised you all, didn't I?'"

An exceptional power forward in basketball as well, McDaniel received the following review from former Agua Fria Union coach, athletic director, and assistant principal, O. K. Fulton: "He was a Charles Barkley-type force. He could jump and do all the things inside like Charles Barkley. But he could not shoot from the outside. He would have had to develop that."

Fulton then added, "He was a wonderful basketball player, but football was where we ultimately thought he would go."

Proving Fulton to be prophetic, McDaniel accepted an athletic scholarship from Arizona State University, where he lettered in football for four years, transitioning from tight end to offensive guard as a sophomore. Performing brilliantly his last two seasons at ASU, McDaniel helped lead the Sun Devils to a 10-1-1 record and a victory over Michigan in the Rose Bowl his junior year, earning in the process First-Team All–Pac-10 and All-America honors. McDaniel followed that up by winning the Morris Trophy as the best lineman in the Pac-10 his senior year, while also gaining consensus All-America recognition.

Yet, despite McDaniel's exceptional play at the collegiate level, pro scouts remained concerned over his relative lack of size heading into the 1988 NFL Draft. Although the Vikings ultimately selected him with the 19th overall pick after he posted a time of 4.6 seconds in the 40-yard dash and registered a 37-inch vertical leap at the NFL combine, the doubts that others expressed over his ability to succeed as a pro due to his somewhat smallish 6'3", 270-pound frame provided McDaniel with additional motivation, as he later revealed when he said, "I knew I was just as strong as all those guys. I just didn't have that size they wanted to see. Everybody assumed that if you're undersized, you're going to wear down. . . . I looked at it the opposite way. I figured if the guys were bigger than me, that meant they're going to wear down because I'm going to be in better shape with my quickness and strength."

McDaniel continued, "I went back to my powerlifting days. I always beat the big guys in the powerlifting meet, and I thought, 'What's going to be different for myself?'"

After assuming the role of a backup in his first game as a pro, McDaniel joined the Vikings' starting unit in Week 2 of the 1988 campaign, performing so well the rest of the year that he not only earned a spot on the NFL All-Rookie Team, but, also, Second-Team All-NFC honors. McDaniel subsequently missed two games in 1989, before beginning a string of 10 consecutive seasons during which he started every game at left guard for the Vikings. Named to the Pro Bowl 11 straight times from 1989 to 1999, McDaniel also gained All-Pro recognition in nine of those seasons, being named to the First Team seven times and the Second Team twice.

McDaniel managed to perform at an elite level even though he employed an unorthodox pre-snap stance that Gary Zimmerman, who played left tackle next to him for five seasons, once called "the worst stance I've ever seen in the NFL." Bending his left leg at an awkward angle, McDaniel squared off against his opponent with his toes pointed back and his ankle practically flat on the ground. Nevertheless, the results proved to be devastating, with Zimmerman adding, "Randall was the strongest man I ever played with and the fastest lineman I ever played with."

Although McDaniel gradually added some 15 pounds of muscle onto his frame, increasing his weight to more than 285 pounds, he continued to display extraordinary quickness, with former Vikings teammate Warren Moon recalling, "One time, against New Orleans at the Metrodome, Randall turned the corner and there was no one for him to block. In that situation, he's taught to turn it upfield and the back will catch up to him. Well, Amp Lee couldn't catch him. It was strange seeing a man that big run that fast. And then he just destroyed some poor defensive back."

Making good use of McDaniel's agility, the Vikings often lined him up as a fullback in short-yardage and goal-line situations, where he excelled as a lead blocker. McDaniel even caught a touchdown pass on a goal-line play in the Pro Bowl. Extremely strong as well, McDaniel had the ability to either outmaneuver or overpower his opponent at the point of attack, with Buffalo Bills Hall of Fame defensive end Bruce Smith saying, "Randall was a beast. I cannot remember facing another guard that possessed the ability, the tenaciousness, the strength; he was just incredible. Once he locked on to you, you weren't going anywhere."

Former Vikings offensive coordinator Brian Billick also had high praise for McDaniel, stating, "Randall is probably the greatest athlete to play guard in the history of the NFL. There wasn't anything you couldn't do with Randall because he could do it all."

Also known for his tenacity and competitive spirit, McDaniel drew comparisons to former Vikings center Mick Tingelhoff from longtime Minnesota offensive line coach John Michels, who suggested, "Randall was a young Mick. He wouldn't say boo to you, but he'd beat you down . . . Mick liked to tangle, and so did Randall. If you went after Randall on the field, he'd come right at you and was ready to fight until one of you was dead. And my money was always on Randall, just like it was with Mick."

Meanwhile, former Vikings and Buccaneers center Jeff Christy spoke of McDaniel's character and leadership ability when he said, "He was the consummate pro. He never seemed out of shape. He did what he had to do in the locker room. When somebody needed to speak up, he spoke up. He was just a great all-around player and person."

Longtime Vikings teammate Anthony Carter added, "Randall was a great player with high expectations for himself and the team. It was as important to him, if not even more, to become a great teacher working with kids."

McDaniel continued to star for the Vikings at left guard until 1999, when the team surprisingly released him at season's end after he had earned his 11th straight Pro Bowl selection. Although the Vikings claimed at the time that they parted ways with him due to salary cap constraints, McDaniel later revealed that he received a letter from team management stating that it no longer felt he had the ability to compete at an extremely high level. McDaniel left Minnesota having started every game in each of the previous 10 seasons, missing just two contests in his 12 years with the Vikings.

Signed by Tampa Bay just one week later, McDaniel drew praise from Buccaneers head coach Tony Dungy, who said, "We feel extremely fortunate to sign a player with Randall's talent, experience, and leadership qualities. Randall is one of the best linemen this league has ever produced, and he will have an immediate impact on our offensive line."

McDaniel ended up spending two seasons in Tampa Bay, helping the Buccaneers advance to the playoffs both years, and earning the last of his 12 Pro Bowl nominations, before announcing his retirement following the conclusion of the 2001 campaign. He subsequently signed a one-day contract with the Vikings on February 27, 2002, that enabled him to officially retire as a member of the team.

Since retiring as an active player, McDaniel, who began working with children while he was still in college, has continued to assist in their development. The day he announced his retirement, McDaniel got his license to work full-time in elementary education. He now lives in Shorewood, Minnesota, where he works as a basic skills instructor at Hilltop Primary School in the Westonka Public School District. A member of that institution's special education department, McDaniel helps instruct a small group of youngsters from the minute they get off the bus in the morning until he puts them back on the bus at the end of the day.

VIKINGS CAREER HIGHLIGHTS

Best Season

It could be argued that McDaniel played his best ball for the Vikings in 1998, when he allowed just 1½ sacks the entire year, in helping them score a then-NFL record 556 points, with his exceptional blocking prompting Pro Football Reference to assign him an "approximate value" of 18 that represents the highest grade of his career. However, with McDaniel earning NFL Offensive Lineman of the Year and NFLPA NFC Offensive Lineman of the Year honors in 1992, we'll identify that as his finest season.

Memorable Moments/Greatest Performances

As is the case with any offensive lineman, McDaniel typically found himself living vicariously through the accomplishments of others. That being the case, the performance of the Minnesota offense must be examined to determine how well McDaniel likely played on any given day.

McDaniel helped the Vikings amass 426 yards of total offense and gain a season-high 209 yards on the ground during a 45–3 manhandling of the New Orleans Saints on December 4, 1988.

McDaniel and his line-mates dominated the Packers at the point of attack during a 26–14 win on October 15, 1989, with the Vikings rushing for a season-high 238 yards.

McDaniel and his cohorts once again controlled the line of scrimmage against Green Bay on November 17, 1991, with the Vikings rushing for 231 yards and amassing 443 yards of total offense during a 35–21 win over the Packers.

McDaniel helped the Vikings amass 436 yards of total offense during a 26–24 win over the Tampa Bay Buccaneers on December 8, 1991, with 296 of those yards coming on the ground.

McDaniel helped pave the way for Vikings running backs to gain a season-high total of 212 yards on the ground during a 42–14 rout of the Bears on September 18, 1994.

McDaniel anchored an offensive line that enabled the Vikings to amass 544 yards of total offense during a 43–24 win over the Saints on November 19, 1995.

Notable Achievements

- Missed just two games in 12 seasons, starting every contest in each of last 10 seasons.
- Four-time division champion (1989, 1992, 1994, and 1998).
- Member of 1988 NFL All-Rookie Team.
- 1992 NFLPA NFC Offensive Lineman of the Year.
- 1992 NFL Offensive Lineman of the Year.
- 11-time Pro Bowl selection (1989, 1990, 1991, 1992, 1993, 1994, 1995, 1996, 1997, 1998, and 1999).
- Seven-time First-Team All-Pro selection (1990, 1992, 1993, 1994, 1995, 1996, and 1998).
- Two-time Second-Team All-Pro selection (1991 and 1997).

- Nine-time First-Team All-NFC selection (1990, 1991, 1992, 1993, 1994, 1995, 1996, 1997, and 1998).
- Two-time Second-Team All-NFC selection (1988 and 1989).
- Pro Football Reference All-1990s First Team.
- NFL 1990s All-Decade First Team.
- Named to NFL 100 All-Time Team in 2019.
- Inducted into Minnesota Vikings Ring of Honor in 2006.
- Elected to Pro Football Hall of Fame in 2009.

6

CRIS CARTER

The Vikings' all-time leader in every major pass-receiving category, Cris Carter overcame serious addictions to alcohol and drugs to establish himself as one of the greatest wide receivers in NFL history. Spending 12 of his 16 years in the league in Minnesota, Carter surpassed 100 receptions twice and 1,000 receiving yards eight times while wearing the Purple and Gold, ending his career second only to Jerry Rice all-time in receptions, receiving yards, and TD catches. Along the way, Carter helped the Vikings make eight playoff appearances and win four division titles, earning in the process eight trips to the Pro Bowl, three All-Pro nominations, and four All-NFC selections. And following the conclusion of his playing career, Carter received the additional honors of having his #80 retired by the Vikings and being inducted into both the team's Ring of Honor and the Pro Football Hall of Fame.

Born in Troy, Ohio, on November 25, 1965, Graduel Christopher Darin Carter attended local Heywood Elementary School, before moving with his mother, three brothers, and two sisters to Middletown, Ohio, at the age of 12. Growing up in poverty in a Middletown housing project, Carter spent much of his youth living in a small four-bedroom apartment that offered little in the way of privacy. After getting his start in football with a group of neighborhood friends, Carter began using the name Cris in the seventh grade, later saying that he did not believe he would ever become famous with the name Graduel.

An outstanding all-around athlete, Carter excelled in multiple sports at Middletown High School, recalling years later, "Besides football, I played basketball in high school. I could have played football or basketball in college. My high school coach told me if I wasn't Isiah Thomas, then I should try to play football. He believed I could make a huge impact as a big receiver. At the time, I was playing quarterback, but he thought I could be a fabulous receiver. He thought I could make first-team high school All-American. I was like, 'I don't want to make All-American. I might not

Cris Carter holds franchise records for most receptions, receiving yards, and TD catches.
Courtesy of George A. Kitrinos

even play football next year.' It was before my junior year of high school. In basketball, I played two guard (shooting guard), three (forward). I could play one (point guard). If I went to college, I would have played one."

Recruited by several major colleges, Carter ultimately accepted an athletic scholarship from Ohio State University, where he initially planned to compete in both football and basketball, before choosing to focus exclusively on the former after performing brilliantly as a freshman, when he set a Rose Bowl record by making nine receptions for 172 yards. Developing a reputation during his time at OSU for his exceptional hands, extraordinary body control, and precise route-running, Carter drew particular attention to himself with an amazing catch he made at the 1985 Citrus Bowl, when he gathered in a pass that quarterback Jim Karsatos intended to throw away. Claiming that he never saw another reception like it, Karsatos later said, "When I finally saw it on film, he was tiptoeing the sidelines and he jumped up and caught the ball left-handed by the point of the football at least a yard out of bounds. Then, he somehow levitated back in bounds to get both his feet in bounds. I swear to this day he actually levitated to get back in bounds. When I saw it on film, it just blew me away."

After gaining All-America recognition as a junior, Carter secretly signed with notorious sports agent Norby Walters prior to the start of his senior year. But, when NCAA officials learned of the secret pact, they ruled Carter ineligible, forcing him to spend his final year of college watching the action from the stands.

Subsequently selected by the Philadelphia Eagles in the fourth round of the 1987 NFL Supplemental Draft, with the third overall pick, Carter saw very little action as a rookie, making just five receptions for 84 yards and two touchdowns. Assuming a far more prominent role in 1988, Carter made 39 receptions for 761 yards and six touchdowns, before catching 45 passes, amassing 605 receiving yards, and finishing third in the NFL with 11 touchdown receptions the following year.

Although Carter performed well for the Eagles his last two seasons in Philadelphia, head coach Buddy Ryan chose to release him following the conclusion of the 1989 campaign, famously saying at the time, "All he did was catch touchdowns." However, Carter later revealed that Ryan based his decision solely on the receiver's preoccupation with partying, drugs, and alcohol, admitting that he drank heavily and used large amounts of ecstasy and marijuana. Speaking to a group of NFL rookies in 2005, Carter said, "When I was in Philadelphia, we used to cash our paychecks after practice and go to Atlantic City. We would party and gamble all night. We'd stay there and drive back to Philadelphia in the morning. We'd sleep in the parking lot and tell the security guards to wake us up when everyone else got there. . . . You guys don't have the market cornered on dumb stuff. It's unbelievable all the dumb stuff I did."

Carter then went on to say, "Buddy Ryan told me he couldn't depend on me. He didn't know if I would flunk a drug test. He didn't know what I might do. . . . I knew exactly what Buddy was doing. He told me he would never reveal my past to anyone. Someone asked him a question, 'Why did you cut him?' And he said, 'Well, he only caught touchdowns. He wasn't a complete receiver.' It was what he decided to do to try to protect me."

Claimed off waivers by the Vikings on September 4, 1990, Carter began to turn his life around after he arrived in Minnesota, attending drug and alcohol counseling sessions that helped him attain sobriety. Meanwhile, Carter spent his first year in the Twin Cities serving primarily as a backup to Anthony Carter and Hassan Jones, making just 27 receptions for 413 yards and three touchdowns, before displacing Jones as a starter the following season. Emerging as one of the league's better wideouts in 1991, Carter caught 72 passes, amassed 962 receiving yards, and scored five touchdowns. He followed that up by making 53 receptions for 681 yards and six touchdowns in 1992, before beginning an exceptional eight-year run during which he posted the following numbers:

YEAR	RECS	REC YDS	TD RECS
1993	86	1,071	9
1994	**122**	1,256	7
1995	122	1,371	**17**
1996	96	1,163	10
1997	89	1,069	**13**
1998	78	1,011	12
1999	90	1,241	**13**
2000	96	1,274	9

In addition to surpassing 1,000 receiving yards all eight years, Carter annually ranked among the league leaders in receptions and TD catches, with his 122 receptions in 1994 setting a new single-season NFL record that Detroit's Herman Moore broke one year later. Carter also topped the circuit in touchdown catches three times, with his brilliant play throughout the period earning him eight straight Pro Bowl selections and three All-Pro nominations. More importantly, the Vikings made the playoffs seven times, capturing the division title in 1994, 1998, and 2000.

Although the 6'3", 205-pound Carter did not possess great running speed, he made up for whatever he lacked in that area with his exceptional athletic ability, soft hands, and ability to use his body to shield defenders from the football. Known for his one-handed diving catches, Carter caught everything within his reach, with former Vikings coach Bud Grant saying, "Some guys worry about catching the ball, but Cris is beyond that. If Cris got a hand or a finger on it, you knew he was going to bring it in. He was concerned about what he would do before he caught the ball and after he caught it, but he didn't have to worry about catching it because he was so instinctive in that area."

One of the league's most acrobatic receivers, Carter also possessed excellent leaping ability and remarkable body control, allowing him to make the sideline or back-of-the-end-zone catch better than anyone else. Capable of manipulating his body like a contortionist, Carter displayed an uncanny ability to extend his entire body out of bounds, while tiptoeing the sideline or end zone marker with his feet. Expressing the belief that this quality separated Carter from the league's other top two wideouts, Jerry Rice and Michael Irvin, Vikings head coach Dennis Green stated, "I think Cris is more acrobatic and will make more difficult catches than those other guys. You see a pass that you think he has no chance to catch because it's too high or will go out of bounds, and then he does something that you don't believe. He'll dive for a ball and make a catch by scooping it, or he will keep the tips of his toes in bounds while reaching over the barrier to make a catch. Nobody else can do it like Cris."

Developing into a tireless worker after he arrived in Minnesota, Carter gradually evolved into an outstanding team leader, later serving as a mentor to Randy Moss after the latter joined the Vikings in 1998. In discussing Carter's leadership ability, fellow Vikings wideout Jake Reed said, "We had a long list of quarterbacks, but it's the receivers that make the QB really feel comfortable. We had a true leader—Cris Carter. He held us accountable as young receivers, and we really had to make sure that we ran our routes, got off the ball fast."

Unafraid to confront anyone on the team who he believed slacked off in any way, Carter stated, "My whole philosophy is it's not okay to make a mental mistake. I know if a guy is hanging out nightclubbing because he is hurting in the fourth quarter. When that's the case, I'm going to have something to say to him because the veterans are depending on him. My whole attitude, performance, and play is designed to get the most out of everyone on the team."

Carter had another solid year for the Vikings in 2001, finishing second on the team with 73 receptions, 871 receiving yards, and six TD catches, before exercising a clause in his contract that enabled him to become a free agent. Choosing to leave Minnesota, Carter left the Vikings having made 1,004 receptions, amassed 12,383 receiving yards, and caught 110 touchdown passes as a member of the team, with each of those figures representing a franchise record. Carter also ranks second in team annals in yards from scrimmage (12,407), all-purpose yards (12,410), and points scored (670).

After spending the spring of 2002 looking for a new team, Carter accepted a position as an analyst on HBO's *Inside the NFL*. However, he later returned to the field as a member of the Miami Dolphins, with whom he appeared in five games in 2002, before retiring for good at season's end with career totals of 1,101 receptions, 13,899 receiving yards, 130 touchdown catches, 13,940 yards from scrimmage, and 14,184 all-purpose yards.

Upon announcing his retirement, Carter expressed his appreciation to the Vikings and the people of the Twin Cities when he said, "When I went to Minnesota, I was a young kid. When I left, I was a full-grown man. I gained my sobriety there. There are so many things about Minnesota I will never forget. I will always be indebted to the people of Minnesota."

Since retiring as an active player, Carter, who now resides in Boca Raton, Florida, has worked on HBO's *Inside the NFL*, ESPN's *Sunday NFL Countdown* and *Monday Night Countdown*, and online at Yahoo Sports. He also owns Cris Carter's FAST Program, a sports training center in South Florida, and is a faculty member and assistant coach at St. Thomas Aquinas High School, where his son played wide receiver in 2008. In 2017, Carter began co-hosting *First Things First* with radio personality Nick Wright and moderator Jenna Wolfe on FS1, before being relieved of his duties following an altercation with station management in 2019. The outspoken and controversial Carter also ran into trouble after he encouraged players that he addressed at the 2014 NFL rookie symposium to get a "fall guy" that they could trust to take the blame if they got into trouble. The NFL subsequently removed the video of the speech from its website and released a statement, part of which read: "The comment was not representative of the message of the symposium or any other league program. . . . The comment was not repeated in the 2014 AFC session or this year's symposium." Carter later apologized for his remarks on Twitter, saying that he realized they offered bad advice, and that everyone should take responsibility for their own actions.

VIKINGS CAREER HIGHLIGHTS

Best Season

Carter earned First-Team All-Pro honors for the only two times in his career in 1994 and 1999, amassing 1,256 receiving yards, scoring seven touchdowns, and leading the NFL with 122 receptions in the first of those campaigns, before catching 90 passes for 1,241 yards and 13 touchdowns in the second. However, Carter proved to be slightly more productive in 1995, finishing second in the league with a total of 122 receptions that equaled the career-high mark he set one year earlier, while also amassing 1,371 receiving yards and leading the NFL with 17 touchdown receptions, which established a single-season franchise record that still stands.

Memorable Moments/Greatest Performances

Carter scored his first two touchdowns as a member of the Vikings during a 32–24 loss to the Philadelphia Eagles on October 15, 1990, collaborating with Rich Gannon on scoring plays that covered 42 and 78 yards. He finished the game with six catches for 151 yards and those two TDs.

Carter contributed to a 42–7 blowout of the Cincinnati Bengals on September 27, 1992, by making 11 receptions for 124 yards and two touchdowns, which came on passes of 15 and 30 yards from Gannon.

Carter played a huge role in Minnesota's 38–35 win over Miami on September 25, 1994, making seven receptions for 81 yards and three touchdowns, the longest of which went for 44 yards.

Although the Vikings lost to the Arizona Cardinals by a score of 17–7 on October 2, 1994, Carter had a big game, making 14 receptions for 167 yards.

Carter had another big day against New Orleans on November 6, 1994, catching 12 passes for 151 yards during a 21–20 win over the Saints.

Carter gave the Vikings a dramatic 33–27 overtime win over the Bears on December 1, 1994, by collaborating with Warren Moon on a 65-yard touchdown pass as time expired in OT. He finished the game with nine receptions for 124 yards and two touchdowns.

Carter contributed to a 30–24 overtime victory over the Arizona Cardinals on November 12, 1995, that the Vikings ended up winning on a 50-yard pass from Moon to Qadry Ismail by making 12 receptions for 157 yards and two touchdowns.

Carter followed that up by making 12 receptions for 137 yards and two touchdowns during a 43–24 win over the Saints on November 19, 1995, with his TDs coming on hookups of 15 and 20 yards with Warren Moon.

Carter starred during a 46–36 victory over the Cowboys on Thanksgiving Day 1998, finishing the game with seven catches for 135 yards and one touchdown, which came on a 54-yard pass from Randall Cunningham.

Carter earned NFC Offensive Player of the Week honors by making eight receptions for 144 yards and two touchdowns during a 23–20 win over the Denver Broncos on October 31, 1999, collaborating with Jeff George on scoring plays that covered 37 and 16 yards.

Carter led the Vikings to a 27–24 overtime victory over the Bears on November 14, 1999, by making nine receptions for 141 yards and three touchdowns.

Carter earned NFC Offensive Player of the Week honors by catching 11 passes for 136 yards and two touchdowns during a 35–27 win over the San Diego Chargers on November 28, 1999.

Carter contributed to a 13–7 win over the Miami Dolphins on September 10, 2000, by making nine receptions for 168 yards.

Carter made history during a 24–17 victory over the Detroit Lions on November 30, 2000, when his 4-yard TD catch made him just the second player ever to record 1,000 career receptions.

Carter helped lead the Vikings to a 34–16 win over the Saints in the divisional round of the 2000 NFC playoffs by making eight receptions for 120 yards and one touchdown, which came on a 17-yard pass from Daunte Culpepper.

Carter topped 100 receiving yards for the final time in his career on October 14, 2001, making eight receptions for 111 yards and one touchdown during a 31–26 win over the Lions, with his TD coming on a 47-yard pass from Culpepper.

Notable Achievements

- Missed just four games in 12 seasons, starting 144 consecutive contests from 1993 to 2001.
- Surpassed 100 receptions twice, topping 90 receptions three other times.
- Surpassed 1,000 receiving yards eight times.
- Scored at least 10 touchdowns five times.
- Scored more than 100 points once.

- Led NFL in receptions once and touchdown receptions three times.
- Finished second in NFL in receptions once and touchdowns once.
- Finished third in NFL in touchdown receptions once and touchdowns once.
- Led Vikings in receptions 10 times and receiving yards six times.
- Holds Vikings single-season records for most receptions (122 in 1994 and 1995) and most touchdown receptions (17 in 1995).
- Holds Vikings career records for most receptions (1,004), receiving yards (12,383), touchdown receptions (110), and touchdowns (110).
- Ranks among Vikings career leaders with 12,407 yards from scrimmage (2nd), 12,410 all-purpose yards (2nd), and 670 points scored (2nd).
- Ranks among NFL career leaders with 1,101 receptions (6th), 130 touchdown receptions (4th), and 131 touchdowns (8th).
- Four-time division champion (1992, 1994, 1998, and 2000).
- Three-time NFC Offensive Player of the Week.
- November 1999 NFC Offensive Player of the Month.
- 1999 NFL Walter Payton Man of the Year.
- Eight-time Pro Bowl selection (1993, 1994, 1995, 1996, 1997, 1998, 1999, and 2000).
- Two-time First-Team All-Pro selection (1994 and 1999).
- 1995 Second-Team All-Pro selection.
- Two-time First-Team All-NFC (1994 and 1999).
- Two-time Second-Team All-NFC selection (1995 and 1996).
- Pro Football Reference All-1990s Second Team.
- NFL 1990s All-Decade First Team.
- #80 retired by Vikings.
- Inducted into Minnesota Vikings Ring of Honor in 2003.
- Elected to Pro Football Hall of Fame in 2013.

7

RANDY MOSS

Perhaps the most naturally gifted wide receiver in NFL history, Randy Moss established himself as one of the most dynamic offensive forces ever to play the game during his 15 years in the league. Blessed with extraordinary physical talent, Moss possessed the ability to score from anywhere on the field, with his 156 career touchdown receptions placing him second only to Jerry Rice all-time. Having many of his finest years for the Vikings, Moss spent parts of eight seasons in Minnesota, during which time he surpassed 100 receptions twice and 1,000 receiving yards six times. The franchise's single-season record holder for most receiving yards and TD catches, Moss ranks extremely high in team annals in every major pass-receiving category, with his exceptional play in the Twin Cities earning him five Pro Bowl selections and three All-Pro nominations. A member of Vikings teams that made four playoff appearances and won two division titles, Moss later received the additional honors of being included on the NFL Network's 2010 list of the 100 Greatest Players in NFL History, being named to the NFL 100 All-Time Team, and being elected to the Pro Football Hall of Fame.

Born in Charleston, West Virginia, on February 13, 1977, Randy Gene Moss moved with his family at a young age to nearby Rand, where his mother provided for her three children by working long hours as a nurse's aide. Hoping to lessen his mother's burden, Moss dreamed of one day playing either football or basketball professionally, first displaying his considerable ability in both sports at DuPont High School, where he also starred as an outfielder in baseball and a sprinter in track. A two-time West Virginia Player of the Year on the hardwood, Moss averaged 30.2 points, 13.7 rebounds, 5.1 steals, 3.8 blocks, and 3.1 assists per game as a senior, ending his three-year career with a school-record 1,713 points scored. Equally proficient on the gridiron, Moss led the DuPont Panthers to back-to-back state championships by excelling as a wide receiver, free safety, and return-man, with his outstanding play in all phases of the game earning him

Randy Moss surpassed 100 receptions twice and 1,000 receiving yards six times as a member of the Vikings.
Courtesy of Mike Morbeck

West Virginia Football Player of the Year and *Parade* magazine High School All-America honors his senior year.

Despite his many athletic contributions to DuPont High, Moss often found himself being viewed as an outsider by his predominantly white class-mates, some of whom formed a group that became known as "Red Neck Alley" for their racial intolerance. Finding particularly objectionable Moss's romantic relationship with a white student named Libby Offutt, the mem-bers of "Red Neck Alley" frequently made life difficult for Moss, who became persona non grata at the school his senior year after he took part in a racially charged fight that left one person hospitalized. Although Moss merely backed a friend in a hallway altercation against a white student who had allegedly used racist comments toward him, he ended up paying a steep price, spending 30 days in jail and being expelled from school for kicking his friend's assailant. Furthermore, Moss, who previously signed a letter of intent to play football for the Notre Dame Fighting Irish, had his scholarship rescinded.

Fortunately for Moss, he had made an extremely favorable impression on Notre Dame head coach Lou Holtz, who called him "the best high school football player I've ever seen." After Holtz urged Florida State head coach Bobby Bowden, who had a reputation for handling troubled players, to give the youngster a chance, Moss received a full scholarship to that institution. However, before he ever took the field for the Seminoles, Moss tested positive for marijuana, prompting Bowden to revoke his scholarship, and forcing him to spend another 90 days in jail.

Contacting Division I-AA Marshall University head coach Bob Pruett upon his release, Moss received good news when the former FSU assistant agreed to give him a third chance. Moss went on to star for the Thundering Herd, earning First-Team All-America, Division I-AA Offensive Player of the Year, and Southern Conference Freshman of the Year honors by scoring 28 touchdowns and amassing 1,074 receiving yards and 1,686 all-purpose yards. Performing even better the following year, Moss made 96 receptions for 1,820 yards, scored 26 touchdowns, and amassed 2,356 all-purpose yards, with his brilliant play earning him First-Team All-America and MAC Offensive Player of the Year honors. Moss also won the Fred Biletnikoff Award, presented annually to college football's top wide receiver.

Choosing to forgo his remaining time at Marshall, Moss declared himself eligible for the 1998 NFL Draft, which he entered as one of the nation's most highly touted prospects. But, with most teams expressing concerns over his off-field behavior, Moss had to wait until the Vikings finally selected him with the 21st overall pick, prompting him to say at the time that those organizations that bypassed him "will regret it once they see what kind of a player I am and what kind of a guy I really am."

Living up to his words, Moss ended up taking the league by storm, earning NFL Offensive Rookie of the Year, Pro Bowl, and First-Team All-Pro honors by making 69 receptions for 1,313 yards and topping the circuit with a franchise-record 17 touchdown receptions, with his extraordinary performance prompting Randall McDaniel to say years later, "That rookie season of 1998 was something special. You knew he was going to be something special from that first game on. You just knew watching him in practice he was going to be one of the Vikings' greats. It was just fun to watch him play."

Marveling over Moss's tremendous physical gifts, then–Vikings offensive coordinator Brian Billick said, "Nobody, and I mean nobody, has all the physical skills Randy has. They just don't. That kid loves to play football."

Moss followed up his virtuoso performance with five more brilliant seasons, compiling the following numbers from 1999 to 2003:

YEAR	RECS	REC YDS	TD RECS
1999	80	1,413	11
2000	77	1,437	**15**
2001	82	1,233	10
2002	106	1,347	7
2003	111	1,632	**17**

In addition to leading the NFL in touchdown receptions in two of those years, Moss finished second in the league in receiving yards twice, with his 1,632 yards gained through the air in 2003 setting a new Vikings record that still stands. That same season, Moss also began to assume more of a role of leadership on the team, taking young receivers Kelly Campbell and Nate Burleson under his wing and teaching them the nuances of excelling at the position in the NFL. Moss's exceptional play over that five-year period earned him four trips to the Pro Bowl and three First-Team All-Pro nominations. Meanwhile, the Vikings advanced to the playoffs twice and won the division title in 2000.

Blessed with great speed, good size, soft hands, and exceptional leaping ability, the 6'4", 210-pound Moss proved to be a mismatch for anyone who attempted to cover him one-on-one. Capable of outrunning or outjumping any defensive back in the league, Moss typically found himself being double- or even triple-teamed, with teammate Cris Carter stating, "I've never seen concentration on one player like Randy faces."

In discussing the manner with which opposing defenses attempted to slow Moss down by assigning him multiple defenders, Brian Billick suggested, "You can stop Randy. But you're going to have to give up the game to do it."

Despite the efforts of opposing teams, Moss remained confident in his ability to positively impact every game in which he played, proclaiming, "Excluding nobody, I'm the best player in the National Football League."

On another occasion, Moss said, "You can't stop me in bump. And you definitely can't stop me playing off. You just try to contain me and stop me from getting a lot of catches."

Moss's Vikings teammates also had a great deal of confidence in him, with backup QB Bubby Brister saying, "He's so confident in himself that, even if he is doubled, he likes his chances. He's probably right. He's so good it's hard to argue with him."

Vikings quarterback Daunte Culpepper stated, "Having someone like Randy in a game-breaking moment is a tremendous advantage."

Reserve wideout Matthew Hatchette added, "Playing football with Randy is like playing basketball with Michael Jordan."

Meanwhile, former Vikings offensive coordinator Scott Linehan spoke of Moss's intelligence when he said, "He has a tremendous football IQ. The guy has the ability to dominate a game even when he's not touching the ball."

Still, Moss had his shortcomings, often drawing criticism for the manner with which he tended to shy away from contact, the lack of discipline he occasionally displayed when running his routes, and the lackadaisical attitude he sometimes exhibited on the playing field. Admitting that he did not always put forth a 100 percent effort, Moss once said, "My concentration and focus level tends to go down sometimes when I'm in a bad mood. . . . If it's early in the game and the team's not doing well, I get frustrated when I don't get the ball, because I think I can spark the team and get the crowd into it."

Moss's questionable attitude caused him to develop a reputation as a selfish player, with New Orleans Saints offensive lineman Kyle Turley stating, "As a player, I like Randy Moss—he's got incredible talent, and I think he's nasty. But, if he was on my team and he pulled the shit he pulls, I'd walk up to him on the sideline and punch him in the face."

More than anything, though, Moss received criticism for his immature behavior, both on and off the playing field. After being fined by the league office twice in 1999—once for abusing a side judge and once for squirting water at an official—Moss found himself being censured in 2001 for telling reporters, "I play when I want to play." Moss subsequently attempted to quell the backlash he received for that remark by explaining, "I don't think people get the meaning of 'I play when I want to play.' You think a guy like Randy Moss is going to blow off a game, as much as I love football? Really, I'm just being smart. I'm not going to go full speed every time when I don't need to." Nevertheless, Moss's statement caused others to view him in a very negative light, making him, in their minds, the embodiment of the spoiled professional athlete.

Moss again drew unwanted attention to himself in September 2002, when he spent a night in jail after being charged with two misdemeanors in connection with an altercation with a traffic officer in Minneapolis, who he knocked down after bumping with his SUV. Police also discovered a small amount of marijuana in the ashtray of his Lexus. Moss provided more fodder for his critics when he walked off the field during the latter stages of a 21–18 loss to the Washington Redskins in the final game of the 2004 regular season, even as the Vikings prepared to attempt an onside kick. Meanwhile, FOX announcers called Moss's "mooning" gesture against Green Bay in the wild card round of the 2004 playoffs "obscene."

Having finally grown weary of Moss's antics, the Vikings worked out a trade with the Raiders in March 2005 in which they sent the enigmatic receiver to Oakland for the seventh overall pick in that year's draft, another late-round selection, and linebacker Napoleon Harris. Moss subsequently spent two years in Oakland, surpassing 1,000 receiving yards for the seventh time in his career in 2005, before eventually wearing out his welcome there as well. Dealt to the Patriots prior to the start of the 2007 campaign, Moss had three extremely productive years in New England, establishing a new NFL record in 2007 by catching 23 touchdown passes, while also making 98 receptions for 1,493 yards. Earning the respect and admiration of Bill Belichick during his time in New England, Moss received high praise from his head coach, who called him "the smartest receiver I've ever been around." Belichick went on to compare Moss's ability to see the field and anticipate plays to that of Tom Brady and Lawrence Taylor, who he coached in New York, saying that he not only knew what he was doing on a play, but what everybody else on the field was doing.

However, prior to the start of the 2010 regular season, Moss told CBS Sports that the Patriots' unwillingness to offer him a contract extension made him feel unwanted in New England. After Moss requested a trade a few weeks later, the Patriots dealt him to the Vikings for a third-round pick in the 2011 NFL Draft. Moss's second stint in Minnesota did not last very long, though, since differences with head coach Brad Childress prompted the Vikings to release him less than four weeks later. Moss subsequently sat out the remainder of the year, before announcing his retirement from football on August 1, 2011. Choosing to return to the game after a one-year layoff, Moss signed with the 49ers on March 12, 2012. But, after making just 28 receptions for 434 yards and three touchdowns in a part-time role in 2012, Moss retired for good, ending his playing career with 982 receptions, 15,292 receiving yards, and 156 touchdown receptions, all of which place him among the NFL's all-time leaders. During his time in Minnesota, Moss caught 587 passes, amassed 9,316 receiving yards, and scored 93 touchdowns.

Since retiring as an active player, Moss has served as an analyst for Fox Sports 1's *Fox Football Daily* show and ESPN's *Sunday NFL Countdown* and *Monday Night Countdown* programs. In 2014, Moss also assumed the position of associate head coach and defensive coordinator at Victory Christian Center High School in Charlotte, North Carolina, for whose football team his son played.

VIKINGS CAREER HIGHLIGHTS

Best Season

Moss performed brilliantly for the Vikings in 1998, earning First-Team All-Pro and NFL Rookie of the Year honors by making 69 receptions for 1,313 yards and a league-leading 17 touchdowns. However, he proved to be even more productive in 2003, once again gaining First-Team All-Pro recognition by finishing second in the NFL with 111 receptions and 1,632 receiving yards, while also topping the circuit with 17 TD catches.

Memorable Moments/Greatest Performances

Moss excelled in his first game as a pro, making four receptions for 95 yards and two touchdowns during a 31–7 victory over the Tampa Bay Buccaneers in the opening game of the 1998 regular season, with his TDs coming on passes of 48 and 31 yards from Brad Johnson.

Moss helped lead the Vikings to a 37–24 win over the Packers on October 5, 1998, by making five receptions for 190 yards and two touchdowns, which came on hookups of 52 and 44 yards with Randall Cunningham.

Moss torched the Green Bay defensive secondary again in the next meeting between the two teams on November 22, 1998, earning NFC Offensive Player of the Week honors by making eight receptions for 153 yards and one touchdown during a 28–14 victory over the Packers, with his TD coming on a 49-yard connection with Cunningham in the fourth quarter that put the game out of reach.

Moss continued his extraordinary play against the Dallas Cowboys four days later, leading the Vikings to a 46–36 Thanksgiving Day win by catching three passes for 163 yards, with all three of his receptions going for touchdowns. Collaborating with Randall Cunningham on scoring plays that covered 51, 56, and 56 yards, Moss once again gained recognition as the NFC Offensive Player of the Week.

Moss turned in another outstanding performance against the Bears on December 6, 1998, making eight receptions for 106 yards and three touchdowns during a 48–22 Vikings win.

Moss proved to be the difference in a 21–14 win over Tampa Bay on October 3, 1999, making four receptions for 120 yards and two touchdowns, which came on first-quarter connections with Randall Cunningham that covered 61 and 27 yards.

Moss amassed 204 yards on 12 receptions during a 27–24 overtime victory over the Bears on November 14, 1999, earning NFC Offensive Player of the Week honors once again in the process.

Although the Vikings ended up losing their December 12, 1999, meeting with the Chiefs by a score of 31–28 on a last-second 38-yard field goal by Pete Stoyanovich, Moss tied the game at 28–28 with just 1:38 remaining in regulation by returning a punt 64 yards for a touchdown.

Moss helped lead the Vikings to a 24–20 win over the Packers on December 20, 1999, by making five receptions for 131 yards and two touchdowns, one of which came on a 57-yard pass from Jeff George.

Moss starred again in the 1999 regular-season finale two weeks later, making five receptions for 155 yards and one touchdown during a 24–17 win over the Lions, with his TD coming on a 67-yard second-quarter connection with George that put the Vikings ahead to stay.

Moss contributed to a 27–10 victory over the Cowboys in the 1999 NFC wild card game by making five receptions for 127 yards and one touchdown, which came on a 58-yard hookup with George just before halftime.

Although the Vikings subsequently lost their 1999 divisional round playoff game matchup with the eventual Super Bowl champion St. Louis Rams by a score of 49–37, Moss starred in defeat, catching nine passes for 188 yards and two touchdowns.

Moss led the Vikings to a 31–24 win over the Lions on October 1, 2000, by making seven receptions for 168 yards and three touchdowns, collaborating with Daunte Culpepper on scoring plays that covered 61, 17, and 50 yards.

Moss continued his success against the Cowboys on Thanksgiving Day 2000, making seven receptions for 144 yards and two touchdowns during a 27–15 Vikings win.

Although Moss made just two receptions during Minnesota's 34–16 victory over New Orleans in the divisional round of the 2000 playoffs, they both went for touchdowns, with the speedy receiver collaborating with Daunte Culpepper on scoring plays that covered 53 and 68 yards.

Moss earned NFC Offensive Player of the Week honors for the fourth and final time by making 10 receptions for 171 yards and three touchdowns during a 28–16 win over the Giants on November 19, 2001, with the longest of his TDs coming on a 57-yard pass from Culpepper.

Moss punctuated a 42–24 victory over the Tennessee Titans on December 9, 2001, by collaborating with backup QB Todd Bouman on a 73-yard scoring play late in the final period. He finished the game with seven catches for 158 yards and that one TD.

Moss helped give the Vikings a dramatic 32–31 win over the Saints on December 15, 2002, by gathering in a 13-yard touchdown pass from Daunte Culpepper with just 10 seconds remaining in regulation. Culpepper's subsequent run up the middle for a two-point conversion gave the Vikings the victory.

Moss helped the Vikings begin the 2003 campaign on a positive note by making nine receptions for 150 yards and one touchdown during a 30–25 win over the Packers in the regular-season opener.

Moss had a huge game against the 49ers on September 28, 2003, catching eight passes for 172 yards and three touchdowns during a 35–7 Vikings win, with his longest TD of the day coming on a 59-yard connection with Gus Frerotte.

Moss helped lead the Vikings to a lopsided 34–7 victory over the Seattle Seahawks on December 7, 2003, by making eight receptions for 133 yards and two touchdowns, which came on hookups of 47 and 45 yards with Daunte Culpepper.

Notable Achievements

- Surpassed 100 receptions twice, topping 80 receptions two other times.
- Surpassed 1,000 receiving yards six times, topping 1,500 yards once.
- Scored at least 10 touchdowns six times.
- Scored more than 100 points twice.
- Returned one punt for a touchdown.
- Led NFL in touchdown receptions three times.
- Finished second in NFL in receptions once, receiving yards twice, and touchdowns once.
- Finished third in NFL in receptions once, receiving yards twice, touchdowns once, and yards per reception once.
- Led Vikings in receptions three times and receiving yards six times.

- Holds Vikings single-season records for most receiving yards (1,632 in 2003) and most touchdown receptions (17 in 1998 and 2003).
- Ranks among Vikings career leaders with 587 receptions (2nd), 9,316 receiving yards (2nd), 9,475 yards from scrimmage (3rd), 9,670 all-purpose yards (4th), 92 touchdown receptions (2nd), 93 touchdowns (3rd), and 564 points scored (6th).
- Ranks among NFL career leaders with 15,292 receiving yards (4th), 156 touchdown receptions (2nd), and 157 touchdowns (4th).
- Two-time division champion (1998 and 2000).
- Four-time NFC Offensive Player of the Week.
- Member of 1998 NFL All-Rookie Team.
- 1998 NFL Offensive Rookie of the Year.
- Five-time Pro Bowl selection (1998, 1999, 2000, 2002, and 2003).
- Three-time First-Team All-Pro selection (1998, 2000, and 2003).
- Four-time First-Team All-NFC selection (1998, 2000, 2002, and 2003).
- Pro Football Reference All-2000s First Team.
- NFL 2000s All-Decade First Team.
- Named to NFL 100 All-Time Team in 2019.
- Number 65 on the NFL Network's 2010 list of the NFL's 100 Greatest Players.
- Inducted into Minnesota Vikings Ring of Honor in 2017.
- Elected to Pro Football Hall of Fame in 2018.

8
JOHN RANDLE

Identified by Brett Favre as the toughest defensive player he ever faced, John Randle spent 11 seasons in Minnesota dominating opposing offensive linemen from his right defensive tackle position. A fierce competitor with a motor that never stopped, Randle provided leadership to his teammates with his on-field intensity and exceptional play, contributing greatly to Vikings teams that made eight playoff appearances and won four division titles. Recording double-digit sack totals eight straight times, Randle led the Vikings in that category on nine separate occasions, ending his career as one of the NFL's all-time sack leaders. A six-time Pro Bowler and six-time All-Pro, Randle later received the additional honors of being named to the NFL 100 All-Time Team and gaining induction into the Pro Football Hall of Fame.

Born in Hearne, Texas, on December 12, 1967, John Anthony Randle grew up in poverty in nearby Mumford, where he faced many hardships as a youth. Growing up without a father in a 20-by-20-foot shack with just a small gas heater and no running water that noted sportswriter Peter King described in a 1998 edition of *Sports Illustrated* as "a shoe box with a corrugated-metal roof, a rectangular wooden box of maybe 400 square feet," Randle lived with his two brothers and mother, who made $23 a week working as a maid. Further hampered by a birth defect that slightly disfigured his spine, Randle had to wear braces as a child, preventing him from competing in sports.

After finally being freed from his constraints, Randle began his athletic career on the basketball court, before gravitating more toward football while in high school. Hoping to follow in the footsteps of his older brother Ervin, a linebacker for the NFL's Tampa Bay Buccaneers, Randle starred on the gridiron as a defensive lineman at tiny Texas A&I University in Kingsville, after transferring there from Trinity Valley Community College prior to the start of his junior year. In addition to earning Lone Star Conference Lineman of the Year honors twice, Randle gained Little All-America

John Randle led the Vikings in sacks nine times.
Courtesy of George A. Kitrinos

recognition as a senior. Nevertheless, he didn't particularly enjoy his time at Kingsville, later revealing that the town offered hardly any nightlife when he said, "A pro scout was visiting down there, and he told me that if some doctor told him he had six months to live, he'd move to Kingsville. Because down here, six months would seem like forever because there ain't nothin' to do. He was right about that. Outside of football, all I did was study and play basketball. Play basketball and study."

Despite his exceptional play at Texas A&I, Randle drew little attention from pro scouts due to his small college background and somewhat smallish 6'1", 245-pound frame. Ultimately bypassed by all 28 teams in the 1990 NFL Draft, Randle received tryouts from the Atlanta Falcons and Tampa Bay Buccaneers. But, when both teams suggested that he consider moving to linebacker, Randle balked at the idea, causing him to remain unsigned until the Vikings finally offered him a free-agent contract.

Commenting on how Randle's hard work and spirited play during training camp ended up landing him a roster spot, Vikings head coach Jerry Burns said at the time, "I don't know if I've ever seen a kid work that hard to make the team."

Revealing years later that the doubts others had in his ability to play in the NFL helped motivate him throughout his career, Randle said, "That was important in how I approached the game, being an undrafted free agent. You never become comfortable as a free agent. It's almost like when you're a draft pick, you were hand-picked because this is what they want. A free agent is like a temporary guy, a guy we're going to put in there until we get something else better."

Randle continued, "It's almost like you were a rental car. When you rent a car, you have it for a few days. It's not something you buy or want, it's what they give you. That's how I felt about myself. I wanted to make the most of it."

Randle then added, "The first thing I wanted to do is make the team. The second thing I wanted to do was make an impact. I wanted to go out and play every play as hard as I could, then walk off the field, look back and say, 'Did I give it my best?'"

Randle ended up spending his first season in Minnesota serving as a backup to starting defensive linemen Chris Doleman, Henry Thomas, Al Noga, and Ken Clarke, while also fulfilling the role of a situational pass-rusher. Yet, even though he didn't receive a significant amount of playing time on game day, Randle made an extremely favorable impression on Randall McDaniel during the team's practice sessions, with the Hall of Fame guard recalling, "He was on the scout team and giving the tackles a hard time. He was just sprinting by them. . . . Your first impression is, 'This kid never stops moving.' He had that motor running. Practices were not fun if you had him over you that day."

Randle assumed a far more prominent role his second year in the league, starting eight games at left defensive end and recording 58 tackles and a team-leading 9½ sacks, before being moved inside to right tackle by new defensive line coach John Teerlinck the following season. Excelling at his new post, Randle began a string of eight consecutive seasons in which he recorded at least 10 sacks, finishing his first year as a full-time starter with 11½ sacks and 59 tackles. Randle followed that up by registering 12½ sacks, 59 tackles, and three forced fumbles in 1993, earning in the process Pro Bowl and First-Team All-Pro honors for the first of six straight times. After totaling 35½ sacks over the course of the next three seasons, Randle recorded a career-high and league-leading 15½ sacks in 1997, making him the first defensive tackle ever to lead the NFL in that category.

Although Randle gradually added some 35 pounds of bulk onto his frame, he typically found himself being outweighed considerably by the men who opposed him at the line of scrimmage. Nevertheless, he made up for whatever he lacked in size with his tenacity, tremendous conditioning, and extraordinary work ethic, with Randall McDaniel saying, "He was the only defensive tackle I know who never missed a play. This day and age, and even back then, every guy came out and took a breather. He would never leave the field. They tried to send someone in and he's like, 'No thanks.' He was like an offensive lineman on defense."

Called virtually "unblockable" by Brett Favre, Randle also drew high praise from Troy Aikman, who stated, "Tenacious is the first word that comes to mind when I think of John. He played hard on every play for 60 minutes."

Former Vikings defensive coordinator and interim head coach Leslie Frazier noted that many current players try to emulate Randle when he said, "They look at the way he played and try to model his play because he was a guy who played 100 miles per hour, every single down."

Randle, who never missed a game in his 11 years with the Vikings, also became known for his intensity and trash-talking, which caused some teammates and coaches to question his sanity at times. In discussing Randle, former Vikings defensive coordinator Brian Billick stated, "If you didn't know him and you just watched him and heard him play, you would swear this guy is nuts. Literally, bona fide certifiable nuts."

Attempting to explain his somewhat peculiar conduct, Randle claimed that he not only hoped to intimidate his opponent, but also boost his own self-esteem, saying, "Being a little small dog, you wanted to have a big bark, so I always started talking."

Randle's unconventional behavior tended to obscure the fact that he paid great attention to detail, studied his opponent carefully, and employed exceptional technique that included his trademark jab punch to linemen and an almost unstoppable spin move. An outstanding team leader, Randle earned the respect of teammates and opponents alike with his high-energy style of play and dedication to his profession.

Randle spent three more seasons in Minnesota, recording another 28½ sacks, before being released by the Vikings following the conclusion of the 2000 campaign. Stating his feelings at the time, Randle said, "The course of me playing for the Vikings finally came to an end. As for me and the defense, we tried everything we could do. I think it was time for me to get out." Leaving Minnesota with career totals of 114 sacks, 25 forced fumbles, nine fumble recoveries, and 486 tackles, Randle ranks among the franchise's all-time leaders in each of the first two categories.

Following his release by the Vikings, Randle signed with the Seattle Seahawks, with whom he spent the next three seasons. Leaving a lasting impression on many of his Seattle teammates, Randle later received words of praise from Hall of Fame guard Steve Hutchinson, who said, "You knew who he was from seeing all the highlights through the years. What you didn't know when you first met him was how hard he worked every day in practice and how much he put into his preparation. . . . I was lucky to see first-hand what a player of his caliber dedicated to his day-to-day routine. You couldn't help but work harder when he was going full-bore every day. He made all of us on the offensive line better by facing him at practice."

Although Randle's streak of 183 consecutive games played came to an end his first year in Seattle, he had three productive seasons for the Seahawks, registering another 23½ sacks and earning the last of his seven Pro Bowl selections as a member of the team, before announcing his retirement at the end of 2003. Retiring with career totals of 137½ sacks, 556 tackles, 29 forced fumbles, and 11 fumble recoveries, Randle currently is tied for 10th in NFL history in the first category.

Since retiring as an active player, Randle has taken up golf as a hobby, frequently hitting the links with Randall McDaniel. In 2015, he also set up the St. David's Center Tee Up for Tomorrow Golf Tournament, which has raised $13.7 million for charity.

VIKINGS CAREER HIGHLIGHTS

Best Season

Randle played his best ball for the Vikings in 1993, 1994, 1996, and 1997, gaining consensus First-Team All-Pro recognition in each of those four seasons. After recording 12½ sacks and a career-high 59 tackles in 1993, Randle registered 13½ sacks, 42 tackles, and two fumble recoveries the following year. Continuing his exceptional play in 1996, Randle recorded 11½ sacks, made 46 tackles, and forced four fumbles. However, Randle proved to be slightly more dominant in 1997, when, in addition to bringing down opposing ball-carriers 58 times, he forced two fumbles, recovered two others, and led the NFL with a career-high 15½ sacks.

Memorable Moments/Greatest Performances

Randle recorded the first sack of his career when he brought down Randall Cunningham behind the line of scrimmage during a 32–24 loss to the Philadelphia Eagles on October 15, 1990.

Randle contributed to a 34–7 win over the Phoenix Cardinals on October 13, 1991, by sacking Tom Tupa three times.

Randle recorded 2½ sacks during a 38–10 victory over the Bears on November 2, 1992.

Randle earned NFC Defensive Player of the Week honors by registering three sacks during a 19–12 win over the Bears on October 25, 1993.

Randle sacked Detroit quarterback Rodney Peete three times during a 13–0 shutout of the Lions on December 5, 1993.

Randle continued to be a thorn in the side of the Lions in the next meeting between the two teams on September 11, 1994, recording 2½ sacks during a 10–3 Vikings win.

Randle turned in a tremendous all-around effort against the 49ers in the final game of the 1994 regular season, earning NFC Defensive Player of the Week honors by recording two sacks, forcing a fumble, and recovering another during a 21–14 Vikings victory.

Randle earned that distinction again by recording a career-high 3½ sacks during a 30–21 win over the Packers on September 22, 1996.

Randle nearly matched that total when he sacked Steve Beuerlein three times during a 21–14 victory over the Carolina Panthers on October 12, 1997.

Although the Vikings lost to the Lions by a score of 14–13 on December 14, 1997, Randle continued his assault on Detroit signal-callers, bringing down Scott Mitchell behind the line of scrimmage three times.

Randle recorded two sacks, forced a fumble, and recovered another during a 21–14 win over Tampa Bay on October 3, 1999, earning in the process NFC Defensive Player of the Week honors.

Randle recorded the only interception of his career during a lopsided 40–16 victory over the 49ers on October 24, 1999.

Randle earned NFC Defensive Player of the Week honors for the fifth and final time by recording three sacks and forcing a fumble during a 24–17 win over the Lions in the final game of the 1999 regular season.

Notable Achievements

- Never missed a game in 11 seasons, appearing in 176 consecutive contests.
- Finished in double digits in sacks eight times.
- Led NFL with 15½ sacks in 1997.
- Led Vikings in sacks nine times.
- Ranks among Vikings career leaders with 114 sacks (3rd) and 25 forced fumbles (2nd).
- Ranks among NFL career leaders with 137½ sacks (tied for 10th).
- Four-time division champion (1992, 1994, 1998, and 2000).
- Five-time NFC Defensive Player of the Week.
- Five-time NFC Defensive Player of the Month.
- Six-time Pro Bowl selection (1993, 1994, 1995, 1996, 1997, and 1998).
- Six-time First-Team All-Pro selection (1993, 1994, 1995, 1996, 1997, and 1998).
- Six-time First-Team All-NFC selection (1993, 1994, 1995, 1996, 1997, and 1998).
- Pro Football Reference All-1990s First Team.
- NFL 1990s All-Decade First Team.
- Named to NFL 100 All-Time Team in 2019.
- Inducted into Minnesota Vikings Ring of Honor in 2008.
- Elected to Pro Football Hall of Fame in 2010.

9
RON YARY

Just the third offensive lineman ever taken with the first overall pick of the NFL Draft, Ron Yary spent 14 years starring at right tackle for the Vikings, contributing greatly to teams that won 11 division titles and appeared in four Super Bowls. Combining size and strength with intelligence, exceptional athletic ability, superb technique, and a nasty disposition, Yary dominated opposing defensive linemen, earning in the process Pro Bowl and All-Pro honors seven times each. A member of the NFL 1970s All-Decade Team, Yary received the additional distinctions of being named the NFL Players Association's NFC Offensive Lineman of the Year three straight times and eventually being inducted into both the Vikings Ring of Honor and the Pro Football Hall of Fame.

Born in Chicago, Illinois, on July 16, 1946, Anthony Ronald Yary grew up in Bellflower, California, where he excelled at multiple positions on the gridiron while attending Bellflower High School, earning All–San Gabriel Valley honors as an offensive tackle in his junior year, before moving to fullback in his final season. Revealing years later that it mattered little to him where he went to college, Yary said, "I just wanted to play football. I didn't care where."

After spending one semester playing offensive tackle at Cerritos Junior College, Yary transferred to USC, recalling, "They said I was just a 'B' player, but they wanted to take a look at me." Making an extremely favorable impression on head football coach John McKay upon his arrival at USC, Yary soon found himself starting at defensive tackle, with McKay stating at the end of his first season, "Ron is as good as I've ever seen. If he continues to develop, he'll be fantastic . . . he is fast and hard to move out, he's so strong."

More than living up to McKay's expectations, Yary gained recognition as the Pac-8 defensive lineman of the year as a sophomore, before spending his final two seasons at USC playing offensive tackle. Establishing himself as the finest collegiate player at that position, Yary earned consensus

Ron Yary gained recognition from the NFL Players Association as NFC Offensive Lineman of the Year on three separate occasions.

All-America honors in both 1966 and 1967, with his exceptional play in the second of those campaigns resulting in him also being named the winner of the Outland Trophy, presented annually to the nation's top interior lineman. Exhibiting his tremendous versatility at the end of his senior year, Yary played offensive tackle in the Rose Bowl and defensive tackle in the Hula Bowl.

Subsequently selected by the Vikings with the first overall pick of the 1968 NFL Draft, Yary became the first offensive lineman to be accorded that honor since the Philadelphia Eagles used the first pick in 1949 to select center/linebacker Chuck Bednarik. In discussing Yary's versatility following the draft, Vikings head coach Bud Grant told reporters, "If he arrived tomorrow, he'd be an offensive tackle. But he could play any one of four positions—defensive tackle, and any position in the offensive line—center, guard, or tackle."

Agreeing with Grant's assessment, USC assistant coach Dan Levy stated, "Lots of kids in college football are big but not athletic. A lot of young men can't handle their growth. Yary is an athlete, a great one. I don't think he has a weakness."

Yary ended up spending the first half of his rookie campaign learning the intricacies of offensive line play at the NFL level, before starting the final seven games at right tackle. Yet even though he remained an unfinished product, Yary made a strong impression on Carl Eller, whom he faced every day in practice, with the future Hall of Fame defensive end saying, "Ron has the strength so that you can't run over him. It's suicide to charge straight at him. Maybe his strongest point is his blocking on the run, straight ahead. That's when he uses his strength to his best advantage."

A full-time starter by the start of his second season, Yary helped the NFL champion Vikings score more points than any other team in the league, with one teammate commenting, "To appreciate Yary, you have to watch the films. He's amazing. He destroys people. I've seen plays where he cleans out the defensive end and takes the linebackers with him."

Another teammate remarked, "Yary is fantastic. How many times has anybody gotten in on the quarterback? He's the best tackle I've ever seen."

Recognized as one of the NFL's premier offensive tackles by 1970, Yary began a string of eight straight seasons in which he gained All-NFC recognition. Also accorded Pro Bowl and All-Pro honors seven consecutive times from 1971 to 1977, Yary drew praise from his opponents throughout the league, with Los Angeles Rams Hall of Fame defensive end Jack Youngblood frequently identifying him as one of the toughest opponents he faced during his career.

Nevertheless, Yary tended to downplay the significance of any individual honors that came his way, stating, "I honestly believe there are five, maybe eight tackles who are as good as one another. It's just a matter of location, the amount of press the player gets that determines a lot of his postseason honors. And how well your team does, that's a big factor. If your team has a very successful year like we did in 1973 and you're playing good football . . . it's easier to get recognition."

A consummate team player, Yary added, "All of your applause comes from your peers inside your team, and not from the audience or media or anything else like that. Your glory comes in other ways; it comes from knowing that you got a good block, even though it's not noticed—it's noticed the following day during films. A lot of times, if a back makes a good run, the offensive lineman was the main cause of that. That's when your glory comes."

Standing 6'5" and weighing 255 pounds, Yary possessed an outstanding combination of size, strength, and agility—all of which he used to impose his will against the men he faced at the line of scrimmage. Yary also played the game with an edge, as Vikings offensive line coach John Michels suggested when he said, "That man had a mean streak on the field. He literally wanted to destroy his opponent. He took it so personally and wanted to dismantle his opponent. And, in most cases, Ron was successful."

Michels continued, "He couldn't wait to get on the field and tear people apart. Ron was sky high. You tried to calm him, but it was a challenge. He wanted to get on the field and use that nastiness."

In addressing his more aggressive side, Yary stated, "Being an offensive lineman is about the most boring job in football. It's just a head-butting contest. . . . The only satisfaction comes from knocking someone on his rear-end. And, if it helps score a touchdown, it is all the more satisfying."

Yary's in-game persona even extended onto the practice field, with longtime teammate Bob Lurtsema saying, "The thing about Ron was he was more focused on football and winning than anyone I played with. He lived for football. He'd get upset when other people weren't as focused on football as he was . . . I hated practicing against him because he was so into football all the time, even in practice. He was brutal to play against. . . . Practicing against Ron Yary was practicing against the best. Getting blocked by him was an honor. You just knew you were competing against the best."

Yary also proved to be an excellent technician, with Pittsburgh Steelers defensive end L. C. Greenwood suggesting, "What Yary does better than anyone is hooking. Especially when Tarkenton is rolling out. He can get inside you and keep you hemmed in. Other linemen don't learn it, or just can't do it. Yary is one of the best at it."

In discussing the technique that he often used to impede the advance of his opponent, Yary explained, "The block is used on a weakside play, and my responsibility is to hook the end, get to the outside, and keep him pinned on the line or move him back. If I can move him back far enough, there's a good chance of him cutting off the middle linebacker. Some tackles have a hard time doing that because the ends are usually lined up outside of you. They're usually on your outside ear, to a foot-and-a-half outside your shoulder. Regardless, I still enjoy it . . . the play is set up so that I just can't miss, and it gives me a chance to get even with some of the great ends who have made me miserable."

Named First-Team All-Pro for the fourth straight time in 1974, Yary received high praise from Bud Grant at season's end, with the Vikings' usually reserved head coach saying, "He should be All-Pro the next 10 years. When you get a great player, the few mistakes he makes become magnified because you get conditioned to his excellence. But, when you add up the big plays he makes, you realize his worth. We think he's the best tackle in football."

Yary remained a pillar of strength on the right side of Minnesota's offensive line for seven more seasons, missing just two games in 1980 due to a broken foot. In explaining his ability to play with the injury the rest of the year, Yary said, "I know myself better than anyone else. I will know when I can't do it anymore. I will know when I am truly on my way out, and that is when I will hang it up."

With the 35-year-old Yary unable to perform at the same lofty level in 1981, the Vikings traded him to the Los Angeles Rams for a 10th-round draft pick at season's end. Leaving Minnesota with a total of 199 games played, Yary continues to rank among the franchise's all-time leaders in that category. Extremely durable, Yary failed to appear in just five games in his 14 years with the Vikings, missing just two of those due to injury (he also missed three games in 1969 due to military obligations).

Yary ended up spending just one season with the Rams, serving them primarily as a backup in 1982, before announcing his retirement. He subsequently remained in Southern California, where he headed a successful construction company.

In discussing some of the qualities that made Yary so special, Bud Grant said, "Ron was one of the great competitors I coached. Ron simply liked to play football. You never had to motivate Ron. He always wanted to be the best, and he was."

Meanwhile, in assessing Yary's career, former Vikings quarterback and current NFL analyst Sean Salisbury stated, "Yary was one of three dominant linemen of his era . . . Yary was an extremely smart player, he had great technique, and there was a special nastiness about him. . . . When you are successful and dominate the offensive line position for as long as Yary did, there comes a time when the knees and the legs start to go. But Yary—and superstars like him—their technique became better. Yary always played on good teams, and he went to four Super Bowls. He could play in today's NFL and succeed because he had the head and the heart to play with anybody."

VIKINGS CAREER HIGHLIGHTS

Best Season

Yary played his best ball for the Vikings from 1971 to 1976, earning six consecutive First-Team All-Pro nominations. Also accorded NFC Offensive Lineman of the Year honors by the NFLPA in 1973, 1974, and 1975, Yary turned in his most dominant performance in the last of those campaigns, when the 1,000-Yard Club named him the NFL's Outstanding Blocker of the Year.

Memorable Moments/Greatest Performances

Yary helped the Vikings earn a hard-fought 23–20 victory over the Los Angeles Rams in the divisional round of the 1969 playoffs by totally neutralizing Hall of Fame defensive end Deacon Jones, who he held to no sacks.

Yary once again excelled against the league's best when he prevented perennial All-Pro defensive end Claude Humphrey from recording a single sack and helped the Vikings gain a season-high total of 257 yards on the ground during a 24–7 win over the Atlanta Falcons on November 28, 1971.

Yary helped the Vikings amass 502 yards of total offense during a 51–10 blowout of the Houston Oilers on October 13, 1974, with Minnesota gaining 357 yards through the air and another 145 on the ground.

Yary and his line-mates once again dominated the opposition at the line of scrimmage during a 35–20 win over the Washington Redskins in the divisional round of the 1976 playoffs, with the Vikings rushing for 221 yards and amassing 384 yards of total offense.

Notable Achievements

- Missed just five games in 14 seasons, appearing in 144 consecutive contests from 1970 to 1979.
- Ranks among Vikings career leaders with 14 seasons played (tied-6th) and 199 games played (6th).
- 11-time division champion (1968, 1969, 1970, 1971, 1973, 1974, 1975, 1976, 1977, 1978, and 1980).

- 1969 NFL champion.
- Three-time NFC champion (1973, 1974, and 1976).
- Three-time NFLPA NFC Offensive Lineman of the Year (1973, 1974, and 1975).
- 1975 1,000-Yard Club NFL Outstanding Blocker of the Year.
- Seven-time Pro Bowl selection (1971, 1972, 1973, 1974, 1975, 1976, and 1977).
- Six-time First-Team All-Pro selection (1971, 1972, 1973, 1974, 1975, and 1976).
- 1977 Second-Team All-Pro selection.
- Eight-time First-Team All-NFC selection (1970, 1971, 1972, 1973, 1974, 1975, 1976, and 1977).
- Pro Football Reference All-1970s First Team.
- NFL 1970s All-Decade Second Team.
- Inducted into Minnesota Vikings Ring of Honor in 2001.
- Elected to Pro Football Hall of Fame in 2001.

10

CHRIS DOLEMAN

An elite pass-rusher who ranks among the NFL's all-time leaders in sacks and forced fumbles, Chris Doleman spent 10 seasons in Minnesota terrorizing opposing quarterbacks. Starring for the Vikings primarily at right defensive end, Doleman recorded double-digit sack totals five times, leading the team in that category on six separate occasions. The franchise's all-time leader in forced fumbles, Doleman also ranks extremely high in team annals in sacks, fumble recoveries, and tackles, with his exceptional all-around play earning him six trips to the Pro Bowl, four All-Pro nominations, and six All-NFC selections. Accorded NFC Defensive Player of the Year honors once as well, Doleman received the additional distinctions of being named to the NFL 1990s All-Decade Team and being elected to the Pro Football Hall of Fame following a career that also included stints with the Atlanta Falcons and San Francisco 49ers.

Born in Indianapolis, Indiana, on October 16, 1961, Christopher John Doleman grew up in York, Pennsylvania, where he excelled on the gridiron while attending William Penn High School. After spending one postgrad year at Valley Forge Military Academy, Doleman accepted an athletic scholarship to the University of Pittsburgh, where he starred at defensive end for four years, helping to lead the Panthers to three Top 20 finishes, including a number two ranking in 1981.

Impressed with Doleman's outstanding play at the collegiate level, the Vikings made him the fourth overall pick of the 1985 NFL Draft, after which he spent his first year in Minnesota playing left-outside linebacker in the team's 3-4 defensive scheme. Performing extremely well at that post, Doleman earned a spot on the 1985 NFL All-Rookie Team by recording 113 tackles, three fumble recoveries, and one interception. Although Doleman returned an interception 59 yards for a touchdown the following year, he experienced a significant decline in overall production, registering only 49 tackles, while sharing playing time with Chris Martin.

Chris Doleman earned NFC Defensive Player of the Year honors in 1992.
Courtesy of MearsOnlineAuctions.com

With the Vikings switching to a 4-3 defense in 1987, Doleman moved to right defensive end, where he found a new home. In addition to recording 57 tackles and a team-high 11 sacks during the strike-shortened campaign, Doleman led the NFL with six forced fumbles, earning in the process Pro Bowl and Second-Team All-Pro honors. Yet, Doleman did not develop an immediate fondness for his new position, telling a writer for the *Boston Globe* in January 1988, "I wouldn't say it was love at first sight. It was like someone asking you to go cover a wedding. It's a job, but you don't fall in love with writing about weddings."

Before long, though, Doleman came to embrace his new role, suggesting, "If I made two tackles at linebacker, you'd say where was I all day? If I made two sacks at defensive end, you'd say I had a great day. Defensive end is where you can just tee off and get the quarterback."

In discussing the logic behind moving Doleman to defensive end, Bud Grant, who was in his final season as Vikings head coach when the talented pass-rusher first arrived in Minnesota, said, "We thought of him as a linebacker at first. When he played on the outside [as an end], he was in on every play. He rushed on every play. His athleticism really lent itself to him being an end rather than a linebacker. He didn't deliver a blow from the linebacker stance. From end, he had the ability to be in on every play, and he didn't have to meet those blocking backs and people pulling. He was stronger and could run over people. At linebacker, he wasn't as adept."

Grant added, "He was hard to block. He was big, fast, strong. He was extremely durable. He just had all the attributes of being a great player."

After gaining Pro Bowl recognition again in 1988 by recording eight sacks and 58 tackles, Doleman turned in a magnificent performance in 1989, earning First-Team All-Pro honors by leading the NFL with 21 sacks and ranking among the league leaders with five forced fumbles and five fumble recoveries. Doleman followed that up by registering 18 sacks and 193 tackles over the course of the next two seasons, before earning First-Team All-Pro and United Press International (UPI) NFC Defensive Player of the Year honors in 1992 by placing near the top of the league rankings with 14½ sacks and six forced fumbles.

A tremendous force on the defensive side of the ball, the 6'5", 285-pound Doleman combined great physical talent with superior technique and a relentless motor to establish himself as one of the dominant players of his era, with former Vikings tight end Steve Jordan saying, "Pound for pound, he was one of the strongest players in the league. He had tremendous talent and was an exceptional defensive end."

Fellow Pro Football Hall of Famer Randall McDaniel said of his long-time teammate, "He was a true leader on the field. Chris was relentless in his attack, and he was an unselfish player. . . . In my opinion, to be a great player you have to be able to do everything well . . . and Chris did them extremely well."

McDaniel continued, "Doleman had that move when he'd work upfield, he could stick that arm out, and the way he leaned into you he could get his arm into the middle of the lineman's chest and just drive him back to the quarterback."

Former Vikings defensive line coach Paul Wiggin further expounded upon Doleman's special qualities when he stated:

> Chris Doleman was the prototypical football player at defensive end, and particularly at pass-rusher for that particular time. First of all, he had an unbelievable get-off. He could explode out of his stance, and you have to do that. He always had the tackle off balance because he could get upfield so fast.
>
> Secondly, he had great lean. I have never coached a football player in my life with the lean that Chris Doleman had, and I think if you ask anybody during that era about Chris Doleman, that's one of the first things they see. He's going wide open with his body leaning almost unbelievably off balance, yet he's in total balance.
>
> And the third thing he had was, every once in a while, he'd drill 'em. He'd overpower them and he'd just collapse the tackle into the quarterback. Chris had the perfect package, and it was all based on his great athleticism.

In addition to his many other attributes, Doleman became extremely adept at stripping the football from opposing quarterbacks, with his career total of 44 forced fumbles representing the sixth-highest total in NFL history. In addressing his former teammate's propensity for creating turnovers, Scott Studwell recalled, "He was so explosive, and he had such great acceleration off the edge, and he was so good at stripping people because he had such great acceleration into contact. He was a freak athlete. He was one of those guys . . . I guess I would compare him to a Randy Moss on the other side of the ball."

Commenting on the problems that Doleman presented to opposing signal-callers, Warren Moon said, "Doleman is one of those rare guys— maybe one of four or five that I played against during my career, right there with Reggie White, Bruce Smith and Derrick Thomas—that you had to know where they were and set your protection accordingly. Doleman was someone you always had to worry about because you knew he could get to the quarterback. The amount of time and attention that went to prepare for Chris Doleman benefitted the other guys on those defensive lines. He was one of those guys that you had to make sure could be blocked in one way or another."

Former Vikings teammate John Randle discussed Doleman's ability to alter the outcome of a game when he stated, "Chris Doleman had the ability to deliver the big play when you needed it. Teams had to keep an eye on him because they knew it was coming, be it at the beginning, middle, or end of the game. He was capable of making that big play."

Pass-rusher extraordinaire Jared Allen also had high praise for Doleman, saying, "He was relentless. He used his hands so well in what he did off the edge . . . I watched a lot of tape on him. There are players in sports who seem to be ahead of the curve. Chris played at a time when you didn't really see a true speed rusher. Chris' ability to get off the ball and turn the corner and bend and use his body like that was honestly ahead of his time. He set the pace for that style of rushing. . . . You've got to include him on the list of players that kind of revolutionized that d-end pass-rushing forte."

A true student of the game, Doleman also possessed a strong work ethic and an extremely high football IQ, with the *Pioneer Press* once writing, "No other Vikings player brought a briefcase into the locker room, and teammates joked the only thing Doleman carried in it was his lunch. Asked about it one day, he said, 'This is where I come to work. This is what you bring to the office.' He opened his briefcase to reveal his playbook. Just the playbook."

Doleman followed up his exceptional 1992 campaign by recording 12½ sacks, 68 tackles, and three forced fumbles in 1993, before signing with the Atlanta Falcons as a free agent at season's end. He subsequently spent two years in Atlanta and three in San Francisco, earning two more Pro Bowl selections by registering 54 sacks, 226 tackles, 13 forced fumbles, eight fumble recoveries and three interceptions. Doleman then returned to Minnesota for one final season, recording eight sacks and 53 tackles in 1999, before announcing his retirement. In addition to his 44 forced fumbles, Doleman ended his career with 150½ sacks, 975 tackles, 24 fumble recoveries, eight interceptions, 121 interception-return yards, three touchdowns, and two safeties. While playing for the Vikings, he recorded 96½ sacks, forced 31 fumbles, recovered 16 others, intercepted five passes, scored two touchdowns, and recorded both of his safeties. Extremely durable, Doleman missed just two games due to injury his entire career, appearing in a total of 232 contests, 213 of which he started.

An honorable man with strong moral fiber, Doleman later discussed his motivation for performing at an elite level, saying, "I played for God, family and teams. My teammates were very important to me, but I always knew that I wanted to honor God. I never wanted to embarrass my family by playing bad, doing something that would bring shame to them, and my teammates, I owed that to them. I owed them the best performance that I could give them, week in, week out."

Following his playing days, Doleman moved to Suwanee, Georgia, where he enjoyed his retirement until January 2018, when he received a diagnosis of glioblastoma, a form of brain cancer, that necessitated the removal of three tumors and a subsequent five-week stay in the hospital. Recalling his thoughts at the time, Doleman revealed, "When a doctor tells you that you have brain cancer, it changes your whole world. Those are the scariest words that you'll ever hear in your life. When I first heard it, I was so devastated by it I couldn't get any words out of my mouth. How many people do you know who survive brain cancer?"

After battling his illness for two years, Doleman finally succumbed to it on January 28, 2020. The news of the 58-year-old Doleman's passing spread quickly, with the Vikings sending out a statement that read: "The Minnesota Vikings express our deepest sympathies to Chris Doleman's family and friends upon his passing. Chris was a great example for players past and present, as he embodied all the best characteristics of a Viking—resilience, toughness, and a competitive spirit. Chris always carried himself with dignity and class. Vikings fans worldwide will greatly miss him."

Hall of Fame president and CEO David Baker expressed his sadness over Doleman's loss by saying, "The entire Pro Football Hall of Fame mourns the passing of Chris Doleman after a prolonged and courageous battle against cancer. I had the honor of getting to know him not only as a great football player, but an outstanding human being. One of the honors of my life was witnessing Chris get baptized in the Jordan River during a Hall of Fame trip to Israel. . . . The legacy of Chris Doleman will live forever in Canton, Ohio, for generations to learn from how he lived a life of courage and character."

Meanwhile, a stunned Keith Millard said of his close friend and former teammate, "This is a guy who never missed a practice, never missed a game, this guy was Superman. If this was going to happen to anybody, this would be the last person you would expect it to happen to. That's what blows me away."

Millard added that he and other former teammates spent the previous two years providing constant encouragement to Doleman, saying, "When we got together, we're all in our late 50s, but it would be like the old times. You don't have to be together all the time to have that bond. . . . I'd let him know that I was thinking about him, and praying, and I loved him. He would text me or call me back when he could—toward the end he had a hard time doing that—but, as long as he got back to me in any way, shape or form, I knew that was enough. It was Chris."

VIKINGS CAREER HIGHLIGHTS

Best Season

Doleman performed brilliantly for the Vikings in 1992, earning UPI Defensive Player of the Year honors by recording 14½ sacks and 64 tackles, forcing six fumbles, recovering three others, and scoring one touchdown on defense. However, he proved to be even more dominant in 1989, when en route to gaining consensus First-Team All-Pro recognition, he led the NFL with 21 sacks, recorded 94 tackles, forced five fumbles, and recovered five others.

Memorable Moments/Greatest Performances

Doleman helped lead the Vikings to a 23–10 win over the Tampa Bay Buccaneers on September 14, 1986, by scoring the game's first points when he returned his interception of a Steve DeBerg pass 59 yards for a touchdown.

Doleman recorded the first sack of his career during a convincing 45–13 victory over Tampa Bay on November 30, 1986.

Doleman earned NFC Defensive Player of the Week honors by recording two sacks during a 31–20 win over the Los Angeles Raiders on November 8, 1987.

Doleman starred during a 44–38 Thanksgiving Day overtime win over the Cowboys in 1987, sacking Dallas quarterback Danny White three times.

Doleman contributed to the Vikings' 36–24 upset victory over the heavily favored San Francisco 49ers in the divisional round of the 1987 playoffs by sacking Joe Montana twice.

Doleman sacked Vinny Testaverde three times during a 24–10 win over Tampa Bay on November 12, 1989.

Doleman earned NFC Defensive Player of the Week honors by recording three sacks during a 43–17 win over the Atlanta Falcons on December 10, 1989.

Doleman earned that distinction again by sacking Boomer Esiason four times during a 29–21 win over the Cincinnati Bengals in the final game of the 1989 regular season.

Doleman recorded two of the five sacks the Vikings registered against Tom Tupa during a 34–7 victory over the Phoenix Cardinals on October 13, 1991, earning NFC Defensive Player of the Week honors once again in the process.

Doleman received that honor for the final time as a member of the Vikings after he sacked Don Majkowski twice during a 23–20 win over the Packers in the 1992 regular-season opener.

Doleman scored the second touchdown of his career when he ran 27 yards to paydirt after picking off a Steve DeBerg pass during a 35–7 victory over Tampa Bay on November 8, 1992.

Notable Achievements

- Missed just two non-strike games in 10 seasons, appearing in 154 out of 156 contests.
- Scored two defensive touchdowns.
- Finished in double digits in sacks five times, topping 20 sacks once (21 in 1989).
- Recorded more than 100 tackles twice.
- Led NFL in sacks once and forced fumbles once.
- Finished second in NFL in forced fumbles twice.
- Led Vikings in sacks six times and tackles three times.
- Holds Vikings career record for most forced fumbles (31).
- Ranks among Vikings career leaders with 96½ sacks (5th), 16 fumble recoveries (tied for 6th), and 737 solo tackles (8th).
- Ranks among NFL career leaders with 150½ sacks (5th) and 44 forced fumbles (6th).
- Two-time division champion (1989 and 1992).
- Five-time NFC Defensive Player of the Week.
- Three-time NFC Defensive Player of the Month.
- Member of 1985 NFL All-Rookie Team.
- 1992 UPI NFC Defensive Player of the Year.
- Six-time Pro Bowl selection (1987, 1988, 1989, 1990, 1992, and 1993).
- Two-time First-Team All-Pro selection (1989 and 1992).
- Two-time Second-Team All-Pro selection (1987 and 1993).
- Four-time First-Team All-NFC selection (1987, 1989, 1992, and 1993).
- Two-time Second-Team All-NFC selection (1988 and 1990).
- Pro Football Reference All-1990s Second Team.

- NFL 1990s All-Decade Second Team.
- Inducted into Minnesota Vikings Ring of Honor in 2011.
- Elected to Pro Football Hall of Fame in 2012.

11

PAUL KRAUSE

Acquired by the Vikings in one of the greatest trades in franchise history, Paul Krause arrived in Minnesota in 1968 after spending the previous four seasons with the Washington Redskins. Starring at free safety for the Vikings for the next 12 years, Krause went on to record more interceptions than any other player in NFL history, while also picking off more passes and amassing more interception-return yards than anyone else in team annals. A key member of Vikings teams that won 10 division titles and appeared in four Super Bowls, Krause earned six Pro Bowl selections and three All-Pro nominations during his time in Minnesota, before being further honored following the conclusion of his playing career by being inducted into the team's Ring of Honor and elected to the Pro Football Hall of Fame.

Born in Flint, Michigan, on February 19, 1942, Paul James Krause attended Bendle High School, where he earned All-State honors in football, baseball, basketball, and track, competing in the latter as a pole vaulter and high jumper. After accepting an athletic scholarship to the University of Iowa, Krause continued to excel in multiple sports, starring on the gridiron as a wide receiver and defensive halfback, while also being accorded All-America honors in baseball at the end of his sophomore year for his outstanding play in center field. Choosing to focus exclusively on football after turning down an offer to play minor-league baseball, Krause spent his last two years at Iowa earning numerous individual accolades, with his exceptional two-way play prompting the Washington Redskins to select him in the second round of the 1964 NFL Draft, with the 18th overall pick.

Making an immediate impact in his first NFL season, Krause led the league with 12 interceptions in 1964, earning in the process Pro Bowl and First-Team All-Pro honors for the first of two straight times. Yet even though Krause picked off another 16 passes over the course of the next three seasons, Washington's coaching staff eventually grew disenchanted with his overall play, prompting the Redskins to trade him to the Vikings

Paul Krause intercepted more passes than any other player in NFL history.

for linebacker Marlin McKeever and a seventh-round draft pick following the conclusion of the 1967 campaign. In trying to explain the deal from the Redskins' perspective, Hall of Fame linebacker Sam Huff said, "They traded Paul Krause because he wasn't a great tackler. I told them, 'Don't trade him. This guy can play weak-side safety like nobody, like Willie Mays in the outfield.' They said, 'He doesn't tackle.' I said, 'I make all the tackles, that's what I get paid for.' They traded him anyway, and he's in the Hall of Fame. But what do coaches know?"

Still somewhat bitter over the trade many years later, Krause stated, "I didn't care for [Redskins head coach] Otto Graham. Graham listened to one of his defensive coaches who didn't know what he was doing. Then Graham traded me, so I don't think he knew what he was doing, either."

Krause then added, "I don't know that it was a blessing that I was traded. But I had 12 good seasons with the Minnesota Vikings, went to four Super Bowls, and had some great years. I would have liked to stay with the Redskins, but that's not the way it worked out."

Washington's loss proved to be Minnesota's gain, as Krause helped the Vikings begin an exceptional 11-year run during which they won 10 division titles, three NFC championships, and one NFL title. After earning Second-Team All-Pro honors in 1968 by picking off seven passes, Krause made his first Pro Bowl appearance as a member of the Vikings the following year. He then gained First-Team All-NFC recognition for the first of four straight times in 1970, before making the Pro Bowl in each of the next five seasons. Performing especially well in 1975, Krause earned First-Team All-Pro honors by recording 10 interceptions and amassing a league-leading 201 interception-return yards.

Although Krause never developed into anything more than an average tackler during his time in Minnesota, he made huge contributions to the Vikings' defense with his ability to diagnose plays, which made him an exceptional ball-hawk. Blessed with good size and speed, the 6'3", 200-pound Krause did an outstanding job of covering receivers deep downfield. But his greatest assets proved to be his instincts, intelligence, sense of timing, and ability to anticipate where the quarterback intended to throw the football, which he addressed when he said, "I knew what I could do, and I also knew the game very well. I also knew what the offense was trying to do to the defense. So, I put myself in the positions I was supposed to be in to get the interceptions."

In discussing his role on the team, Krause stated, "I'm plain and simple the safety man, the guy who has to stop the play when the others don't, and that's the way I like it."

Often referred to as the Vikings' center fielder because of his baseball background and ability to create turnovers, Krause explained how his experience playing center field in college helped him patrol the secondary as a free safety when he said, "I was a centerfielder in baseball, and Bud Grant said I was the best centerfielder he's ever seen. That was in football. Basically, if you can find a centerfielder in baseball that plays football too, he would be a good free safety."

Krause continued, "It's the timing that, all of a sudden, you notice how high the ball is going, or how fast the ball is going, you have to take the angles and determine in a split second if you're going to go for the interception or not go for the interception. If you go for it and miss it, it's a touchdown. There are a lot of things that centerfielders and free safeties can do alike. It's all angles, timing, and knowing what you can do with the abilities that you have. I feel like I was blessed with that ability."

Krause remained the Vikings' last line of defense until 1978, when he lost his starting job to Tom Hannon. After sharing playing time with Kurt Knoff the following year, Krause announced his retirement, ending his career with an NFL-record 81 interceptions, which he returned a total of 1,185 yards. Krause also recovered 19 fumbles and scored six touchdowns on defense. During his time in Minnesota, Krause recorded 53 interceptions, amassed 852 interception-return yards, recovered 11 fumbles, and scored four touchdowns, with the first two figures both representing franchise records. An extremely durable player, Krause missed just two games his entire career, appearing in 172 consecutive contests as a member of the Vikings.

Since retiring as an active player, Krause has worked in a variety of fields, including real estate development and insurance. He has also owned a golf course and several restaurants. However, Krause made his greatest contribution to society by spending 20 years serving on the Board of County Commissioners for Dakota County, Minnesota.

On a more personal level, Krause and his family experienced a major setback several years ago when an automobile accident left his wife severely injured, putting her in a coma for five and a half months. In describing how the unfortunate incident has affected his life, Krause told TheGoal .com in 1998:

About two and a half years ago, my wife was in a car accident. A friend called to say she hadn't arrived and, when I went out to look for her, I found a helicopter rushing her to a nearby hospital. She had to be revived twice on the way there. Somehow, I knew she would live, but, for five and a half months, she was in a coma. The battles did not end when she left the hospital, either. An injury to her brainstem has changed her personality some, and she has to have care 24 hours a day. I have experienced just about every emotion you can imagine during all of this, and I still don't know why it happened. But I trust that God knows and, when I get to heaven, I'll ask Him. For now, I know that my wife and I have grown closer, and our whole family continues to pray for her recovery. The doctors tell us that the brainstem can heal, and we have hope.

VIKINGS CAREER HIGHLIGHTS

Best Season

Krause earned Second-Team All-Pro honors twice as a member of the Vikings, doing so for the first time in 1968, when he ranked among the league leaders with three fumble recoveries and seven interceptions, setting a franchise record by picking off passes in six straight games at one point during the season. Krause gained that distinction again in 1972, when he intercepted six passes, amassed 109 interception-return yards, and scored two touchdowns on defense. However, Krause played his best ball for the Vikings in 1975, earning his lone First-Team All-Pro nomination by finishing second in the NFL with 10 interceptions and leading the league with 201 interception-return yards, with his 10 picks establishing a single-season franchise record that still stands.

Memorable Moments/Greatest Performances

Krause recorded his first interception as a member of the Vikings when he picked off a Bart Starr pass during a 26–13 win over the Packers on September 22, 1968.

Krause intercepted two passes during a 52–14 rout of the Steelers on November 23, 1969, returning one of his picks 77 yards for a touchdown.

Although the Vikings lost their 1970 divisional round playoff game matchup with the 49ers by a score of 17–14, Krause recovered two fumbles, one of which he returned 22 yards for a touchdown.

Krause contributed to a 24–7 victory over the Atlanta Falcons on November 28, 1971, by picking off two passes, which he returned for a total of 22 yards.

Krause recorded another pair of interceptions during a 23–20 win over the Denver Broncos on October 15, 1972, returning his two picks a total of 52 yards.

During a 27–13 win over the Packers on October 29, 1972, Krause put the Vikings ahead to stay in the fourth quarter when he returned his interception of a Scott Hunter pass 32 yards for a TD.

Krause lit the scoreboard again on November 19, 1972, when he returned a fumble 30 yards for a touchdown during a 45–41 victory over the Los Angeles Rams.

Krause recorded two of the five interceptions the Vikings registered during a 38–0 blowout of the Falcons on November 9, 1975, returning his picks a total of 31 yards.

Although the Vikings lost to the Lions by a score of 17–10 on December 14, 1975, Krause intercepted two passes and returned a fumble 86 yards for Minnesota's only TD of the game.

Krause, who spent most of his time in Minnesota serving as the holder on field goal and extra-point attempts, gave the Vikings a 22–16 overtime win over the Bears on October 16, 1977, when he delivered an 11-yard touchdown pass to Stu Voigt following a botched field goal attempt.

Krause made history during a 27–21 overtime loss to the Rams on December 2, 1979, recording the final two interceptions of his career, the first of which enabled him to surpass former New York Giants great Emlen Tunnell as the NFL's all-time leader in that category.

Notable Achievements

- Scored four defensive touchdowns.
- Recorded at least five interceptions six times, picking off 10 passes once.
- Amassed more than 100 interception-return yards three times, topping 200 yards once.
- Led NFL with 201 interception-return yards in 1975.
- Finished second in NFL in interceptions once and fumble-return yards once.
- Led Vikings in interceptions three times.
- Holds Vikings single-season record for most interceptions (10 in 1975).
- Holds Vikings career records for most interceptions (53) and most interception-return yards (852).
- Holds NFL career record for most interceptions (81).
- Ranks seventh in NFL history with 1,185 interception-return yards.
- 10-time division champion (1968, 1969, 1970, 1971, 1973, 1974, 1975, 1976, 1977, and 1978).
- 1969 NFL champion.
- Three-time NFC champion (1973, 1974, and 1976).
- Six-time Pro Bowl selection (1969, 1971, 1972, 1973, 1974, and 1975).
- 1975 First-Team All-Pro selection.
- Two-time Second-Team All-Pro selection (1968 and 1972).
- Five-time First-Team All-NFC selection (1970, 1971, 1972, 1973, and 1975).
- Pro Football Reference All-1970s Second Team.
- Inducted into Minnesota Vikings Ring of Honor in 1998.
- Elected to Pro Football Hall of Fame in 1998.

12

MICK TINGELHOFF

dentified by legendary Chicago Bears linebacker Dick Butkus as the toughest center he ever faced, Mick Tingelhoff anchored Minnesota's offensive line from his center position for 17 seasons, starting every game the Vikings played during that time. One of only six players to have his jersey number retired by the team, Tingelhoff appeared in a total of 240 regular-season contests for the Vikings, placing him second in franchise history only to Jim Marshall. A member of Vikings teams that won 10 division titles and made four Super Bowl appearances, Tingelhoff gained Pro Bowl and All-Pro recognition six times each, before being further honored following the conclusion of his playing career by being inducted into the Vikings Ring of Honor and elected to the Pro Football Hall of Fame. Amazingly, Tingelhoff accomplished all he did after entering the NFL in 1962 as an undrafted free agent linebacker.

Born to German immigrant parents in Lexington, Nebraska, on May 22, 1940, Henry Michael Tingelhoff grew up on a farm, where he developed a love for the sport of football by listening to Cornhusker games while milking cows with his dad in the barn. Although Tingelhoff excelled on the gridiron for four years while attending Lexington High School, he never seriously considered pursuing a career in football, revealing, "I had no idea that I would be able to when I was in high school. Then, I got into college and people said that I might have a chance. Things worked out."

Tingelhoff added, "Dad thought football was a waste of time. Mom and dad were from Germany. Mean Germans. They weren't real happy that I got a scholarship to Nebraska. They wanted me to stay on the farm."

Despite the resistance he met from home, Tingelhoff ended up lettering for three years at Nebraska, starting for the Cornhuskers at linebacker and center as a senior, while serving as team co-captain. Nevertheless, Tingelhoff failed to make much of an impression on pro scouts, with all 14 teams subsequently bypassing him in the 1962 NFL Draft. The Vikings, though, showed some interest, with Tingelhoff recalling, "The Vikings were the only

Mick Tingelhoff ranks second only to Jim Marshall in franchise history in games played.

team interested in me, to tell you the truth. After the draft, a couple of days later, I got a phone call. It was the Vikings, and they wanted to talk to me."

After signing with the Vikings as a linebacker for the sum of $11,000, Tingelhoff received his big break when head coach Norm Van Brocklin waived his starting center during training camp and moved him to the offensive side of the ball. Making a seamless transition to his new post, Tingelhoff proved to be a natural at the center slot, saying years later, "It was about the only position I ever played. As the center, we had to call out the defenses. Whether it was even defense or 4-3 defense, or over or under. I enjoyed it."

Developing into one of the league's finest players at his position before long, Tingelhoff earned Pro Bowl and All-Pro honors six straight times from 1964 to 1969, a period during which the Vikings gradually emerged as championship contenders. And, as the Vikings rose to prominence, Tingelhoff established himself as one of the most important figures on the team, with Stu Voigt stating, "Mick was the undisputed leader of the Vikings with Jim Marshall for years and years . . . Mick held his own with some of the game's best—Ray Nitschke, Mike Lucci, and Dick Butkus."

Tingelhoff performed at an extremely high level even though, at only 6'2" and 237 pounds, he lacked the size of an ideal center—even for his day. A quick and tenacious blocker, Tingelhoff had the ability to surge off the ball and knock a linebacker off his feet or engage a defensive tackle when the guard pulled.

In discussing his former teammate, Jim Marshall said, "He never quit. I think that's one of the things that you could always say about him. . . . He would do whatever was necessary to advance the ball. I think Fran Tarkenton summed it up best when he said that he's one of the greatest centers ever to play football. I totally agree with that."

Longtime Vikings trainer Fred Zamberletti suggested, "In his era, he was the best center playing football at that time. . . . He was someone that you could always depend upon. Not only was he a great center, he was a great snapper. And he probably made more tackles snapping the ball and going down on the punting team than anybody on the special teams."

Known for his mental and physical toughness, Tingelhoff, said Vikings head coach Bud Grant, "played center with the mentality of a linebacker. I have no doubt that, had he not played center, he would have been a Hall of Fame linebacker. . . . His intangibles were the thing that made him so great. He was the captain the whole time I coached him, and guys looked at him as an example of how to do things right."

Ed White, who spent nine seasons playing alongside Tingelhoff on the Vikings' offensive line, claimed, "Mick was tough as nails. He played well against all middle linebackers. . . . He was every bit as good as [Mike] Webster. None were any better than Mick."

Meanwhile, Fran Tarkenton wrote in his autobiography, "Mick Tingelhoff was as tough a player as any who ever played. If I gathered every football player that I knew or played with in my life and put them all in a room with the instructions to fight their way out, I would put my money on Mick to get there first."

Tarkenton continued, "He was absolutely ferocious as a blocker and pass protector. He even snapped the ball for punts, field goals, and extra points. If they kept the records for how many tackles he made after interceptions and on punts, his numbers would be staggering. . . . On the field, when I was scrambling, Mick made some of the most devastating blocks imaginable. He took people out of plays—and sometimes out of games. He would make tough hits, clean hits that were absolutely shocking to watch."

Tingelhoff's consecutive games played streak only added to his mystique, with teammate Dave Osborn saying, "Mick Tingelhoff was as durable as they come. He never missed a game. He was an extremely hard worker and full of determination."

Osborn also spoke of Tingelhoff's legendary temper, suggesting that, while he was one of the nicest, quietest guys on the team, "You don't wanna get Mick mad."

Vikings offensive line coach John Michels expressed similar sentiments when he called Tingelhoff "the toughest guy I ever coached," and stated, "This guy was just a warrior. You didn't want to tangle with Mick Tingelhoff."

And, as for Tingelhoff's ability to play with pain, Michels recalled, "There was one game when his leg was basically just hanging there. I told Mick he wasn't going to play. He looked at me and said, 'Forget about it. I'm playing.' You know what? He went on and just clobbered his opponent. Mick was just the toughest guy I knew."

Revealing that Tingelhoff's toughness left a lasting impression on legendary Green Bay Packers head coach Vince Lombardi, Sid Hartman of the *Minneapolis Star Tribune* once wrote:

> One of Tingelhoff's biggest boosters was the late Vince Lombardi, who was a personal friend and told me after one of the Vikings' victories over the Packers in Green Bay, "That number 53 played one of the greatest games I've ever witnessed a center play." And, when I told Lombardi that Tingelhoff played with a torn muscle, he laughed. So, to prove my point, I got Don Lannon, the Vikings' doctor at the time, to send Lombardi an X-ray of Tingelhoff's knee. The Packers coach was shocked and brought it up the next time I saw him.

When the Vikings retired his jersey in 2001, longtime Vikings trainer Fred Zamberletti verified what I told Lombardi when he told the *Star Tribune*: "I remember once he tore a leg muscle. We taped him all the way from his toes to his buttocks, and he played every play against Green Bay. I remember another time he had a separated shoulder. The doctor said there was no way he could play, but, somehow, he had a miraculous recovery and played Sunday."

Tingelhoff continued to start every game at center for the Vikings until the end of 1978, when, after 17 seasons, he decided to announce his retirement. In addition to the many individual accolades Tingelhoff earned over the course of his career, he helped Vikings running backs earn 13 trips to the Pro Bowl. Meanwhile, Tingelhoff's snaps allowed placekicker Fred Cox to score more points than anyone else in franchise history.

Yet, despite his many accomplishments, it took Tingelhoff more than three decades to gain induction into the Pro Football Hall of Fame, with the Senior Committee finally electing him in 2015. Upon learning of his longtime teammate's election, Alan Page said, "After all these years, he's finally getting the recognition he deserves. Absolutely, he should be in. He, certainly at the time I was playing, was one of the best centers in the game. I think he was as good a center as any center who played after that. . . . You have to be good, and you have to be healthy, not just every game, but every week and every year. He was both."

Following his playing days, Tingelhoff became a stockbroker and dealt in commercial real estate development. Unfortunately, he began experiencing memory loss around 2005 and has since been diagnosed with dementia.

CAREER HIGHLIGHTS

Best Season

Tingelhoff earned six consecutive trips to the Pro Bowl from 1964 to 1969, turning in his most dominant performance in the last of those campaigns. In addition to gaining First-Team All-Pro recognition for the fifth and final time, Tingelhoff earned the distinction of being named NFL Offensive Lineman of the Year by the 1,000-Yard Club in Columbus, Ohio.

Memorable Moments/Greatest Performances

Tingelhoff anchored an offensive line that enabled the Vikings to amass 549 yards of total offense during a convincing 42–21 victory over the San Francisco 49ers on October 24, 1965.

Tingelhoff and his line-mates dominated the San Francisco defensive front once again on October 30, 1966, with the Vikings gaining 246 yards on the ground and amassing 559 yards of total offense during a 28–3 win over the 49ers.

Tingelhoff's stellar blocking at the point of attack helped the Vikings amass 622 yards of total offense during a 52–14 rout of the defending NFL champion Baltimore Colts in Week 2 of the 1969 campaign.

Notable Achievements

- Never missed a game his entire career, starting 240 consecutive games at center.
- Ranks second in franchise history with 17 seasons played and 240 games played.
- 10-time division champion (1968, 1969, 1970, 1971, 1973, 1974, 1975, 1976, 1977, and 1978).
- 1969 NFL champion.
- Three-time NFC champion (1973, 1974, and 1976).
- Six-time Pro Bowl selection (1964, 1965, 1966, 1967, 1968, and 1969).
- Five-time First-Team All-Pro selection (1964, 1965, 1966, 1968, and 1969).
- 1967 Second-Team All-Pro selection.
- 1970 First-Team All-NFC selection.
- Pro Football Reference All-1960s Second Team.
- #53 retired by Vikings.
- Inducted into Minnesota Vikings Ring of Honor in 2001.
- Elected to Pro Football Hall of Fame in 2015.

13

JIM MARSHALL

The heart and soul of the Vikings' defense for nearly two decades, Jim Marshall spent 19 seasons in Minnesota, serving as one of the most significant figures in the franchise's rise to prominence. A member of Vikings teams that won 10 division titles and made four Super Bowl appearances, Marshall proved to be a model of consistency during his time in Minnesota, starting 270 consecutive games at defensive end following his arrival in the Twin Cities in 1961. The Vikings' all-time leader in games played, seasons played, and fumbles recovered on defense, Marshall also recorded a total of 127 sacks that represents the second-highest figure in team annals. A consummate team player, Marshall contributed to the development of fellow Purple People Eaters Alan Page and Carl Eller, helping both men reach their full potential. Selected to two Pro Bowls, honored by having his #70 retired by the Vikings, and inducted into the team's Ring of Honor in 1999, Marshall has received numerous individual accolades for the many contributions he made to the Purple and Gold through the years. Yet, the one honor that continues to elude him is election to the Pro Football Hall of Fame.

Born in Danville, Kentucky, on December 30, 1937, James Lawrence Marshall moved with his family to Columbus, Ohio, where he attended East High School. After starring in football at East High, Marshall spent three years at Ohio State University, earning All-America honors as a junior, before leaving prior to the start of his senior year to play for the Saskatchewan Roughriders of the Canadian Football League. Dealt to the Cleveland Browns, who had selected him in the fourth round of the 1960 NFL Draft, following the conclusion of the 1959 campaign, Marshall spent one year in Cleveland serving as a part-time player, before being included in a trade that sent six players to the expansion Minnesota Vikings for a pair of picks in the 1962 NFL Draft.

Joining the Vikings in their inaugural season, Marshall spent his first few years in Minnesota playing for mostly losing teams, with the club

Jim Marshall holds franchise records for most seasons played, games played, and fumbles recovered on defense.

posting a winning mark just once from 1961 to 1967. Nevertheless, Marshall soon established himself as one of the NFL's better defensive ends, leading the Vikings in sacks in each of their first six years in the league, while also recovering a total of 15 fumbles. After playing on the left side of Minnesota's defense in 1961, Marshall moved to right defensive end the following year, beginning in the process a string of 18 consecutive seasons during which he manned that post for the Vikings.

The 6'4" Marshall, who entered the NFL weighing only 220 pounds, spent most of his career playing at a listed weight of 248 pounds, although that figure seems somewhat generous when it is considered that many sources suggest that he weighed somewhere between 220 and 235 pounds. Yet, despite his relative lack of size, Marshall possessed several qualities that enabled him to gradually emerge as one of the league's top players at his position, as Vikings head coach Bud Grant noted years later when he said, "Jim was the epitome of what a defensive end could do, and how the position could change a game. He was a guy who was gifted beyond belief with ability to play the position. His toughness to play through injuries and conditions is what people remember the most about Marshall. He was a guy who players gravitated to because he was simply better than them at everything. Run faster, jump higher, hit harder—Marshall just did it better than everyone else and did it better for a long time."

Fran Tarkenton further elaborated on his longtime teammate's unique gifts when he stated, "Jim was the leader of the team, unequivocally, for 19 years. He made everyone around him better. He was as good a pass rusher as there was during all 19 years. He had enormous talent, relentless competitiveness, and was respected by everyone in football. No offensive lineman could keep Jim Marshall from harassing the quarterback."

In addition to excelling as a pass-rusher, Marshall played the run extremely well, recording an unofficial total of 988 tackles as a member of the Vikings that places him ninth in franchise history. Yet, Marshall's greatest strength may well have been his extraordinary leadership ability, which made him arguably the Vikings' most respected player. In discussing the impact that Marshall had on the other players around him, Bobby Bryant said, "To those of us who played with him, he was a godlike figure. He did it all, was very intelligent and a great player."

Alan Page, who spent parts of 12 seasons playing immediately next to Marshall on the Vikings' defensive line, stated, "Jim was the consummate team player, an inspiration to offensive and defensive players. His enthusiasm was infectious, and he led by word and deed. To do the things he could do, for as long and as well as he did, I sit in awe, and I was able to see it up close. He was considered in the same class as a Deacon Jones or a Carl Eller and was respected as much as any defensive end of the time."

Page continued, "Jim Marshall is what football is all about, both from the inside and visibly from the outside. He had a really strong sense of what it took to get the job done. He could play against people that outweighed him by 30 or 40 pounds and bend them over backwards. He could work over an offensive tackle or a running back, or whoever was in the way, and he knew what was important in the game. He knew that the object was to stop the other team from advancing the ball, and he literally would do whatever it took."

Persevering through the lean years that lasted from 1961 to 1967, Marshall proved to be a key figure in the greatest period in franchise history, helping the Vikings win 10 division titles, three NFC championships, and one NFL title from 1968 to 1978. Starting every game at his familiar position of right defensive end, Marshall ended up setting an NFL record for defensive players that still stands by making 270 consecutive starts. In addition to playing with ankle sprains and concussions that might have sidelined a lesser man, Marshall twice left his hospital bed to take the field for the Vikings, once while recuperating from pneumonia, and another time while battling ulcers. On another occasion, Marshall kept his streak intact by playing after he accidentally shot himself in the side while cleaning a shotgun.

In discussing his extraordinary streak years later, Marshall told the *Minneapolis Star Tribune*, "I was blessed. When it got close to game time, regardless of whether I was in the hospital or how badly banged up I was, something always seemed to happen to allow me to play."

In trying to explain Marshall's amazing durability and tremendous longevity, longtime Vikings trainer Fred Zamberletti commented, "Jim would say it's the vitamins he takes or transcendental meditation or something else, but it's not true. I've seen all that stuff come and go with him. He's just one of those people who has been blessed with a great body."

Meanwhile, Marshall suggested that his career lasted so long simply because he wanted it to, saying, "Why can't I play football until I'm 42? Only because someone my age isn't supposed to be able to. That's the mind's negative programming. The human body is the only thing we have that we can control to some degree, and the mental controls the physical. There are things we are physically capable of doing but push away from because our minds tell us to."

Finally deciding to leave the game he loved at the end of the 1979 season, Marshall announced his retirement shortly after celebrating his 42nd birthday. Pleased with her husband's decision, Marshall's wife, Anita, said at the time, "I'm glad it's done. It has been fun, but inside you knew it had to end sometime. There were two ways that it could end—on top with dignity, or the other way. I like the 'on top with dignity.'"

Meanwhile, Marshall stated, "I always said I would play as long as I could contribute and the team needed me, and I still feel like I could play another year or two, but it's time for a change. I'm a talented individual, and now I have to let those talents take me elsewhere."

In addition to his 270 consecutive starts, Marshall played in 282 straight games, which represents the second-longest streak in NFL history. Marshall also recovered the second-most fumbles of any NFL player on defense, with all but one of his 30 fumble recoveries coming as a member of the Vikings.

Looking back with amazement on Marshall's career, Bob Lurtsema, who spent parts of six seasons during the 1970s serving the Vikings as a backup defensive lineman, told *Sports Headliners*, "He instigated the consistency for the 'Purple People Eaters.' He is a lot of the reason that Page and Eller are in the Hall of Fame. . . . You gotta realize how good he was. I couldn't beat him out of his job. What he did the best was consistency."

Meanwhile, Pro Football Hall of Famer Paul Krause expressed disbelief that his former teammate had yet to join him in Canton when he said, "Jim Marshall was a great team leader. He was also a great pass-rusher. He never missed a game his entire career, and that tells me that he did things in a game that really dominated the game. And why Jim Marshall is not in the Hall of Fame I do not know."

VIKINGS CAREER HIGHLIGHTS

Best Season

Marshall had his finest season for the Vikings in 1969, when he recorded 14 sacks, earning in the process one of his two trips to the Pro Bowl and Second-Team All-Pro recognition from the Newspaper Enterprise Association, United Press International, and the *New York Daily News*.

Memorable Moments/Greatest Performances

Marshall scored the only touchdown of his career when he ran the ball in from 12 yards out after recovering a fumble during a lopsided 45–14 victory over the San Francisco 49ers on September 29, 1963.

Marshall recorded a safety when he sacked Bart Starr in the end zone during a 26–13 win over the Packers on September 22, 1968.

Marshall registered his lone career interception during a 27–0 victory over the Lions on November 27, 1969, subsequently returning the ball 30 yards into Detroit territory.

Marshall contributed to the Vikings' 23–20 win over the Los Angeles Rams in the divisional round of the 1969 playoffs by recording one of the three sacks they registered against Roman Gabriel.

Marshall helped lead the Vikings to a 10–3 victory over the Buffalo Bills on December 9, 1979, by sacking Joe Ferguson twice in the final home game of his illustrious career. Marshall, who even played offensive tackle during Minnesota's final series, subsequently found himself being carried off the field by his teammates. Vikings head coach Bud Grant further honored Marshall following the conclusion of the contest by presenting him with the first game ball he ever awarded to a member of the team.

Despite his many on-field achievements, Marshall is perhaps remembered most for the blunder he committed during a 27–22 win over the San Francisco 49ers on October 25, 1964. After recovering a fumble on the Minnesota 34 yard line, Marshall lost his bearings and ran the wrong way 66 yards into his own end zone. Thinking that he had scored a touchdown for the Vikings, Marshall tossed the ball into the air in celebration. With the ball landing out of bounds, officials awarded two points to the 49ers, crediting them with a safety. Fortunately for Marshall, the Vikings ended up winning the game, with the final margin of victory provided by a Carl Eller touchdown return of a fumble caused by a Marshall sack. Looking back on his miscue years later, Marshall said, "I was so intent on picking the ball up and doing something with it that I wasn't even aware of what I had done until the ball had been whistled dead. It was the perfect example of a young player using energy without thinking." In 2019, Marshall's gaffe received a number 54 ranking on the list of the NFL's 100 Greatest Plays.

Notable Achievements

- Never missed a game in 19 seasons, starting franchise record 270 consecutive contests.
- Scored one defensive touchdown.
- Recorded 14 sacks in 1969.
- Led Vikings in sacks six times.
- Holds Vikings career records for most seasons played (19), games played (270), and fumble recoveries (29).
- Ranks among Vikings career leaders with 127 sacks (2nd) and 988 tackles (8th).
- Ranks second in NFL history with 30 fumbles recovered on defense.
- Holds second-longest consecutive games played streak in NFL history (282).

- 10-time division champion (1968, 1969, 1970, 1971, 1973, 1974, 1975, 1976, 1977, and 1978).
- 1969 NFL champion.
- Three-time NFC champion (1973, 1974, and 1976).
- Two-time Pro Bowl selection (1968 and 1969).
- 1971 Second-Team All-NFC selection.
- Pro Football Reference All-1960s Second Team.
- Pro Football Reference All-1970s Second Team.
- #70 retired by Vikings.
- Inducted into Minnesota Vikings Ring of Honor in 1999.

14

CHUCK FOREMAN

The focal point of the Vikings' offense for much of the 1970s, Chuck Foreman proved to be arguably the NFL's most versatile running back during his seven seasons in Minnesota. A swift and elusive runner who became known as "The Spin Doctor" for his ability to avoid defenders with his patented spin move, Foreman gained more than 1,000 yards on the ground three times, leading the Vikings in rushing in each of his first six seasons. An exceptional receiver as well, Foreman caught more than 50 passes four times, becoming in 1975 just the second running back in NFL history to lead the league in receptions. Amassing more than 1,000 yards from scrimmage on six separate occasions, Foreman earned five Pro Bowl selections and three All-Pro nominations, before being further honored following the conclusion of his playing career by being named to the Pro Football Reference All-1970s Second Team and inducted into the Vikings Ring of Honor.

Born in Frederick, Maryland, on October 26, 1950, Walter Eugene Foreman attended Frederick High School, where he starred in football, basketball, and track, excelling in the latter as a hurdler. A standout wide receiver at Frederick, Foreman, who grew up rooting for the Washington Redskins, Baltimore Colts, and Baltimore Bullets, began incorporating the spin move into his running style after watching Bullets Hall of Fame guard Earl Monroe employ the same maneuver on the basketball court. After being recruited by several colleges for his skills on the hardwood, Foreman ultimately accepted a football scholarship from the University of Miami, where he displayed his versatility by playing three different positions.

Forced to move to the defensive side of the ball due to a rash of injuries, Foreman spent his sophomore campaign playing cornerback for the Hurricanes, before being shifted to running back the following year. Excelling at his new post, Foreman earned All-America honors by gaining 951 yards on the ground and another 72 yards through the air. Foreman then spent his senior year at wide receiver, making 37 receptions for 557 yards, while also

Chuck Foreman amassed more than 1,000 yards from scrimmage six times for the Vikings.
Courtesy of Wikimedia Commons

carrying the ball 107 times for 484 yards. Impressed with Foreman's ability to navigate his way past would-be tacklers, Miami head coach Fran Curci noted, "Chuck Foreman has that extra move you don't teach; you have to be born with it."

Selected by the Vikings in the first round of the 1973 NFL Draft, with the 12th overall pick, Foreman initially had strong reservations about going to Minnesota, recalling years later, "All I could think of was the game I'd seen where they'd used flamethrowers at Metropolitan Stadium to thaw out the field. I said, 'Damn, it's cold up there.'"

However, Foreman eventually came to enjoy the time he spent in the Twin Cities, adding, "But going to Minnesota was the best thing that happened because people treated you with respect. Once, I dropped a $100 bill on the sidewalk and a kid said, 'Hey mister, you dropped your money.'"

Inserted into the Vikings' starting backfield immediately upon his arrival in Minnesota, Foreman manned both running back positions at different times, concluding his first pro season with 801 yards rushing, 37 receptions, 362 receiving yards, 1,163 yards from scrimmage, and six touchdowns, with his exceptional play earning him Pro Bowl and NFL Offensive Rookie of the Year honors. And, with Foreman's quickness, elusiveness, and pass-receiving ability adding a new dimension to their offense, the Vikings improved their record from 7-7 to 12-2 and won the NFC championship, before losing to the Miami Dolphins in Super Bowl VIII.

Foreman followed up his brilliant rookie campaign with five more outstanding seasons, posting the following numbers from 1974 to 1978:

YEAR	YDS RUSHING	RECS	REC YDS	YDS FROM SCRIMMAGE	TDS
1974	777	53	586	1,363	15
1975	1,070	73	691	1,761	22
1976	1,155	55	567	1,722	14
1977	1,112	38	308	1,420	9
1978	749	61	396	1,145	7

After leading the NFL with 15 touchdowns in 1974, Foreman topped the circuit with 73 receptions the following year, setting in the process a new single-season record for running backs. That same season, Foreman became the first Vikings player to rush for more than 1,000 yards. He also finished second in the league in yards from scrimmage, touchdowns, and points scored (132), with his fabulous performance earning him First-Team All-Pro honors. Foreman followed that up by ranking among the league leaders in seven different offensive categories in 1976, prompting the United Press International (UPI) to name him its NFC Offensive Player of the Year. Foreman appeared in the Pro Bowl in four of those five seasons, made three All-Pro three teams, and gained All-NFC recognition four times. More importantly, the Vikings won the division title all five years and made two Super Bowl appearances.

Standing 6'2" and weighing 210 pounds, Foreman possessed good size and strength, making it extremely difficult for defenders to bring him down one-on-one. Also blessed with tremendous stamina, Foreman seemed to grow stronger over the course of a game, with teammate Bob Lurtsema stating, "The thing about Chuck was he got better as the game went on. Chuck was nearly unstoppable in the fourth quarter. The other team would be tired, and he was getting stronger. He just ran over people as the game wore on."

Extremely quick and elusive as well, Foreman employed a rather unique running style in which he often used powerful stiff arms and wide-legged spin moves that frequently left would-be tacklers grasping for air. In discussing his patented spin move, Foreman said, "Carrying the ball, I would see a place where I wanted to be on the field, and the only way to get there was to spin. It worked."

Meanwhile, Alan Goldstein of the *Baltimore Sun* described Foreman's running style as having "the grace of a ballet dancer and the elusiveness of a greased pig."

Foreman's exceptional running ability, combined with his superior pass-catching skills, made him invaluable to the Vikings' offense, which served as a precursor of the West Coast Offense that Bill Walsh installed in San Francisco during the 1980s. Responsible for nearly 25 percent of the yards the Vikings gained on offense during his time in Minnesota, Foreman proved to be the one indispensable member of the unit, with offensive line coach John Michels stating, "What a horse. He absolutely carried us at times. Chuck was a load. It was a pleasure having my guys block for him. Chuck made it easy for all of us at times."

But, with the Vikings depending so heavily on Foreman, the star running back began to wear down in 1979, rushing for only 223 yards, amassing just 370 yards from scrimmage, and scoring only two touchdowns while trying to play through injuries. Dealt to the New England Patriots at season's end, Foreman left Minnesota with career totals of 5,887 yards rushing, 336 receptions, 3,057 receiving yards, 8,944 yards from scrimmage, 8,978 all-purpose yards, 52 rushing touchdowns, 23 TD catches, 75 touchdowns, and 450 points scored, with many of those figures continuing to place him among the franchise's all-time leaders.

Foreman ended up spending just one season in New England, assuming a backup role for the Patriots in 1980, before announcing his retirement at the end of the year. He subsequently became involved with numerous business ventures, including a Twin Cities–based trucking company that dissolved in 1994. After being sentenced to probation in 2000 for his involvement in a mail fraud scheme, Foreman began public speaking at schools and became a substitute teacher in Bloomington. He also owns a commercial cleaning company and a memorabilia business. Now 70 years of age, Foreman lives in Eden Prairie, Minnesota, where he says he spends most of his time "playing golf and riding my bike, 15 or 20 miles at a time, on trails around here."

Looking back on his playing career, Foreman says, "I think my versatility defined my career more than one single play did. I could do things other guys couldn't do. I could go out for a pass and catch the ball with one hand behind my head. Nobody else could do that. I was the first guy to be used out of the backfield as a receiving threat."

VIKINGS CAREER HIGHLIGHTS

Best Season

Foreman had a tremendous year for the Vikings in 1976, earning UPI NFC Offensive Player of the Year honors by leading the NFL with 14 touchdowns and placing near the top of the league rankings with 1,155 yards rushing, 1,722 yards from scrimmage, 1,723 all-purpose yards, 55 receptions, and 13 rushing touchdowns. However, he posted slightly better overall numbers the previous season, earning his lone First-Team All-Pro selection in 1975 by leading the league with 73 receptions and ranking among the leaders with 1,070 yards rushing, 1,761 yards from scrimmage, 1,765 all-purpose yards, 13 rushing touchdowns, nine TD receptions, 22 touchdowns, and 132 points scored, with his 22 TDs setting a single-season franchise record that still stands.

Memorable Moments/Greatest Performances

Foreman scored the first touchdown of his career in his first game as a pro when he hauled in a 9-yard pass from Fran Tarkenton during a 24–16 win over the Oakland Raiders in the opening game of the 1973 regular season.

Foreman followed that up in Week 2 by rushing for 116 yards and making four receptions for 46 yards during a 22–13 victory over the Chicago Bears.

Foreman helped lead the Vikings to a 31–7 win over the Packers on December 8, 1973, by carrying the ball 19 times for 100 yards and one touchdown, which came on a season-long 50-yard run.

Foreman proved to be a thorn in the side of the Packers once again in the opening game of the 1974 regular season, rushing for three touchdowns during a 32–17 Vikings win.

Foreman led the Vikings to a 23–21 victory over the Dallas Cowboys on October 6, 1974, by amassing 203 yards from scrimmage and scoring two touchdowns. In addition to gaining 72 yards on the ground, Foreman made five receptions for 131 yards and two TDs, the longest of which came on a 66-yard pass from Fran Tarkenton.

Foreman excelled during a 30–14 win over the St. Louis Cardinals in the divisional round of the 1974 playoffs, rushing for 114 yards and one touchdown, while also making five receptions for 54 yards.

Foreman provided much of the offensive firepower when the Vikings defeated the Jets by a score of 29–21 on October 12, 1975, rushing for 96 yards and one touchdown, and making nine receptions for 105 yards and another two TDs.

Foreman turned in another outstanding all-around effort against the Packers on November 2, 1975, rushing for 72 yards, gaining another 93 yards on nine pass receptions, and scoring a touchdown during a 28–17 Vikings win.

Foreman followed that up by rushing for 102 yards and scoring three touchdowns during a 38–0 rout of the Atlanta Falcons on November 9, 1975.

Foreman led the Vikings to a 28–13 win over the San Diego Chargers on November 23, 1975, by gaining a season-high 127 yards on the ground and scoring three touchdowns.

Foreman capped off his exceptional 1975 campaign by rushing for 85 yards, making 10 receptions for 87 yards, and scoring a career-high four touchdowns during a 35–13 victory over the Buffalo Bills in the regular-season finale.

Foreman proved to be the difference in a 17–6 win over the Pittsburgh Steelers on October 4, 1976, finishing the game with 148 yards rushing and two touchdowns.

Foreman starred during a 24–7 victory over the Giants on October 17, 1976, rushing for 83 yards and making eight receptions for 118 yards and one touchdown, which came on a 41-yard pass from Fran Tarkenton.

Picking up right where he left off the following week, Foreman scored two touchdowns and established career-high marks with 200 yards rushing and 265 yards from scrimmage during a 31–12 win over the Philadelphia Eagles on October 24, 1976, with his 265 yards from scrimmage representing a single-game franchise record.

Foreman helped lead the Vikings to a 35–20 victory over the Washington Redskins in the divisional round of the 1976 playoffs by rushing for 105 yards and two touchdowns, one of which came on a 30-yard scamper.

Foreman followed that up by rushing for 118 yards, making five receptions for 81 yards, and scoring one touchdown during the Vikings' 24–13 win over the Los Angeles Rams in the 1976 NFC championship game, with his 199 yards from scrimmage accounting for nearly 75 percent of Minnesota's offense.

Foreman led the Vikings to a 22–16 overtime win over the Bears on October 16, 1977, by rushing for 150 yards and one touchdown.

Foreman contributed to a 42–10 rout of the Cincinnati Bengals on November 13, 1977, by rushing for 133 yards and scoring three touchdowns.

Foreman helped lead the Vikings to a 30–21 win over the Lions in the final game of the 1977 regular season by rushing for 156 yards and two touchdowns.

Foreman gained more than 100 yards on the ground for the final time in his career during a 21–10 win over the Cowboys on October 26, 1978, finishing the game with 101 yards on 22 carries.

Notable Achievements

- Rushed for more than 1,000 yards three times.
- Surpassed 50 receptions four times and 500 receiving yards three times.
- Amassed more than 1,000 yards from scrimmage six times, topping 1,500 yards twice.
- Scored more than 10 touchdowns three times, registering more than 20 TDs once.
- Scored more than 100 points once.
- Led NFL in receptions once and touchdowns twice.
- Finished second in NFL in yards from scrimmage once, rushing touchdowns once, touchdowns once, and points scored once.
- Finished third in NFL in rushing attempts once, yards from scrimmage once, all-purpose yards once, rushing touchdowns twice, and receiving touchdowns once.
- Led Vikings in rushing six times and receptions three times.
- Holds Vikings single-season record for most touchdowns scored (22 in 1975).
- Ranks among Vikings career leaders with 1,533 rushing attempts (3rd), 5,887 yards rushing (3rd), 8,944 yards from scrimmage (4th), 8,978

all-purpose yards (6th), 52 rushing touchdowns (tied for 2nd), 75 touchdowns (5th), and 450 points scored (10th).

- Six-time division champion (1973, 1974, 1975, 1976, 1977, and 1978).
- Three-time NFC champion (1973, 1974, and 1976).
- 1973 NFL Offensive Rookie of the Year.
- 1974 Kansas City Committee of 101 NFC Offensive Player of the Year.
- 1976 UPI NFC Offensive Player of the Year.
- Five-time Pro Bowl selection (1973, 1974, 1975, 1976, and 1977).
- 1975 First-Team All-Pro selection.
- Two-time Second-Team All-Pro selection (1974 and 1976).
- Three-time First-Team All-NFC selection (1974, 1975, and 1976).
- 1977 Second-Team All-NFC selection.
- Pro Football Reference All-1970s Second Team.
- Inducted into Minnesota Vikings Ring of Honor in 2007.

15

MATT BLAIR

One of the most athletically gifted players ever to don the Purple and Gold, Matt Blair spent 12 seasons in Minnesota starring for the Vikings on both defense and special teams. A nine-year starter at left-outside linebacker, Blair proved to be equally effective against the run and the pass, recording the second-most tackles in franchise history, while also intercepting more passes than any other Vikings linebacker. An exceptional performer on special teams as well, Blair ranks among the NFL's all-time leaders in blocked kicks, with his tremendous versatility helping the Vikings win six division titles and two NFC championships. Accorded Pro Bowl and All-Conference honors six times each, Blair received the additional distinction of being inducted into the Vikings Ring of Honor following the conclusion of his playing career.

Born in Hilo, Hawaii, on September 20, 1950, Matthew Albert Blair lived a nomadic existence as a youngster, with his father's service in the US Air Force forcing his family to relocate many times. Finally settling in Ohio as a teenager, Blair finished his high school days at Columbus East High, where he began playing football in his junior year as a means of obtaining a college scholarship. Yet, despite making All-City as a senior, Blair failed to receive a single scholarship offer from a major university due to his struggles in the classroom. Ultimately choosing to enroll at tiny Northeast Oklahoma Junior College, Blair earned a half scholarship through football and received his other half scholarship by playing basketball. Fortunate enough to grow three inches and gain 45 pounds over the summer following his freshman year, Blair recalled, "I had grown so much that my sister had to sew flairs [sic] on the bottom of my jeans so they would look right. I still had those jeans when I played for the Vikings."

Subsequently recruited by several major colleges, including Florida, Florida State, Oklahoma, Oklahoma State, Alabama, and Iowa State, Blair ended up choosing Iowa State over Florida State, saying years later, "I settled on Iowa State because then-coach Johnny Majors said I would have to

Matt Blair excelled for the Vikings on both defense and special teams for 12 seasons.
Courtesy of MearsOnlineAuctions.com

work for my spot on the team, and I love a challenge. Florida State said I would be a starter right away, but I had heard that before. I liked the idea of having to go in and earn my way, and I did that at Iowa State."

A two-time letter winner at ISU, Blair performed brilliantly for the Cyclones in his junior year, recording 121 tackles, en route to earning

All-America honors. However, a knee injury forced him to miss most of the 1972 season, prompting him to return to the school as a fifth-year senior in 1973, when he once again gained All-America recognition by registering 77 tackles, one interception, and three fumble recoveries.

Impressed with Blair's outstanding athleticism and exceptional play at the collegiate level, the Vikings made him the 51st overall pick of the 1974 NFL Draft when they selected him in the second round, with Blair recounting years later, "I got the call, and back then there was not a lot of hype over the draft. Anyway, the Vikings called me and said, 'We are taking you in the second round,' and I said, 'Cool, this is good,' and me and my dog Slick walked down to Burger King and I bought him two burgers, and I had one, and that is how we celebrated."

Looking back on the team's selection of Blair, Vikings head coach Bud Grant recalled, "When we saw him on film and scouted him, I told our coaches that we needed that young man in Minnesota. He was recruited by other teams, but he actually got hurt his first senior year, and that may have scared a few teams away from him. We wanted to take the chance because we liked what we saw, so, when he was there in the second round, we had to take him."

Realizing that he faced many obstacles once he arrived in Minnesota, Blair later said, "The Vikings took [linebacker] Fred McNeill in the first round, and, of course, I got picked in the second. There were already five backers on the roster, so I knew I had to work my butt off to make this team."

Blair continued, "I think a telling moment was when I forced Fran Tarkenton into a bad pass, because I covered a lot of ground and took away his short passes that he was so good at. I believe I immediately gained his respect."

In discussing his former teammate, Carl Eller said, "I tell you what— Matt was a great football player. He came in and showed that he had the interest to learn, and it didn't take long for him to build that relationship you need out on the field."

Blair ended up spending most of his first two seasons in Minnesota playing on special teams, while also backing up veteran Roy Winston at left-outside linebacker. Yet, even in his somewhat limited role, Blair performed well enough in 1974 to earn a spot on the NFL All-Rookie Team. After taking over for Winston in 1976, Blair started all but two games over the course of the next eight seasons, a period during which he established himself as one of the finest all-around linebackers in the game.

Blessed with good size and speed, the 6'5", 235-pound Blair did an excellent job of supporting the run, recording more than 100 tackles seven times, with his 1,452 career stops and 20 fumble recoveries both placing him among the franchise's all-time leaders. Excellent in pass coverage as well, Blair picked off 16 passes, which he returned a total of 119 yards. And, although the NFL did not begin keeping an official record of sacks until 1982, Blair did an outstanding job of applying pressure to opposing quarterbacks coming off the edge.

Nevertheless, Blair's most unique gift lay in his ability to block kicks, which he likened to going for a slam dunk in basketball, saying, "You take a running start, you leap, and you make it happen. . . . Playing basketball at a small college in Oklahoma, I developed the ability to jump, and jump pretty high. That really helped me, along with my timing, to block kicks."

In all, Blair thwarted 20 field goal, extra-point, or punt attempts over the course of his career—more than any other Vikings player. And, with another three blocked kicks in postseason play, Blair's total of 23 blocks places him second in NFL history.

Extremely durable, Blair, who spent his final seven seasons in Minnesota serving as defensive captain, missed just two games his first 10 years in the league. But, after undergoing arthroscopic surgery on his left knee, Blair sat out the first five games of the 1984 campaign. Failing to regain his earlier form upon his return to action, Blair lost his starting job the following year, prompting him to announce his retirement at season's end. In addition to his 1,452 tackles, 16 interceptions, 20 fumble recoveries, and 20 blocked kicks, Blair scored two touchdowns—with one of those coming on defense and the other on special teams.

After retiring as an active player, Blair took up golfing, which, along with photography, became one of his two great passions. Unfortunately, Blair was diagnosed in 2015 as being in the early stages of dementia, likely brought on by the many hits he took to the head during his playing career. Having lost his close friend and former teammate Fred McNeill to CTE that same year, Blair said at the time, "He was my best friend. I just don't know what he went through."

Cared for by his wife as his condition continued to worsen over the course of the next few years, Blair later said, "Each day that I'm living, she's taking care of me. I just can't remember a lot of things that she tells me to do. And most of the time, when she tells me when to do things, I try and write things down."

Finally admitted to hospice care, Blair died on October 22, 2020, just one month after he turned 70 years of age. Upon learning of his former teammate's passing, Scott Studwell stated, "He'd been suffering for a while, so I guess maybe it's a blessing in disguise. But it's still too young. It's a sad day."

Meanwhile, Vikings owner Mark Wilf released a statement that read: "Matt Blair was a great presence at Vikings events and a tremendous teammate long after playing. He embodied the best of what it means to be a Viking. Matt is a Ring of Honor player whose legacy will live on forever with the franchise and in the community he loved."

CAREER HIGHLIGHTS

Best Season

Blair had a tremendous all-around year for the Vikings in 1981, earning Second-Team All-NFC honors by recording six sacks, successfully defending 12 passes, blocking four kicks, and registering more than 150 tackles. However, he performed even better the previous season, gaining First-Team All-Pro recognition for the only time in his career and being named the NFC's Most Valuable Linebacker after recording 220 combined tackles, which represents the third-highest single-season total in franchise history.

Memorable Moments/Greatest Performances

Blair recorded the first interception of his career during a 17–10 win over the Bears on November 3, 1974.

Although the Vikings lost Super Bowl IX to the Steelers by a score of 16–6, Blair gave them their only points of the game when he blocked Bobby Walden's punt, which Minnesota teammate Terry Brown subsequently recovered in the end zone for a touchdown.

Blair proved to be a huge factor in the 1976 NFC championship game, helping the Vikings record a 24–13 victory over the Los Angeles Rams by recovering two fumbles and blocking a field goal attempt that teammate Bobby Bryant subsequently returned 90 yards for a touchdown.

Blair scored the first points of his career when he returned a blocked punt 10 yards for a touchdown during a 10–7 loss to the Bears on November 20, 1977.

Blair lit the scoreboard again during a 24–20 win over the Bears on September 25, 1978, when he ran 49 yards for a touchdown after having the ball lateraled to him following a fumble recovery.

Blair helped lead the Vikings to a 10–3 victory over the Buffalo Bills on December 9, 1979, by picking off two passes in one game for the only time in his career.

Notable Achievements

- Scored one touchdown on defense and another on special teams.
- Recorded more than 100 tackles seven times, registering more than 200 stops once.
- Finished third in NFL with five fumble recoveries in 1976.
- Holds Vikings career record for most blocked kicks (20).
- Ranks among Vikings career leaders with 1,452 tackles (2nd) and 20 fumble recoveries (3rd).
- Six-time division champion (1974, 1975, 1976, 1977, 1978, and 1980).
- Two-time NFC champion (1974 and 1976).
- Member of 1974 NFL All-Rookie Team.
- Six-time Pro Bowl selection (1977, 1978, 1979, 1980, 1981, and 1982).
- 1980 First-Team All-Pro selection.
- Two-time First-Team All-NFC selection (1978 and 1980).
- Four-time Second-Team All-NFC selection (1977, 1979, 1981, and 1982).
- Inducted into Minnesota Vikings Ring of Honor in 2012.

16

JOEY BROWNER

A ferocious hitter who possessed good speed, excellent mobility, and outstanding ball-skills, Joey Browner spent nine seasons in Minnesota intimidating the opposition from his post in the Vikings' defensive secondary. One of the finest safeties of his time, Browner recorded more than 100 tackles in each of his seven seasons as a full-time starter, while also picking off at least five passes on five separate occasions. Ranking among the franchise's all-time leaders in several defensive categories, including interceptions, tackles, and forced fumbles, Browner earned six trips to the Pro Bowl, four All-Pro nominations, and five All-NFC selections, before being further honored by being named to the NFL 1980s All-Decade Team and inducted into the Vikings Ring of Honor.

Born in Warren, Ohio, on May 15, 1960, Joey Matthew Browner attended local Warren G. Harding High School for two years, before transferring to Southwest High School after he moved with his family to Atlanta, Georgia, prior to the start of his junior year. Excelling in multiple sports at Southwest High, Browner earned All-State honors as a defensive lineman, played basketball with future NBA forward Gerald Wilkins, and ran track and field, twice qualifying for the state track meet. Particularly impressive on the gridiron in his senior year, Browner recorded 120 unassisted tackles and three interceptions, with his exceptional play gaining him recognition as a *Parade* All-American, the Georgia Class 3-A Lineman of the Year, and the Atlanta Area Player of the Year.

Although his three older brothers all attended the University of Notre Dame, Browner instead decided to accept an athletic scholarship to the University of Southern California, where he spent his collegiate career playing alongside future NFL stars Ronnie Lott and Dennis Smith in the Trojans' defensive secondary. Recording 243 tackles, nine interceptions, and three touchdowns in his four seasons at USC, Browner earned First-Team All–Pac-10 and First-Team All-Coast honors twice, making him a coveted commodity heading into the 1983 NFL Draft.

Joey Browner ranks among the Vikings' all-time leaders in interceptions, tackles, and forced fumbles.
Courtesy of George A. Kitrinos

Selected by the Vikings in the first round, with the 19th overall pick, Browner spent his first season in Minnesota playing mostly on special teams, although he also managed to record two interceptions, two sacks, and four fumble recoveries in a backup role on defense. Browner then started eight games at left cornerback in 1984, before being moved permanently to strong safety the following year. Excelling at that spot, Browner earned Pro Bowl honors for the first of six straight times by recording 188 tackles, beginning in the process a string of seven consecutive seasons in which he registered more than 100 stops. Establishing himself as arguably the league's finest all-around player at his position during that time, Browner also picked off a total of 34 passes from 1985 to 1991. Performing especially well in 1987, 1988, and 1990, Browner earned First-Team All-Pro honors in each of those seasons by recording at least five interceptions and 120 tackles.

Known for his aggressive style of play and willingness to sacrifice his body for the team, the 6'2", 221-pound Browner proved to be one of the league's hardest hitters, often making opposing receivers think twice before coming across the middle of the field. An outstanding open-field tackler, Browner possessed the quickness to track down speedy wide receivers and the strength to engage tight ends and running backs mano-a-mano. Rarely allowing ball-carriers to escape his grasp, Browner became known for his powerful hands, which he often used to "horse-collar" his opponent, a technique that has since been outlawed by the league. In discussing the banning of one of his favorite maneuvers, Browner says, "You could play football back then. Now, there's a rule for everything." Browner also claims that the leverage and hand-to-hand fighting skills he developed in martial arts helped make him a better tackler.

Excelling on special teams as well, Browner played on every punt and kick-coverage unit, ending his career with 111 special team tackles, with his 38 stops in 1989 representing a single-season franchise record.

After earning the last of his All-Pro nominations in 1990, Browner recorded 102 tackles, picked off five passes, and amassed 97 interception-return yards the following year. Nevertheless, the Vikings released him prior to the start of the 1992 campaign after saying that he failed his physical due to a shoulder injury he suffered the previous season. Browner then signed with the Tampa Bay Buccaneers, joining in the process former Vikings teammate, Darrell Fullington, who had a different perspective on Browner's departure from Minnesota, suggesting at the time, "Joey became expendable. There was a guy who had done everything for that organization, all the Pro Bowls and All-Pros. Then, they come back and put a knock on his shoulder. If there was something wrong with it, he wouldn't be here."

Fullington continued, "It was economics. They didn't want to pay him. But even though it was business, if I were Joey Browner, in the back of my mind, I would have taken it very, very personally. Because you think about the things that led up to Joey's release."

Claiming that Browner angered Vikings management by asking for better, more equitable pay for the players and speaking out against what he termed as racist treatment by the organization, Fullington added, "A lot of players shared the same views, but, when Joey made the statements, nobody else came forward. Everyone else stepped back in the shadows."

Browner ended up spending just one season in Tampa Bay, appearing in only seven games, before announcing his retirement following the conclusion of the 1992 campaign. Ending his time in Minnesota with 1,098 tackles, 37 interceptions, 465 interception-return yards, three touchdown interceptions, four defensive touchdowns, 18 forced fumbles, 17 fumble recoveries, and 9½ sacks, Browner continues to rank among the franchise's all-time leaders in all but the last category. Extremely durable, Browner missed just two non-strike games in his nine years with the Vikings, appearing in 138 out of 140 contests.

Choosing to remain in the Twin Cities following his retirement, Browner works with a foundation that helps prepare young children for school. He also works with the University of St. Thomas in St. Paul in a national youth sports program.

VIKINGS CAREER HIGHLIGHTS

Best Season

Browner earned the first of his six consecutive Pro Bowl nominations in 1985 by making a career-high 188 tackles, recovering three fumbles, and intercepting two passes, one of which he returned for a touchdown. He subsequently gained First-Team All-Pro recognition in both 1987 and 1988 by recording at least five interceptions and 120 tackles in each of those campaigns. However, Browner had his finest all-around season in 1990, once again earning First-Team All-Pro honors by establishing career-high marks with seven interceptions, 103 interception-return yards, and three sacks.

Memorable Moments/Greatest Performances

Browner recorded the first interception of his career during a 20–17 win over the Lions on September 25, 1983.

Although the Vikings lost to the San Diego Chargers by a score of 42–13 in the opening game of the 1984 regular season, Browner scored his first career touchdown on a 63-yard fumble return.

Browner crossed the opponent's goal line again when he returned his interception of a Steve DeBerg pass 15 yards for a touchdown during a 31–16 win over the Tampa Bay Buccaneers on September 15, 1985.

Browner contributed to a 21–17 victory over the Chargers on October 20, 1985, by recording an interception and a sack.

Browner scored the first points of a 24–10 victory over the Lions on November 9, 1986, when he returned his interception of an Eric Hipple pass 39 yards for a touchdown.

Browner performed brilliantly in defeat on November 23, 1986, recording an interception and a career-high 20 tackles during a 24–20 loss to the Cincinnati Bengals.

Browner picked off another two passes against the Lions during a 17–14 Vikings win on December 20, 1987.

Browner recorded two of the six interceptions the Vikings registered against Vinny Testaverde during a 49–20 win over Tampa Bay on October 23, 1988.

Browner proved to be a huge factor when the Vikings defeated the Los Angeles Rams by a score of 28–17 in the 1988 NFC wild card game, recording a sack and picking off two Jim Everett passes, which he returned a total of 40 yards.

Browner contributed to a 27–22 win over the Denver Broncos on November 4, 1990, that ended Minnesota's five-game losing streak by returning his interception of a Gary Kubiak pass 26 yards for a touchdown.

Browner helped lead the Vikings to a 17–7 victory over the Lions on November 11, 1990, by recording a pair of interceptions, which he returned a total of 59 yards.

Notable Achievements

- Missed just two non-strike games in nine seasons, appearing in 138 out of 140 contests.
- Scored four defensive touchdowns.
- Recorded at least five interceptions five times.
- Amassed more than 100 interception-return yards once.
- Recorded more than 100 tackles seven times.
- Finished second in NFL with six interceptions in 1987.
- Finished third in NFL with seven interceptions in 1990.
- Led Vikings in interceptions four times and tackles twice.
- Ranks among Vikings career leaders with 37 interceptions (4th), 465 interception-return yards (4th), three touchdown interceptions

(tied-2nd), 18 forced fumbles (3rd), 17 fumble recoveries (5th), and 1,098 tackles (6th).

- 1989 division champion.
- November 1990 NFC Defensive Player of the Month.
- Six-time Pro Bowl selection (1985, 1986, 1987, 1988, 1989, and 1990).
- Three-time First-Team All-Pro selection (1987, 1988, and 1990).
- 1989 Second-Team All-Pro selection.
- Three-time First-Team All-NFC selection (1987, 1988, and 1990).
- Two-time Second-Team All-NFC selection (1985 and 1989).
- NFL 1980s All-Decade Second Team.
- Inducted into Minnesota Vikings Ring of Honor in 2013.

17

KEVIN WILLIAMS

Part of what became known as the "Williams Wall," Kevin Williams combined with fellow defensive tackle Pat Williams to give the Vikings a dominant interior to their defensive front from 2005 to 2010. Spending 11 of his 13 NFL seasons in Minnesota, the massive Williams established himself as a force-to-be-reckoned-with at the line of scrimmage, preventing opposing teams from running the ball inside against the Vikings, while also leading the team in sacks twice. A member of Vikings teams that made four playoff appearances and won two division titles, Williams earned six trips to the Pro Bowl, five All-Pro nominations, and six All-NFC selections, before being further honored by being named to the NFL 2000s All-Decade Team.

Born in Arkadelphia, Arkansas, on August 16, 1980, Kevin Williams starred in multiple sports at Fordyce High School, earning All-State honors in basketball, while also excelling at tight end and defensive tackle in football. After recording 60 tackles, 20 tackles for loss, five sacks, and two touchdowns his senior year, Williams accepted an athletic scholarship to Oklahoma State University, where he continued his exceptional play on the gridiron. Starting 42 games for the Cowboys, Williams registered 160 tackles, 38 tackles for loss, and 18½ sacks, in helping them gradually improve their record from 3-8 in 2000 to 8-5 in 2002.

Considered one of the top prospects heading into the 2003 NFL Draft, Williams ended up being selected by the Vikings with the ninth overall pick, after much deliberation. In fact, the Vikings, who were originally slotted to pick seventh, put so much thought into their selection of Williams that their 15 minutes on the clock expired, allowing two other teams to jump ahead of them, with the Jacksonville Jaguars choosing quarterback Byron Leftwich at number seven and the Carolina Panthers claiming offensive tackle Jordan Gross with the eighth pick.

After experiencing a bizarre beginning to his NFL career on draft day, Williams made an immediate impact upon his arrival in Minnesota, earning

Kevin Williams combined with fellow defensive tackle Pat Williams to form what
became known as the "Williams Wall."
Courtesy of Shawn Ford via Wikimedia Commons

a spot on the 2003 NFL All-Rookie Team by recording 10½ sacks and registering 51 tackles, including 15 of the solo variety, while splitting his time
between left defensive end and nose tackle. Particularly effective during the
latter stages of the campaign, Williams earned NFC Defensive Rookie of
the Month honors in December by making 18 tackles, registering five sacks,

forcing a fumble, and picking off a pass. Moved to defensive tackle full-time the following year, Williams gained Pro Bowl and First-Team All-Pro recognition by recording 70 tackles and a team-high 11½ sacks, with the last figure placing him sixth in the league rankings. After a somewhat less productive 2005 campaign, Williams began a string of four straight seasons in which he earned Pro Bowl and First-Team All-Pro honors, establishing himself during that time as arguably the most dominant player in the league at his position. Performing especially well in 2008, Williams helped the Vikings capture the division title by recording 8½ sacks and 62 tackles, 15 of which resulted in a loss.

Standing 6'5" and weighing 311 pounds, Williams provided a tremendous physical presence in the middle of Minnesota's defensive front. While teammate Pat Williams typically manned the nose tackle position, Kevin generally played under tackle in the Vikings' 4-3 defensive scheme, with the duo, which also became known as the "Williams Wrecking Crew," helping the Purple and Gold finish first in the league against the run three straight times from 2006 to 2008. Blessed with outstanding quickness for a man his size, Williams excelled in all phases of the game, with Detroit Lions head coach Jim Schwartz praising him for his all-around excellence when he said, "He's wrecked some games that I've been a part of on the other side. A lot of respect for him as a player. . . . He's a guy that's good against the run, good against the pass, doesn't have a weak spot in his game."

In addition to his exceptional on-field play, Williams contributed to the success of the Vikings with his leadership ability and willingness to help others. Extremely approachable and humble, Williams aided immeasurably in the development of many of his teammates, with defensive end Everson Griffen, who he took under his wing when the latter arrived in Minnesota in 2010, recalling, "When I first came in the league, I played a lot of inside. I was three-technique. I played on pass-rushing downs, so when they were throwing everything at me, he said, get me on the field, 'Young buck, I got you.' So, he used to tell me what to do, so I love Kevin. But, also, Kevin, he was a humble man. He didn't say too much."

Vikings nose tackle Remi Ayodele also spoke of Williams's generosity when he said, "He's a great player. He's a great teammate. He helped me out a lot during camp, making sure I knew all my plays and everything when I got down. A lot of vets don't do that. They don't have time for that. You've got to learn yourself. He made sure I knew every call before I got down."

Former Vikings head coach Leslie Frazier also had kind words for Williams, saying, "He is a quiet guy and his personality is low key, but he's one of those guys that, when he does speak up, the entire room listens because of his credibility and how great of a player he is. But also, he's a very bright guy and has a great feel for people and situations. . . . Guys really listen, and they try to adhere to his suggestions."

An excellent pass-rusher his first few years in Minnesota, Williams became more of a run-stopper during the second half of his career, registering just 11½ sacks from 2010 to 2013. Yet, he remained one of the most respected players in the league at his position, earning his fifth consecutive trip to the Pro Bowl in 2010. After serving a two-game suspension at the beginning of 2011 for testing positive for performance-enhancing drugs two years earlier, Williams started all but one contest over the course of the next three seasons, before signing with the Seattle Seahawks as a free agent prior to the start of the 2014 campaign. Ending his time in Minnesota with 60 sacks, four defensive touchdowns, 465 tackles, 104 tackles for loss, eight forced fumbles, 13 fumble recoveries, and five interceptions, Williams ranks among the franchise's all-time leaders in each of the first two categories. Extremely durable, Williams missed just five games as a member of the team, starting 171 out of 176 contests.

In discussing his ability to remain on the field, Williams said, "It had to be the grace of God. Some guys are blessed to play without a lot of injuries, and I was blessed to be one of those guys. I just showed up, it's time to go to work, and I wanted to make sure I was there. What better way to lead the guys than to show up to work and work hard, put your hard hat on."

After leaving Minnesota, Williams spent one year in Seattle, before ending his playing career with the New Orleans Saints in 2015. Williams subsequently signed a one-day contract with the Vikings on July 27, 2016, that allowed him to officially retire as a member of the team. Upon inking his deal with the Vikings, Williams released a statement that read: "I had a great time with the Vikings and appreciate them giving me a chance. They drafted a small-town kid from Arkansas and the organization, the city, the whole state really helped raise me into a man. I appreciate them for that and look forward to coming back and doing some things with the team."

Vikings GM Rick Spielman thanked Williams for his contributions to the team by saying, "Kevin was one of the most respected players in Vikings history by his teammates and by opponents. He set a high standard for himself and led by example instead of words. We thank him for everything he gave the Vikings and the legacy he leaves."

Vikings owner/chairman Zygi Wilf added, "Kevin Williams was an established team leader when we bought the Vikings, and his presence was crucial to our success. His consistency and durability make him a Viking for the ages. We wish Kevin and his family all the best as they enjoy retirement."

VIKINGS CAREER HIGHLIGHTS

Best Season

Williams had a tremendous year for the Vikings in 2008, earning one of his five First-Team All-Pro nominations by recording 8½ sacks, 60 tackles, 15 tackles for loss, and 18 quarterback hits. He also performed extremely well in 2006, when, in addition to registering five sacks, 36 tackles, and three fumble recoveries, he scored one touchdown on defense. But Williams had his finest all-around season in 2004, earning Pro Bowl, First-Team All-Pro, and First-Team All-NFC honors for the first time by establishing career-high marks with 11½ sacks and 70 tackles, while also picking off a pass, forcing two fumbles, and recovering three others, one of which he returned for a touchdown.

Memorable Moments/Greatest Performances

Williams recorded the first two sacks of his career during a 35–7 win over the San Francisco 49ers on September 28, 2003.

Although the Vikings lost to the Arizona Cardinals by a score of 18–17 in the final game of the 2003 regular season, Williams starred in defeat, recording three sacks, eight tackles, and the first of his five career interceptions.

Williams earned NFC Defensive Player of the Week honors for his performance during a 27–16 win over the Jacksonville Jaguars on November 28, 2004. After recording a sack earlier in the game, Williams sealed the victory late in the fourth quarter by recovering a fumble that he subsequently returned 77 yards for a touchdown.

Williams contributed to a 31–13 win over the Seattle Seahawks on October 22, 2006, by recording a sack and scoring a touchdown when he recovered a fumble in the end zone.

In addition to recording a sack during Minnesota's 24–3 victory over Atlanta in the opening game of the 2007 campaign, Williams scored the Vikings' first points of the season when he returned his interception of a Joey Harrington pass 54 yards for a touchdown.

Williams gave the Vikings an early 7–0 lead over the 49ers on December 9, 2007, when he returned his interception of a Trent Dilfer pass 18 yards for a touchdown on the very first play from scrimmage. The Vikings went on to win the game by a score of 27–7.

Williams recorded a career-high four sacks during a 12–10 victory over the Lions on October 12, 2008.

Notable Achievements

- Missed just five games in 11 seasons, starting 171 out of 176 contests.
- Scored four defensive touchdowns.
- Finished in double digits in sacks twice.
- Led Vikings in sacks twice.
- Ranks among Vikings career leaders with 60 sacks (tied for 8th).
- Two-time division champion (2008 and 2009).
- 2004 Week 12 NFC Defensive Player of the Week.
- Member of 2003 NFL All-Rookie Team.
- Six-time Pro Bowl selection (2004, 2006, 2007, 2008, 2009, and 2010).
- Five-time First-Team All-Pro selection (2004, 2006, 2007, 2008, and 2009).
- Five-time First-Team All-NFC selection (2004, 2006, 2007, 2008, and 2009).
- 2010 Second-Team All-NFC selection.
- Pro Football Reference All-2000s Second Team.
- NFL 2000s All-Decade Second Team.

18

GRADY ALDERMAN

The first player selected by the Vikings in the 1961 expansion draft, Grady Alderman spent 14 years anchoring Minnesota's offensive line from his left tackle position. Excelling as both a run-blocker and pass-protector, Alderman proved to be a pillar of strength for the Vikings on offense, missing just three games as a member of the team. An outstanding leader, Alderman served as offensive captain his last eight years in Minnesota, during which time the Vikings won six division titles, two NFC championships, and one NFL title. Earning numerous individual accolades along the way, Alderman appeared in six Pro Bowls and gained All-Pro recognition twice, with his consistently excellent play also landing him a spot on the Pro Football Reference All-1960s Second Team.

Born in Detroit, Michigan, on December 10, 1938, Grady Charles Alderman grew up in the city's housing projects, where he first began competing in sports. Recalling his earliest days as an athlete, Alderman said, "All we did was play sports in the housing projects. We would have two to three players on a side and go at it. By suppertime, we usually had enough for full teams."

Receiving his introduction to organized sports after his family moved to the Detroit suburb of Madison Heights during his teenage years, Alderman starred in football and basketball at Madison High School, proving to be particularly proficient on the gridiron, where he excelled as both an offensive and defensive lineman. Subsequently offered scholarships to Hillsdale College in Michigan and Michigan State University, Alderman instead chose to remain close to home and attend the University of Detroit. After continuing his outstanding two-way play in college, Alderman turned pro when the Detroit Lions selected him in the 10th round of the 1960 NFL Draft, with the 111th overall pick.

With Alderman having received a limited amount of playing time as a rookie in 1960, the Lions left him unprotected in the 1961 expansion draft, allowing the Vikings to claim him with the first overall pick. Laying claim

Grady Alderman missed just three games in his 14 years with the Vikings.

to the starting left tackle job immediately upon his arrival in Minnesota, the 6'2", 247-pound Alderman went on to start every game at that post for the Vikings in 10 of the next 14 seasons, missing a total of only three contests during that time, despite serving in the US Army for much of 1962. And, as Alderman established himself as one of the foundations upon which the fledgling Vikings could build their franchise, he became known throughout the league as one of the finest players at his position, gaining Pro Bowl recognition five straight times from 1963 to 1967. A masterful technician who always took on the opposing team's best pass-rusher, Alderman never entered a game unprepared, carefully studying his opponent before each contest, and then implementing the lessons he learned to neutralize men who often outweighed him by 15 or 20 pounds.

Commenting on Alderman's cerebral approach to his craft years later, longtime Vikings offensive line coach John Michels said, "He was one of the easiest players I ever coached. I never had to tell him anything. He was like having an extra coach on the field."

Michels then added, "Coaching Grady is one of the most memorable parts of my career. Not many people give him credit, but he was really the glue to those great lines."

Making good use of his intelligence, quickness, and excellent technique, Alderman also drew praise from Minnesota head coach Bud Grant, who credited his left tackle for much of the success the Vikings experienced during the second half of his career when he stated, "Grady was a valuable member of those teams that helped us rise from nothing to be a playoff team year-in and year-out. He was a big part of that core of players who made the Vikings in that era. He was a great leader, respected, smart and played left tackle, which is a very valuable position on the field, and was good at it. He was very, very intelligent, and it showed in how he played."

Fran Tarkenton, who benefitted greatly from Alderman's ability to pass-protect, discussed his teammate's many attributes when he said, "Grady played left tackle for us, and he was everything you would want in a player. He was smart, had great talent, and was a team-first guy . . . Grady was as sound a football player as was ever made, a terrific offensive lineman, and as steady as a rock . . . Grady was a leader. He was a player. He probably was the best offensive lineman of those early years when I was in Minnesota. He played against people that were bigger, stronger, and faster, but he never lost. He always protected me."

Then, in addressing the overall impact that Alderman had on the team, Tarkenton suggested, "Those early Vikings teams had a foundation on the offensive and defensive lines—they were Grady Alderman and Jim Marshall. Those two men are how this franchise was built. Grady was a man of integrity, smart, kind, and generous. He was the best guy you could ever be around."

After helping the Vikings advance to the playoffs in five of the previous six seasons, Alderman finally surrendered his starting job to Charles Goodrum in 1974, spending most of the year assuming a backup role, before being released at season's end. The last of the original Vikings to play for the team, Alderman subsequently tried out for the Bears in 1975, but announced his retirement at the end of training camp. Alderman ended his

15-year NFL career having appeared in a total of 204 games, 193 of which came as a member of the Vikings.

After retiring as an active player, Alderman returned to Minnesota, where he spent four seasons serving as a color commentator for Vikings games on radio station WCCO, before becoming the team's director of planning and development. While serving in that capacity, Alderman, who became a certified public accountant during the early stages of his playing career, oversaw the construction of Winter Park, which served as the Vikings headquarters from 1981 to 2018, and managed the $25 million investment that resulted in the construction of the Hubert H. Humphrey Metrodome.

Choosing to accept the position of general manager of the Denver Broncos in 1981, Alderman moved his family to Evergreen, Colorado, where he spent the next two years fulfilling that role, before joining the private business sector. Alderman then spent several years working in banking as an asset-based lender, before retiring to private life. He lived until April 5, 2018, passing away at 79 years of age at Life Care Center of Evergreen. Upon learning of Alderman's passing, Vikings owners Zygi Wilf and Mark Wilf issued a statement that read: "We are saddened to hear of the loss of Grady Alderman. His impact on the Vikings was three-fold—as a great player, as a member of the front office, and as a member of our radio broadcasts. Grady epitomized the Vikings work ethic on the field as a Pro Bowl offensive tackle in the early days of the franchise, and he was a foundation piece for the success of the 1960s and 1970s. Our sympathies are with his family and friends."

VIKINGS CAREER HIGHLIGHTS

Best Season

Alderman had the finest season of his career in 1969, when he earned his lone First-Team All-Pro nomination with his consistently excellent blocking, which helped the NFL champion Vikings score the most points of any team in the league.

Memorable Moments/Greatest Performances

Alderman anchored an offensive line that enabled the Vikings to amass 441 yards of total offense during a 42–21 win over the Los Angeles Rams on December 3, 1961, with 210 of those yards coming on the ground.

Alderman and his line-mates once again dominated the Rams at the point of attack on October 21, 1962, with the Vikings rushing for a season-high 214 yards and amassing 407 yards of total offense during a 38–14 victory.

Alderman helped the Vikings gain 313 yards on the ground and amass 463 yards of total offense during a 34–24 win over the Baltimore Colts in the opening game of the 1964 regular season.

Excelling once again in the 1964 regular-season finale, Alderman anchored an offensive line that enabled the Vikings to gain a total of 432 yards on offense during a lopsided 41–14 victory over the Bears, with 250 of those yards coming on the ground.

Notable Achievements

- Missed just three games in 14 seasons, appearing in 193 out of 196 contests.
- Ranks among Vikings career leaders with 14 seasons played (tied for 6th) and 193 games played (7th).
- Six-time division champion (1968, 1969, 1970, 1971, 1973, and 1974).
- 1969 NFL champion.
- Two-time NFC champion (1973 and 1974).
- Six-time Pro Bowl selection (1963, 1964, 1965, 1966, 1967, and 1969).
- 1969 First-Team All-Pro selection.
- 1965 Second-Team All-Pro selection.
- Pro Football Reference All-1960s Second Team.

19

ROBERT SMITH

L abeled a "bust" during the early stages of his career after being selected by the Vikings with the 21st overall pick of the 1993 NFL Draft, Robert Smith found himself being plagued by injuries that prevented him from reaching his full potential his first four years in Minnesota. However, over the course of the next four seasons, Smith established himself as one of the most dynamic running backs in franchise history, amassing more than 1,000 yards on the ground each year, en route to earning two Pro Bowl selections and one All-Pro nomination. The second-leading rusher in team annals, Smith helped lead the Vikings to seven playoff appearances and three division titles, before surprisingly announcing his retirement following the conclusion of the 2000 campaign.

Born in the Cleveland suburb of Euclid, Ohio, on March 4, 1972, Robert Scott Smith first displayed his exceptional running ability at Euclid High School, where he became the first player to win Ohio's Mr. Football Award twice. After rushing for 1,564 yards as a junior, Smith gained 2,042 yards on the ground and scored 31 touchdowns his senior year, with his extraordinary performance prompting the Touchdown Club of Atlanta to name him its Bobby Dodd National Back of the Year.

Having rushed for a total of 5,038 yards and scored 67 touchdowns in high school, Smith received scholarship offers from several major colleges, before narrowing his choices down to Miami, USC, UCLA, and Ohio State. Ultimately choosing to remain in his home state, Smith spent two seasons starring in the backfield for the Buckeyes, gaining a total of 1,945 yards on the ground, despite sitting out his sophomore year to participate in track and field and focus on academics. Excelling in those two areas as well, Smith posted a personal-best time of 10.24 seconds in the 100-meter dash and studied biology, chemistry, and physics in the hope of eventually pursuing a career in medicine.

Altering his plans after the Vikings made him the 21st overall pick of the 1993 NFL Draft, Smith chose to go to Minnesota, where he spent his

Robert Smith ranks second in franchise history in rushing.
Courtesy of SportsMemorabilia.com

first year as a pro sharing playing time with Barry Word, Roger Craig, and Scottie Graham. Appearing in just 10 games, Smith, who missed the final few weeks of the season after injuring his right knee, rushed for only 399 yards and scored just two touchdowns, even though he averaged a robust 4.9 yards per carry. Taking a step backward in 1994, Smith ran for just 106 yards and one touchdown, causing many people within the organization to wonder if they had properly gauged his talent when they selected him in the first round of the draft.

Although Smith missed a significant amount of playing time due to injury in each of the next two seasons, he began to deliver somewhat on his untapped potential. Despite sitting out the second half of the 1995 campaign with a badly sprained ankle, Smith led the Vikings with 632 yards rushing and scored five touchdowns. He followed that up by rushing for 692 yards, amassing 731 yards from scrimmage, and scoring three touchdowns in 1996, even though a serious injury to his left knee forced him to the sidelines for the season's final eight games.

Fully healthy for the first time in his career, Smith subsequently emerged as a tremendous offensive weapon in 1997, beginning an outstanding four-year run during which he posted the following numbers:

YEAR	YDS RUSHING	RECS	REC YDS	YDS FROM SCRIMMAGE	TDS
1997	1,266	37	197	1,463	7
1998	1,187	28	291	1,478	8
1999	1,015	24	166	1,181	2
2000	1,521	36	348	1,869	10

Ranking among the NFL leaders in rushing in two of those four seasons, Smith finished as high as second in 2000, when he also placed near the top of the league rankings in yards from scrimmage and rushing average (5.2). Meanwhile, Smith posted the third-highest rushing average in the league in both 1997 and 1998, averaging 5.5 yards per carry in the first of those campaigns, before averaging 4.8 yards per carry in the second. And Smith's 1999 numbers would have been even better had he not missed three games after undergoing hernia surgery. In addition to earning two trips to the Pro Bowl, Smith gained All-Pro and All-NFC recognition in 2000. More importantly, the Vikings made the playoffs all four years, winning the division title in both 1998 and 2000.

Despite being blessed with exceptional foot speed, the 6'2", 212-pound Smith employed an aggressive running style in which he often ran to contact. A true power back, Smith preferred to run over his opponent, rather than around him, rarely using flashy moves or jukes to outmaneuver would-be tacklers. Smith also proved to be quite different than many of his peers off the playing field, with his outside interests including astronomy, genetic research, and, of course, medicine.

Demonstrating the uniqueness of his character, Smith chose to leave the game at the peak of his career, announcing his retirement on February 7, 2001, at only 28 years of age, after undergoing surgery on his right knee one month earlier. Saying at the time that he wished to retire while still in relatively good health, Smith released a statement, part of which read: "I want to thank my teammates and coaches for believing in me throughout my career. You know how much I appreciate all of you, but I could never express how much your presence through the highs and lows has meant to me. I wish the Vikings continued success under Coach Green and his staff."

Commenting on his teammate's decision, Chris Walsh told the *Minneapolis Star Tribune* in 2001, "I was perplexed at the time. After the season, he was pretty sure that's what he was going to do. He said, 'The thing that's sad to me is a guy who stays too long.'"

Vikings offensive line coach Mike Tice stated, "Robert is different, and he showed that by retiring when he still had so much time left as a player. I respect him for it. He wanted to move on, and he did."

Head coach Dennis Green offered, "Robert's decision to retire, as everyone knows, comes off his best season ever as a running back for the Minnesota Vikings. He leaves the game on top and is looking forward to his next challenge."

Green added, "Robert has always been a guy that the National Football League has been able to count on as a shining example of quality character off the field and 100 percent effort on the field."

Smith, who retired with career totals of 6,818 yards rushing, 178 receptions, 1,292 receiving yards, 8,110 yards from scrimmage, 8,574 all-purpose yards, 32 rushing touchdowns, and 38 touchdowns, subsequently began a career in broadcasting, serving as a college football analyst for ESPN from 2005 to 2015, before joining Fox Sports and the Big Ten Network in 2016. Smith has also made significant contributions outside of football, creating the Robert Smith Foundation, which is dedicated to providing financial assistance to cancer research and children's hospitals. An outspoken voice against the violent nature of football, Smith also wrote a tell-all book entitled *The Rest of the Iceberg: An Insider's View on the World of Sport and Celebrity*, which details the brutality of the sport, its obsession with celebrity, and why he chose to retire when he did.

Believing that he made the right decision, Smith told the *Willoughby* (Ohio) *News-Herald* in 2011, "I couldn't be happier with my health considering what I went through for eight years. My right knee gets sore for a while when the weather turns, and my right foot is sore every once in a while, but that's about it. I feel lucky."

Yet, Smith is not without his own demons, revealing during a November 1, 2013, interview on ESPN's *SportsCenter* that he has spent much of his adult life battling alcoholism. Stating that his troubles began back in high school, Smith admitted to driving drunk to the Vikings' practice facility "stinking like alcohol," although he somehow managed to conceal his problem from team officials. After seeking counseling, Smith remained sober for four years, before relapsing in 2011.

Speaking once again of his condition in 2019, Smith, who now lives in Texas with his wife and young son, said, "I am an alcoholic—I always have been and always will be. It's not my fault, but it's my problem. Today marks seven years of sobriety, but that can change if I believe for a second that I'm different from every other alcoholic. I'm grateful I know that today. One day at a time."

CAREER HIGHLIGHTS

Best Season

Smith's final NFL season proved to be the finest of his career. En route to earning Pro Bowl honors and his only All-Pro nomination in 2000, Smith established career-high marks with 1,521 yards rushing, 1,869 yards from scrimmage, and 10 touchdowns, with his 1,521 yards gained on the ground and average of 5.2 yards per carry both placing him second in the league rankings.

Memorable Moments/Greatest Performances

Smith scored the first touchdown of his career on a 26-yard run during a 19–12 victory over the Bears on October 25, 1993, finishing the game with 14 carries for 80 yards and that one TD.

Although the Vikings blew a 27–13 fourth quarter lead the following week and ended up losing to the Lions by a score of 30–27, Smith went over 100 yards rushing for the first time as a pro, gaining 115 yards on 23 carries and scoring one touchdown.

Smith helped lead the Vikings to a 44–24 win over the Steelers on September 24, 1995, by carrying the ball 15 times for 115 yards and scoring one TD, which came on a 58-yard run.

Smith gave the Vikings a 23–17 victory over the Houston Oilers on October 8, 1995, when he scored the game-winning touchdown on a 20-yard run some six minutes into overtime.

Smith led the Vikings to a 34–13 win over the Buffalo Bills in the opening game of the 1997 regular season by carrying the ball 16 times for 169 yards and one touchdown, which came on a career-long 78-yard run.

Smith contributed to a 28–19 victory over the Philadelphia Eagles on September 28, 1997, by rushing for 125 yards and one touchdown, which came on a 14-yard scamper.

Smith starred during a 39–28 win over the Colts in the final game of the 1997 regular season, carrying the ball 17 times for 160 yards, with nearly half those yards coming on a 76-yard sprint.

Smith rushed for 179 yards and two touchdowns during a 38–31 win over the St. Louis Rams on September 13, 1998, scoring his TDs on runs of 24 and 74 yards.

Smith gave the Vikings an early 7–0 lead over the Bears on September 27, 1998, when he gathered in a 67-yard touchdown pass from Randall Cunningham on the game's opening possession. The Vikings went on to win the contest by a score of 31–28, with Smith rushing for 76 yards and scoring that one touchdown.

Smith earned NFC Offensive Player of the Week honors by rushing for 134 yards and one touchdown during a 34–13 win over the Lions on October 25, 1998, with his TD coming on a 57-yard run late in the third quarter.

Smith helped lead the Vikings to a 31–24 victory over the Saints on November 8, 1998, by carrying the ball 20 times for 137 yards and one touchdown, which came on a 61-yard run.

Smith proved to be too much for the Giants to handle on December 26, 1999, rushing for 146 yards and one touchdown during a 34–17 Vikings win, with his TD coming on a 70-yard run midway through the fourth quarter that put the game out of reach.

Continuing his strong play in that year's postseason, Smith rushed for 140 yards and caught a 26-yard touchdown pass during Minnesota's 27–10 victory over Dallas in the wild card round of the 1999 NFC playoffs.

Smith proved to be the difference in a 31–24 win over the Lions on October 1, 2000, carrying the ball 16 times for 134 yards and one touchdown, which came on a 65-yard run with just over six minutes remaining in regulation that increased the Vikings' lead to 14 points.

Smith starred again during a 28–16 win over the Bears two weeks later, rushing for 170 yards and scoring a touchdown on a 72-yard scamper.

Smith continued his banner year by rushing for 103 yards, making three receptions for 70 yards, and scoring two touchdowns during a 31–17 victory over the Carolina Panthers on November 19, 2000, with the longest of his TDs coming on a 53-yard pass from Daunte Culpepper.

Smith followed that up four days later by rushing for 148 yards and one touchdown during a 27–15 Thanksgiving Day win over the Dallas Cowboys.

Notable Achievements

- Rushed for more than 1,000 yards four times, topping 1,500 yards once.
- Scored 10 touchdowns in 2000.
- Averaged more than 5 yards per carry twice.
- Finished second in NFL in rushing yards once and rushing average once.
- Finished third in NFL in rushing average twice.
- Finished fourth in NFL with 1,869 yards from scrimmage in 2000.
- Led Vikings in rushing six times.
- Ranks among Vikings career leaders with 1,411 rushing attempts (4th), 6,818 yards rushing (2nd), 8,110 yards from scrimmage (6th), 8,574 all-purpose yards (7th), 32 rushing touchdowns (6th), and 38 touch-downs (11th).
- Three-time division champion (1994, 1998, and 2000).
- 1998 Week 8 NFC Offensive Player of the Week.
- November 2000 NFC Offensive Player of the Month.
- Two-time Pro Bowl selection (1998 and 2000).
- 2000 Second-Team All-Pro selection.
- 2000 First-Team All-NFC selection.

20

GARY ZIMMERMAN

One of the most dominant offensive linemen of his era, Gary Zimmerman spent 14 seasons starring at left tackle for three different teams. After beginning his pro career with the Los Angeles Express of the United States Football League in 1984, Zimmerman arrived in Minnesota two years later when the Vikings acquired his signing rights from the New York Giants. Zimmerman subsequently went on to start every game for the Vikings in each of the next seven seasons, helping them win two division titles and advance to the playoffs four times. Along the way, Zimmerman earned four trips to the Pro Bowl and two All-Pro selections, before being dealt to the Denver Broncos prior to the start of the 1993 season. Continuing his exceptional play in Denver, Zimmerman earned three more Pro Bowl selections and another three All-Pro nominations, with his entire body of work eventually gaining him induction into the Pro Football Hall of Fame.

Born in Fullerton, California, on December 13, 1961, Gary Wayne Zimmerman grew up rooting for the Pittsburgh Steelers and his favorite player, Jack Lambert, who he tried to emulate by playing middle linebacker at Walnut High School. Although Zimmerman lived just outside Los Angeles, he never considered going to college in Southern California, saying years later, "I don't like L.A. I don't like cities."

Choosing instead to accept a scholarship offer from the University of Oregon, Zimmerman explained, "The reason I wound up going to Oregon was they told me I could play defense."

But Zimmerman, who also played center in high school, soon realized that the Ducks had other plans for him, recalling, "When I got there, I saw my number was 75, and I thought, 'That's funny.' I guess I could have quit. I just made the best of it."

Zimmerman ended up playing center and guard at Oregon, performing so well at both positions that he won the Morris Trophy as the best lineman in the Pac-10 as a senior in 1983. Making an extremely favorable

Gary Zimmerman started every game for the Vikings in each of his seven seasons in Minnesota.
Courtesy of MearsOnlineAuctions.com

impression on pro scouts during his time at Oregon, Zimmerman drew praise from longtime Dallas Cowboys player personnel director Gil Brandt, who said prior to the 1983 NFL Draft, "He's an outstanding player. He has the size and speed we're looking for, and he has outstanding athletic ability. I think he can play center or guard, and I'm not so sure he couldn't play tackle."

Later selected by the Giants with the third overall pick of the 1984 NFL Supplemental Draft, Zimmerman elected to sign instead with the Los

Angeles Express of the United States Football League, who claimed him as a territorial pick in that year's USFL Draft. Moved to left tackle by the Express, Zimmerman proved to be a natural at the position, earning All-League honors in each of the next two seasons.

Commenting on Zimmerman's exceptional play for his team, Express head coach John Hadl, who earlier starred at quarterback for the San Diego Chargers and Los Angeles Rams, said, "He was obviously gonna be a great player. He was a great guy who came from good stock. He was steady and smart. He and a guard named Walt Sweeney were the two best linemen I was ever around. . . . Looking back, Gary was definitely as good as anyone who ever played his position."

With the USFL folding after the 1985 season, Zimmerman appeared headed for New York and the Giants, who retained his NFL rights. But, with Zimmerman showing little interest in playing in the Big Apple, the Giants traded him to the Vikings for two second-round picks in the 1986 NFL Draft.

Earning the starting left tackle job immediately upon his arrival in Minnesota, Zimmerman began a string of 108 straight games in which he started every contest for the Vikings. Quickly establishing himself as one of the league's top offensive linemen, Zimmerman earned All-NFC honors for the first of four straight times in 1986, before gaining Pro Bowl recognition in each of the next three seasons.

Crediting much of his success to the players he faced every day in practice, Zimmerman suggested, "A lot of my development goes to those early days with the Vikings. I had to go against [Chris] Doleman and [Keith] Millard every day. Those guys were great defensive linemen, and, back then, practice was a full-out scrimmage every day. It wasn't the country club-type deals teams have now. I learned to be a tough guy."

Most of Zimmerman's accomplishments, though, should be attributed directly to him. Blessed with outstanding physical talent, the 6'6", 294-pound Zimmerman possessed good size, strength, and quickness. However, his greatest assets proved to be his intelligence and superb technique, which former Vikings quarterback Rich Gannon addressed when he said, "Gary was such a technician. He was so good with his hands and his feet. He was hardly ever out of position. He was so competitive. If he missed an assignment, the guy literally would be sick to his stomach."

Jerry Burns, who served as Vikings head coach Zimmerman's first six years with the team, stated, "I remember him as being about as good an offensive lineman as I've ever seen. He wasn't the biggest lineman in the league, but he was smart, sound, and just plain excellent."

Longtime Vikings offensive line coach John Michels added, "Gary is the best technician I've ever seen as an offensive lineman. It's hard to say an offensive lineman dominated. But Gary dominated nearly every player he ever faced."

In addition to his exceptional play, Zimmerman became known for his refusal to interact with the media during his time in Minnesota. Having developed a disdain for the press after one of its members made public negative comments that he made about some of his teammates following a difficult loss, Zimmerman subsequently refused to speak to the media for the rest of his career.

Zimmerman remained in Minnesota until the end of 1992, when, after earning Pro Bowl and All-NFC honors once again, he found himself heading to Denver when a clash of personalities with new Vikings head coach Dennis Green prompted the team to trade him to the Broncos just prior to the start of the 1993 regular season. Choosing not to dwell negatively on the past, Zimmerman says, "I had a personal issue with Dennis, but I don't want to get into it."

Arriving in Denver at less than peak physical condition, Zimmerman recalls, "When I first got traded to Denver and went through the team physical, they said, 'You need a new hip, right?' All those years playing in Minnesota . . . that was back when the [artificial] turf they rolled out really tore you up."

Nevertheless, Zimmerman maintained a high level of play after he joined the Broncos, earning Pro Bowl and All-Pro honors three times each over the course of the next five seasons, in helping his new team win one Super Bowl and advance to the playoffs twice. And during his time in Denver, Zimmerman made a strong impression on former Broncos guard and current NFL analyst Mark Schlereth, who described his onetime teammate as, "Very intelligent, very educated, very determined, a great work ethic."

Schlereth then proceeded to delve into Zimmerman's psyche when he said, "He was as paranoid as anybody I ever played by. I think that was one of the things that made him great is that he always had convinced himself by Sunday that the guy he was going against was the best player he ever lined up against in his whole life."

Schlereth continued, "I was always a guy that studied and prepared and got myself ready to play, and, when I got to Denver and played beside Gary, I grew in my preparation, and I grew in the way I practiced because Gary was a consummate professional. So, playing beside him helped me in my last six years go become a better football player."

Schlereth added, "Again, it comes down to his paranoia, his fear of failure, and I've always felt that's what sets really good football players apart. And even when he was at the top of his game, as good as he could possibly be, he did not want to fail, he did not want to make a mistake, he did not want to get beat. And he would lose sleep over the thought of getting beat."

Despite the success that he experienced as a member of the Broncos, Zimmerman now looks back on his time in Denver with mixed emotions, saying, "I probably played two years too long. My shoulder started going. I had to sneak in and lift weights so nobody knew how weak I was. . . . The last two years, I was getting injections to play. There was kind of a dread in advance, but, once the shot was done, I had a great time. . . . For three hours on Sunday, I had a clear mind. It was being with your buddies. It was, 'All right, let's play ball.'"

Choosing to announce his retirement after the Broncos defeated Green Bay in Super Bowl XXXII, Zimmerman recalls, "I just couldn't do it anymore. The shoulder was just really bad."

Ending his career with seven trips to the Pro Bowl, five All-Pro nominations, and nine All-Conference selections, Zimmerman, who now lives in Bend, Oregon, later became one of the few players to be named to more than one NFL All-Decade Team, earning spots on both the 1980s and 1990s squads. Zimmerman also received football's ultimate honor when he gained induction into the Pro Football Hall of Fame in 2008.

VIKINGS CAREER HIGHLIGHTS

Best Season

Zimmerman played his best ball for the Vikings in 1987 and 1988, gaining First-Team All-Pro recognition in each of those campaigns. With the NFLPA according Zimmerman NFC Offensive Lineman of the Year honors in 1988, we'll identify that as the finest season of his career.

Memorable Moments/Greatest Performances

Zimmerman helped the Vikings amass 463 yards of total offense during a 45–13 rout of Tampa Bay on November 30, 1986, with 342 of those yards coming through the air and the Buccaneers failing to record a single sack during the contest.

Zimmerman and his line-mates dominated the Dallas defense at the line of scrimmage on Thanksgiving Day 1987, with the Vikings amassing 476 yards of total offense during a 44–38 overtime win over the Cowboys.

In addition to recovering a fumble during Minnesota's 44–10 victory over New Orleans in the wild card round of the 1987 NFC playoffs, Zimmerman anchored an offensive line that enabled the Vikings to gain a total of 210 yards on the ground.

Zimmerman's superior blocking at the point of attack helped the Vikings amass 533 yards of total offense during a 44–17 win over the Lions on November 6, 1988.

Notable Achievements

- Started 108 consecutive non-strike games from 1986 to 1992.
- Two-time division champion (1989 and 1992).
- 1988 NFLPA NFC Offensive Lineman of the Year.
- Four-time Pro Bowl selection (1987, 1988, 1989, and 1992).
- Two-time First-Team All-Pro selection (1987 and 1988).
- Three-time First-Team All-NFC selection (1987, 1988, and 1992).
- Two-time Second-Team All-NFC selection (1986 and 1989).
- NFL 1980s All-Decade Second Team.
- NFL 1990s All-Decade First Team.
- Pro Football Reference All-1990s Second Team.
- Elected to Pro Football Hall of Fame in 2008.

21

BILL BROWN

The very personification of the physical and aggressive style of play the Vikings came to embrace during the 1960s and early-1970s, Bill Brown helped set the tone for his teammates with his punishing running style and selfless attitude. A true warrior who not only excelled at fullback, but, also, on special teams, Brown missed just two games in his 13 seasons with the Vikings, appearing in 180 out of 182 contests. The fourth-leading rusher in franchise history, Brown gained more than 800 yards on the ground three times, leading the team in that category on four separate occasions. An outstanding receiver coming out of the backfield as well, Brown amassed more than 1,000 yards from scrimmage four times, with his solid all-around play earning him four trips to the Pro Bowl and two All-Pro nominations. A member of Vikings teams that won six division titles and appeared in three Super Bowls, Brown later received the additional honor of being inducted into the team's Ring of Honor.

Born in Mendota, Illinois, on June 29, 1938, William Dorsey Brown attended Mendota Township High School, where he starred in football and track and field, winning the state shotput title in his junior year with a toss of 55 feet, 2 inches, and finishing second to future NFL center Mike Pyle the following year. Recruited by several major colleges for his skills on the gridiron, Brown eventually narrowed the field down to Illinois, Wisconsin, and Western Illinois, before finally making his decision, which he explained years later: "I made a decision, and it wasn't really hard because my brother Jim was down at Illinois, so that helped. My brother ended up backing me up at Illinois."

Continuing to excel in multiple sports in college, Brown earned All–Big Ten Conference honors for his play at fullback, while also winning the Big Ten shotput title with a then-school record toss of 54 feet, 10.5 inches. Drawing attention to himself with his outstanding play on the football field, Brown received offers from the Canadian Football League, the Chicago Bears, who selected him in the second round of the 1961 NFL Draft,

Bill Brown earned four trips to the Pro Bowl and two All-Pro nominations during his 13 years in Minnesota.

with the 20th overall pick, and the New York Titans, who claimed him with the 42nd overall pick of that year's AFL Draft. Choosing to sign with the Bears even though the CFL offered him more money, Brown spent one season in Chicago, before being dealt to the Vikings for a fourth-round draft pick just prior to the start of the 1962 campaign.

Recalling his one year in the Windy City, Brown said, "I was a backup fullback and played maybe eight to 10 plays a game. I didn't see eye to eye with Mr. Halas, so I told him I wanted him to either play me or trade me. Well, he decided to trade me. He talked me into signing the second year but traded me to the Vikings just before training camp broke."

Although Brown arrived in Minnesota just two days before the start of the regular season, he found himself being pressed into action in Week 1, later detailing the events that transpired at the time: "I got here like on a Friday night, and we were playing the Packers on Sunday. I got the playbook on Saturday. . . . We got behind 17 points early, I remember. Somebody yelled, 'Brown' and I looked around and it was [Norm] Van Brocklin. I looked around because I had just gotten there and didn't know if there was another Brown. Nobody got up, so I ran up there. Van Brocklin said we were going to throw the ball a lot, and, because I was a good blocker, I could release and run the patterns."

Brown continued, "I didn't even know the patterns. All we ran was special teams on Saturday morning when we practiced, so I knew none of the plays. I ended up reading as much of the playbook as I could Saturday night, and I got coaching from Tommy Mason and Fran Tarkenton on what I was supposed to do when I got out there, so that helped quite a bit."

Brown, who ended up playing nearly three quarters of the game, added, "That was not expected when you show up two days before. You'd like to get acclimated first—well, I got acclimated in a hurry. . . . It worked out. I got my feet wet and did fairly well in that game, so I played most of the year then."

Although Brown appeared in all 14 games for the Vikings in 1962, he started just two, finishing the year with only 103 yards rushing and 227 yards from scrimmage. Assuming a far more prominent role the following season, Brown rushed for 445 yards, gained another 109 yards on 17 pass receptions, and scored eight touchdowns, one of which came on a 78-yard kickoff return. A full-time starter by 1964, Brown began an excellent five-year run during which he established himself as one of the NFL's better all-around backs, compiling the following numbers during that time:

YEAR	YDS RUSHING	RECS	REC YDS	YDS FROM SCRIMMAGE	TDS
1964	866	48	703	1,569	16
1965	699	41	503	1,202	7
1966	829	37	359	1,188	6
1967	610	22	263	873	5
1968	805	31	329	1,134	14

After finishing fourth in the NFL in rushing and ranking second in the league in touchdowns, yards from scrimmage, and all-purpose yards (1,637) in 1964, Brown placed near the top of the league rankings in rushing, rushing touchdowns, and yards from scrimmage in three of the next four seasons, earning in the process four Pro Bowl selections and two All-Pro nominations. And, as Brown rose to elite status among NFL running backs, the Vikings gradually established themselves as contenders, capturing their first division title in 1968.

Contributing greatly to the Vikings' improvement as a team, Brown inspired the other players around him with his "take no prisoners" mentality and punishing running style that he described thusly: "I didn't have a lot of fancy moves, so I never used them. I tried that for a while, but it didn't work very well. I got laid out a lot that way. I wasn't good at turning my side to somebody and trying to go around them. I was better off going over them."

The 5'11", 228-pound Brown, whose fondness for contact earned him the nickname "Boom-Boom," also once said, "Well, I feel that a good full-back should go straight ahead and go for the goal line in a direct route or a direct line, and this is the way I feel that I can get the most out of it and get there quicker. I'm not fancy like a halfback, so I'd rather go right at it and get to where I can."

In discussing his longtime teammate, Mick Tingelhoff stated, "Bill is the toughest guy I think that ever played in the NFL. I really believe that. He had no concern for his body at all. I think Van Brocklin gave him the nickname 'Hammerhead' because one day he was going in for a touchdown and he either stumbled or got tripped or something, and he ran right into the goal post with his head and put a big dent in the helmet, and they had to carry him off the field. But he came back and finished that game."

Vikings receiver Gene Washington said, "When you think about somebody being tough, and you need those three yards, if it's a pass play or it's a running play, he would get the yards."

Fran Tarkenton called Brown "Neanderthal man" and stated, "Never been one like him. Today, he still has his crew cut. Came into the league with a crew cut and bole legs. Was willing to do anything. Was the typical hard-nosed football player."

Tarkenton continued, "A great blocker. Could run with the best of them—inside or outside. I think one year when I played there, he set a league record for backs catching touchdown passes. I think he caught 10 touchdown passes out of the backfield. Ended his career as captain of the special teams. He went down, and he was the wedge-buster in his middle-30s on our special teams."

In addressing his willingness to serve on special teams, Brown said, "I did not take it as being disgraceful to play on the special teams the way a lot of people did. That was my time to get back at some of the dudes who were hitting me all day . . . I think it was probably in my temperament and my way of thinking when I grew up that that's the way you play the game. I liked to go out, and I liked to play the sport where you learn to stick your helmet in the middle of their stomach. I never felt it was degrading to play on those teams. And I think, if you get a chance, you'd love to play anytime. Hell, if I could have played defense, I'd love to have played defense too."

Perhaps no one in the organization appreciated Brown more than head coach Bud Grant, who expressed his gratitude for everything the fullback brought to the team when he stated:

Bill was the epitome of what a football player should be. I mean, Bill Brown was one of the few people I know who enjoyed training camp. He loved training camp. He loved to play football. If you walked in and said, "Okay, everybody's gonna take a 50 percent cut in salary," half the players would have left. Bill Brown would have never left. He'd have played for nothing. He loved football. When we got the cold weather, Bill never put on a sweatshirt in his life. He never played in anything but short sleeves. I don't care how cold it was. And he really didn't feel like he'd accomplished anything until his face was bloody. He was a throwback.

Bill had the durability to play every down, and he was the kind of runner that, if you approached him to tackle him, you better be ready because he's not gonna avoid you. He's gonna take you on. For a fullback, with all the blocking and tough inside running that he did, he was a great pass receiver. His hands were as good as anybody's we had on the team. And, even at the end of his career, he was captain of our special teams at one time. He was an all-around football player—could run, could catch, could block, and could tackle. He had all the . . . ingredients that make a great football player. Boom-Boom was as good as we ever had.

Despite missing the only two games of his career in 1969, Brown had his last truly productive season for the Vikings on offense, helping them win the NFL title by rushing for 430 yards, amassing 613 yards from scrimmage, and scoring three touchdowns. Yet even though Brown assumed a backup role in each of the next five seasons, he continued to make significant contributions to the success of the team on both offense and special teams. Performing especially well in 1972, Brown amassed 561 yards from scrimmage and scored eight touchdowns. After serving the Vikings almost exclusively on special teams the next two years, Brown announced his retirement following the conclusion of the 1974 campaign, ending his 13-year stint in Minnesota with 5,757 yards rushing, 284 receptions, 3,177 receiving yards, 8,934 yards from scrimmage, 9,198 all-purpose yards, 52 rushing touchdowns, 23 TD catches, 76 total touchdowns, and a rushing average of 3.5 yards per carry.

After retiring as an active player, Brown served as an analyst on Vikings radio broadcasts for three years, before taking a job in the insurance industry. He later spent more than two decades at the John Roberts Company, a printing business, while also doing promotional work for the Vikings. Brown remained active on both fronts until a diagnosis of dementia forced him to retire to private life. Finally losing his battle with the dreaded disease on November 4, 2018, Brown passed away at 80 years of age.

Following her husband's passing, Darlene Brown said, "It's one of those things, you know it's going to happen, but you're never ready. The last few years, it's been going downhill for him. . . . With all the concussions, his body took a lot of beating, so we're going to donate his brain to Boston University. Until they do an autopsy, they can't be sure that he had CTE."

Meanwhile, Vikings owners Zygi and Mark Wilf released a statement that read: "For 13 years as a Minnesota Viking, Bill 'Boom-Boom' Brown led the team's rushing attack and established himself as one of the most physical players in the NFL. He embodied all the characteristics the Vikings continue to instill in players today—tough, disciplined, selfless—and became an immediate fan favorite. After his playing days were over, Bill stayed in Minnesota and proudly represented the franchise as an active alum. He will be greatly missed by Vikings alumni, staff, and fans. Our prayers are with the entire Brown family at this time."

VIKINGS CAREER HIGHLIGHTS

Best Season

Brown posted excellent numbers for the Vikings in 1968, earning Pro Bowl and Second-Team All-Pro honors by rushing for 805 yards and placing near the top of the league rankings with 1,134 yards from scrimmage, 11 rushing touchdowns, and 14 total touchdowns. However, he had his finest season in 1964, when he established career-high marks with 866 yards rushing, 48 receptions, 703 receiving yards, 1,569 yards from scrimmage, 1,637 all-purpose yards, 16 touchdowns, and 96 points scored.

Memorable Moments/Greatest Performances

Brown scored his first career TD on a 15-yard pass from Fran Tarkenton during a 42–17 loss to the Colts in the 1962 regular-season finale.

Although the Vikings lost to the Los Angeles Rams by a score of 27–24 on October 20, 1963, Brown gave them a 17–14 lead when he returned the second-half kickoff 78 yards for a TD.

Brown turned in a tremendous all-around effort against the Colts in the 1964 regular-season opener, leading the Vikings to a 34–24 victory by amassing 187 yards from scrimmage. In addition to rushing for 103 yards and one touchdown, Brown made three receptions for 84 yards and one TD, which came on a 48-yard pass from Fran Tarkenton.

Brown helped lead the Vikings to a 30–10 win over the Pittsburgh Steelers on October 18, 1964, by rushing for 73 yards and one touchdown and making four receptions for 86 yards and two TDs, the longest of which came on a 59-yard connection with Tarkenton.

Brown had another outstanding all-around game on December 6, 1964, gaining 102 yards on the ground and making three receptions for 55 yards and one touchdown during a 30–21 victory over the Giants, with his 30-yard TD reception in the fourth quarter putting the Vikings ahead to stay.

Brown followed that up by amassing a career-high 226 yards from scrimmage and scoring three touchdowns during a 41–14 rout of the Bears in the final game of the 1964 regular season. In addition to rushing for 98 yards and two touchdowns, Brown made three receptions for 128 yards and one TD, which came on a 20-yard pass from Fran Tarkenton.

Brown led the Vikings to a 27–17 win over the Browns on October 31, 1965, by rushing for a career-high 138 yards, gaining another 46 yards on five pass receptions, and scoring two touchdowns.

Brown contributed to a 47–7 thrashing of the Atlanta Falcons in the opening game of the 1968 regular season by rushing for 38 yards, gaining another 65 yards on six pass receptions, and scoring three touchdowns, one of which came on a 37-yard pass from Joe Kapp.

Demonstrating that he still had something left at 34 years of age, Brown amassed 116 receiving yards and scored three touchdowns during a 45–41 victory over the Los Angeles Rams on November 19, 1972, with one of his TDs coming on a 76-yard pass from Fran Tarkenton.

Brown rushed for more than 100 yards for the final time in his career during a 28–7 win over the Lions on November 11, 1973, finishing the game with 101 yards on the ground and one TD.

Notable Achievements

- Missed just two games in 13 seasons, appearing in 180 out of 182 contests.
- Rushed for more than 800 yards three times.
- Surpassed 40 receptions and 500 receiving yards twice each.
- Amassed more than 1,000 yards from scrimmage four times, topping 1,500 yards once.
- Scored more than 10 touchdowns twice.
- Returned one kickoff for a touchdown.
- Finished second in NFL in rushing touchdowns once, touchdowns twice, yards from scrimmage once, and all-purpose yards once.
- Finished third in NFL in rushing touchdowns once.
- Finished fourth in NFL in rushing twice, yards from scrimmage once, and touchdown receptions once.
- Led Vikings in rushing four times, receptions twice, and receiving yards once.
- Ranks among Vikings career leaders with 1,627 rushing attempts (2nd), 5,757 yards rushing (4th), 8,934 yards from scrimmage (5th), 9,198 all-purpose yards (5th), 52 rushing touchdowns (tied for 2nd), 76 touchdowns (4th), and 456 points scored (9th).
- Six-time division champion (1968, 1969, 1970, 1971, 1973, and 1974).

- 1969 NFL champion.
- Two-time NFC champion (1973 and 1974).
- Four-time Pro Bowl selection (1964, 1965, 1967, and 1968).
- Two-time Second-Team All-Pro selection (1964 and 1968).
- Inducted into Minnesota Vikings Ring of Honor in 2004.

22

BOBBY BRYANT

Atrue shutdown corner before the term became a regular part of football parlance, Bobby Bryant spent his entire 13-year NFL career in Minnesota, helping to lead the Vikings to 11 division titles and four trips to the Super Bowl. Starting at right cornerback for the Purple and Gold for 11 seasons, Bryant recorded the second-most interceptions and amassed the third-most interception-return yards in franchise history. An extremely opportunistic player who displayed a nose for the football throughout his career, Bryant also ranks among the Vikings' all-time leaders in fumble recoveries, with his excellent all-around play earning him Pro Bowl and All-NFC honors twice each.

Born in Macon, Georgia, on January 24, 1944, Bobby Lee Bryant starred in multiple sports while attending Willingham High School, excelling in baseball, football, basketball, and track and field. Despite being limited by injury to just a handful of games on the gridiron in his senior year, Bryant previously made enough of an impression on college scouts to earn an athletic scholarship to the University of South Carolina, where he lettered for three years in football and baseball. An outstanding left-handed pitcher, Bryant earned All-ACC honors as a senior, when he became the first Gamecocks hurler to strike out 100 batters in a season. Among his more notable performances, Bryant fanned 16 batters in a win over Virginia, threw 13 innings of shutout ball against Maryland, and allowed just one hit during a 1–0 win over North Carolina. Equally proficient on the football field, Bryant gained All-America recognition in his senior year, with his exceptional play in both sports earning him ACC Athlete of the Year honors in 1966 and 1967.

Drafted by the New York Yankees following his junior year and the Boston Red Sox at the end of his senior year, Bryant instead chose to pursue a career in football, signing with the Vikings after they selected him in the seventh round of the 1967 NFL Draft, with the 167th overall pick. After injuring his knee during the preseason, Bryant spent the entire 1967

Bobby Bryant recorded the second-most interceptions and the third-most interception-return yards in franchise history.
Courtesy of FootballCardGallery.com

campaign on injured reserve, before serving the Vikings primarily on special teams the following year. Yet even though he received a limited amount of playing time on defense, Bryant managed to record two interceptions, recover three fumbles, and score the first touchdown of his career.

Laying claim to the starting right cornerback job in 1969, Bryant excelled in his first year as a full-time starter, finishing second in the NFL with eight interceptions despite missing four games due to injury. Continuing to perform extremely well in each of the next four seasons, Bryant recorded a total of 17 interceptions, two of which he returned for touchdowns. Bryant also returned one of his five fumble recoveries for a TD.

Bryant managed to establish himself as one of the NFL's top cover corners even though he lacked ideal size and elite speed. Standing 6'1" and weighing only 170 pounds, Bryant became known to his teammates and fans as "Bones." Nevertheless, he played the game with reckless abandon, throwing his body around all over the field. And, whatever Bryant lacked in straight-ahead speed, he made up for with quickness, intelligence, instincts, and an ability to read the minds of opposing quarterbacks—all of which made him one of the league's top playmakers on defense. Extremely popular with Vikings fans, Bryant often displayed his appreciation for their support by blowing them kisses after he made a big play.

After a broken arm prevented him from playing in Super Bowl VIII, Bryant missed virtually the entire 1974 campaign due to an injury he sustained in the opening game of the regular season. However, he bounced back the following year to earn Second-Team All-NFC honors and his first trip to the Pro Bowl by picking off six passes and recovering five fumbles. Bryant continued to start for the Vikings at right cornerback for five more years, during which time he recorded another 18 interceptions. After picking off three passes at the rather advanced age of 35 in 1980, Bryant announced his retirement, ending his career with 51 interceptions, 749 interception-return yards, 14 fumble recoveries, and three pick-sixes, all of which place him among the Vikings' all-time leaders. Bryant also amassed a total of 841 yards returning punts and kickoffs. An outstanding postseason performer, Bryant intercepted six passes and scored two touchdowns in playoff competition.

After retiring as an active player, Bryant remained in Minnesota for five years, before returning to Columbia, South Carolina, where he began working in the auto glass replacement business. Now 77 years of age, Bryant remains active in that industry.

CAREER HIGHLIGHTS

Best Season

Despite missing four games due to injury, Bryant performed exceptionally well for the Vikings in 1969, finishing second in the league with a career-high eight interceptions, which he returned for a total of 97 yards. Bryant had another outstanding season in 1973, earning Second-Team All-NFC honors by picking off seven passes, which he returned for a total of 105 yards and one touchdown. But Bryant played his best ball for the Vikings in 1975, gaining Pro Bowl and Second-Team All-Conference recognition by recording six interceptions, amassing 111 interception-return yards, and finishing second in the NFL with five fumble recoveries.

Memorable Moments/Greatest Performances

Although the Vikings suffered a 20–17 defeat at the hands of the New Orleans Saints on October 13, 1968, Bryant recorded the first two interceptions of his career, one of which he returned 51 yards for a touchdown.

Bryant picked off another two passes during a 31–0 win over the Bears on October 12, 1969.

Bryant recorded three interceptions in one game for the first time in his career during a 51–3 mauling of the Cleveland Browns on November 9, 1969, returning his three picks a total of 62 yards.

Bryant preserved a 9–7 win over the Packers on November 16, 1969, by intercepting a Bart Starr pass deep inside Vikings territory in the final minute of regulation and returning the ball 20 yards. The Vikings subsequently ran out the clock, giving them a hard-fought victory over their division rivals.

Bryant scored the second touchdown of his career when he returned his interception of a Bill Munson pass 39 yards for a TD during a 30–17 win over the Lions on November 1, 1970.

Bryant contributed to a 23–10 victory over the Bears on December 3, 1972, by intercepting a pass and returning a fumble 24 yards for a touchdown.

Bryant intercepted three passes during a 31–7 win over the Packers on December 8, 1973, returning one of his picks 46 yards for a touchdown.

Bryant starred during the Vikings' 27–10 victory over the Cowboys in the 1973 NFC championship game, picking off two Roger Staubach passes, one of which he returned 63 yards for a touchdown.

Bryant helped lead the Vikings to a 35–13 win over the Buffalo Bills in the final game of the 1975 regular season by recording two interceptions, which he returned for a total of 59 yards.

Bryant served as a central figure in the Vikings' 24–13 victory over the Los Angeles Rams in the 1976 NFC championship game, intercepting two passes and scoring the game's first points when he returned a blocked field goal attempt 90 yards for a touchdown.

Notable Achievements

- Scored four defensive touchdowns.
- Recorded more than five interceptions four times.
- Amassed more than 100 interception-return yards twice.
- Finished second in NFL in interceptions once and fumble recoveries once.
- Led Vikings in interceptions four times.
- Ranks among Vikings career leaders with 51 interceptions (2nd), 749 interception-return yards (3rd), three touchdown interceptions (tied-2nd), and 14 fumble recoveries (tied for 9th).
- 11-time division champion (1968, 1969, 1970, 1971, 1973, 1974, 1975, 1976, 1977, 1978, and 1980).
- 1969 NFL champion.
- Three-time NFC champion (1973, 1974, and 1976).
- Two-time Pro Bowl selection (1975 and 1976).
- Two-time Second-Team All-NFC selection (1973 and 1975).

23

SCOTT STUDWELL

A smart and instinctive player who joined the Vikings toward the tail end of their glory days of the 1970s, Scott Studwell spent 14 seasons in Minnesota anchoring the team's defense from his middle linebacker position. One of only five Vikings to appear in more than 200 games as a member of the team, Studwell recorded more than 100 tackles 10 times, amassing more stops than anyone else in franchise history over the course of his career. A key contributor to Vikings teams that won four division titles, Studwell earned two Pro Bowl selections and four All-NFC nominations, before spending nearly three decades serving the Purple and Gold in a front office capacity following his retirement.

Born in Evansville, Indiana, on August 27, 1954, John Scott Studwell developed a love of sports at an early age, recalling, "I grew up in a river town with two sisters and an older brother who was a better athlete than me. My parents were very athletic, and my dad played college baseball at Wesleyan College. . . . Sports were big for me as a kid. My true love was baseball. It was my favorite . . . I spent so much time outside as a youngster that I didn't get very exposed to professional football."

Beginning his career on the gridiron at William Henry Harrison High School, Studwell recollected, "I wasn't real big before high school, and I recall around the eighth grade I was 5'2" and weighed 110 pounds. But I grew fast—about a foot—and gained a lot of weight by the time I got to high school. I was a quarterback, running back, and a linebacker on defense."

After accepting an athletic scholarship to the University of Illinois, Studwell sat out his freshman year due to college rules, before gradually transitioning from defensive tackle to linebacker over the course of the next three seasons. Excelling at his new post as a senior in 1976, Studwell led the Big Ten conference in tackles, leaving him with high hopes heading into the 1977 NFL Draft. But Studwell had to wait until the ninth round to hear his name called, with the Vikings finally selecting him with the 250th overall pick.

Scott Studwell recorded more tackles than anyone else in franchise history.
Courtesy of George A. Kitrinos

Recalling his feelings at the time, Studwell said, "When the Vikings took me in the ninth round of the player draft, I was really disappointed. I sincerely thought I would be taken in the earlier rounds. All I concentrated on was football. I didn't work in the off-season. I just trained to be ready for the season to begin."

Bud Grant later revealed that he fought extremely hard with the team's scouts during the draft process for the Vikings to select Studwell, remembering, "We went down the list and I'd say, 'What about this Studwell?' And 'Well, he isn't big enough.' And then, 'What about this Studwell?' in the next round—'Well, he's not fast enough.'—and go down to the next round, and I said, 'What about this Studwell?' And they said, 'Well, he doesn't have good hands.' I said, 'Yeah, but he makes all these tackles. So, what's the matter with him?' 'Well, he's not fast enough, not good enough, doesn't have good hands, blah, blah, blah.' But I said, 'Yeah, but the tackles. How many games has he missed?' 'None.'"

Grant continued, "They kept giving me all these excuses, and then when the ninth round came around, I said, 'I don't care what names you have on your board. We're drafting Studwell.' And that's how Studwell got here. I had never seen him on film, but I read that he made all these tackles, he played every game, and he never got hurt. He came here and did the same thing."

Longtime Vikings scout Jerry Reichow claimed that former University of Minnesota head coach, and then-Vikings assistant, Murray Warmath also played a pivotal role in the selection of Studwell, noting, "He [Studwell] went to the East-West Shrine Game and we thought, 'Studwell, he's a good-looking kid and all this stuff.' But the guy that loved him was Murray Warmath. He said, 'This is a tough guy here.' Well, OK, there were a lot of tough guys, but the thing you didn't know about Studwell was the intelligence factor and how he could lead that defense. That didn't show up then like it did afterwards."

After arriving in Minnesota in 1977, Studwell spent his first three seasons playing mostly on special teams and backing up starting linebackers Jeff Siemon, Matt Blair, and Fred McNeill. But, with Studwell displaying extraordinary hustle and outstanding leadership ability, he ended up replacing Siemon as the starter at middle linebacker during the latter stages of the 1979 campaign. Remaining at that post the following year, Studwell recorded more than 100 tackles for the first of 10 times, while also establishing himself as the leader of a defense once spearheaded by the Purple People Eaters.

Continuing to excel at right-inside linebacker after the Vikings switched to a 3-4 defense in 1981, Studwell recorded a single-season franchise record 230 tackles, including 156 of the solo variety. However, he subsequently spent one month at Hazelton Rehabilitation Center in the summer of 1982, telling the *Pioneer Press* upon his release, "Alcohol was the drug of my choice. I have tried cocaine on occasion, but that was not the reason I was there. It's not a big issue as far as I'm concerned."

Picking up right where he left off when he returned to action, Studwell performed well once again during the strike-shortened 1982 campaign, earning the first of his four All-NFC selections, before beginning an outstanding three-year run during which he registered more than 200 combined tackles each season. The 6'2", 235-pound Studwell managed to compile those lofty totals even though he lacked superior foot speed, with former teammate Greg Coleman saying, "Nobody would outhustle him. Listen, Stud was not the fastest linebacker, and he was not gifted with great speed. But his play recognition . . . he studied the game. He knew tendencies and would call out where the ball was going before the play would even start."

Coleman continued, "There were a few players that had that uncanny ability, and he was one of them because he did the homework and the classwork. That's why he was always around the ball. He was just there, bloody and all. It didn't matter what game and what color uniform, whether it was purple or white, Stud was going to get bloody."

Former Vikings defensive tackle Doug Sutherland also had fond memories of Studwell, recalling, "Stud liked to hit people and was just a little bit crazy. And he was a good leader. When he stepped in there, it was still Carl Eller, Jim Marshall, Alan Page . . . . and they didn't like rah-rah guys. But he had some fire and kept everybody going and kept us all in line. . . . He was a great hitter and was so intense all the time. That's probably the word that comes to mind. He had these eyes that would stare right through you. If he gave you that look, you knew you were in trouble, especially on the other team. He didn't take much crap from anybody."

With the Vikings transitioning back to a 4-3 defense in 1986, Studwell spent the next five seasons playing middle linebacker, gaining Pro Bowl recognition in 1987 and 1988, before announcing his retirement following the conclusion of the 1990 campaign. Ending his career with a franchise-record 1,981 combined tackles, Studwell led the Vikings in that category on eight separate occasions. He also intercepted 11 passes, registered nine sacks, and recovered 16 fumbles.

After retiring as an active player, Studwell moved into the Vikings' front office, where he spent 11 years serving the team as a scout, before becoming director of college scouting in 2002. He remained in that post until April 23, 2019, when, after 42 years of uninterrupted service, he chose to retire to private life, saying at the time, "I want to spend more time with my family. I know for a fact that, personally, I cannot do this on a part-time basis. I'm either all-in or I'm out. This is not a part-time job, and this is not a part-time business. For me, it was either continue doing what you're doing, or you have to call it quits. I want to spend more time with my wife, my family, my grandkids . . . it just feels like the right time to do it."

Studwell added, "I've been one of the lucky ones. To have been able to play here and stay here as an employee of the Vikings, it's been a dream come true. . . . I've been chasing a dream for the last 42 years of winning a championship here. But now it's time to help the people that I love pursue their dreams and spend more time with them and be around them."

Vikings general manager Rick Spielman subsequently paid tribute to Studwell by saying, "You can't replace a Scott Studwell in your organization. That's an impossible task to do."

CAREER HIGHLIGHTS

Best Season

Although Studwell earned his only two trips to the Pro Bowl in 1987 and 1988, he played the best ball of his career from 1981 to 1985, with his franchise-record 230 tackles in 1981 making that his most dominant season.

Memorable Moments/Greatest Performances

Studwell recorded the first of his 11 career interceptions during a 27–7 loss to the St. Louis Cardinals on November 6, 1977.

Studwell registered his first sack as a pro when he brought down Joe Ferguson behind the line of scrimmage during a 23–22 loss to the Buffalo Bills on September 16, 1982.

Studwell starred during a 16–13 win over the Lions on November 3, 1985, helping to limit Detroit to just 69 yards rushing and 153 yards of total offense by recording a single-game franchise-record 24 tackles.

Studwell contributed to a 36–24 win over the heavily favored San Francisco 49ers in the divisional round of the 1987 playoffs by recording one of the four sacks the Vikings registered against Joe Montana.

Studwell excelled against the Lions once again on November 6, 1988, anchoring a Vikings' defense that surrendered just 68 yards rushing and 89 yards of total offense to their division rivals during a lopsided 44–17 victory.

Studwell made another big play during the Vikings' 28–17 victory over the Los Angeles Rams in the wild card round of the 1988 playoffs when he picked off a Jim Everett pass.

Notable Achievements

- Recorded more than 100 tackles 10 times, registering more than 200 stops on four occasions.
- Led Vikings in tackles eight times.
- Holds Vikings single-game record for most tackles (24 vs. Detroit on November 3, 1985).
- Holds Vikings single-season record for most combined defensive and special team tackles (230 in 1981).
- Holds Vikings career records for most combined tackles (1,981) and defensive tackles (1,928).
- Ranks among Vikings career leaders with 14 seasons played (tied for 6th), 201 games played (5th), and 16 fumble recoveries (tied for 6th).
- Four-time division champion (1977, 1978, 1980, and 1989).
- Two-time Pro Bowl selection (1987 and 1988).
- Four-time Second-Team All-NFC selection (1982, 1984, 1988, and 1989).
- Inducted into Minnesota Vikings Ring of Honor in 2009.

24

STEVE HUTCHINSON

C alled "the best guard I've played with" by Hall of Fame quarterback Brett Favre, Steve Hutchinson arrived in Minnesota in 2006 having already established himself as one of the NFL's premier offensive linemen. Beginning his pro career in Seattle in 2001, Hutchinson gained Pro Bowl and All-Pro recognition three times each over the course of the next five seasons, before signing with the Vikings as a free agent. Continuing his dominant play in the Twin Cities, Hutchinson earned Pro Bowl and All-Pro honors another four times, in helping the Vikings win two division titles. A two-time NFL Offensive Lineman of the Year, Hutchinson later received the additional honors of being named to the NFL 2000s All-Decade Team and elected to the Pro Football Hall of Fame.

Born in Fort Lauderdale, Florida, on November 1, 1977, Steven J. Hutchinson grew up in nearby Coral Springs, where he attended Coral Springs High School. After starring on the gridiron as a two-way lineman for the Coral Springs Colts, Hutchinson accepted an athletic scholarship to the University of Michigan, where he spent his college career playing for head coach Lloyd Carr. A four-year starter at Michigan, Hutchinson initially played defensive tackle, before transitioning to offensive guard during his freshman year, when he helped the Wolverines capture the National Championship. A dominant force at the collegiate level, Hutchinson did not allow a sack his final two seasons, with his exceptional play earning him four All–Big Ten selections, two All-America nominations, and Big Ten Offensive Lineman of the Year honors as a senior in 2000, when he also won the Jim Parker Award from the Touchdown Club of Columbus (Ohio) and received consideration for the Outland Trophy, presented annually to college football's best interior lineman.

Selected by the Seahawks with the 17th overall pick of the 2001 NFL Draft, Hutchinson excelled in his first year as a pro, earning a spot on the NFL All-Rookie Team by helping running back Shaun Alexander rush for 1,318 yards and 14 touchdowns from his left guard position. Continuing

Steve Hutchinson earned NFL Offensive Lineman of the Year honors twice as a member of the Vikings.
Courtesy of SportsMemorabilia.com

to perform at an elite level the next four seasons, Hutchinson earned three trips to the Pro Bowl and three All-Pro nominations, with his superior blocking at the point of attack helping to pave the way for Alexander to gain 1,880 yards on the ground and score 28 touchdowns in 2005.

Subsequently named Seattle's transition player for 2006, Hutchinson remained free to negotiate with other teams, although the Seahawks retained the rights to match any offer he received. But, when the Vikings offered Hutchinson a seven-year deal worth $49 million, the Seahawks had no choice but to allow the perennial All-Pro guard to leave for Minnesota.

Making an immediate impact his first year in the Twin Cities, Hutchinson helped the Vikings vastly improve their running game in 2006, with his dominant blocking earning him Pro Bowl and All-Pro honors for the fourth of seven straight times and gaining him recognition as the NFL Offensive Lineman of the Year. Two years later, Hutchinson helped Adrian Peterson rush for a league-leading 1,760 yards, before being named NFL Offensive Lineman of the Year once again in 2009.

Standing 6'5" and weighing close to 315 pounds, Hutchinson possessed outstanding size and strength, allowing him to control his man at the line of scrimmage in both running and passing situations, with former Vikings center Matt Birk, who lined up next to him for 48 consecutive regular-season games from 2006 to 2008, saying, "Hutch was a physical force . . . one of the few interior linemen who could physically dominate his opponent. In the run game, he moved guys off the line of scrimmage. He would just shut guys down in the passing game. . . . Never had to worry about Hutch and his matchup. You could always rely on him to play winning football."

Also known for his superb technique, tremendous work ethic, and influence in and around the locker room, Hutchinson drew praise from Vikings head coach Brad Childress, who stated, "He comes to work every day. He grinds. Just what you want offensive linemen to be."

Former Vikings defensive tackle Kevin Williams is another who holds Hutchinson in extremely high esteem, saying, "I knew we had signed a great player. I played against Hutch when he was in Seattle, and I already knew what type of player we were getting. I was excited, and the respect was there. We hit the ground running in practice and made each other better. It was fun. I got to see him lock down a bunch of guys."

Williams continued, "He was one of the most patient guards you were ever going to face. He had such a wide base. As a D-lineman, we want you to give us something that we're going to counter when we're rushing, but he would hold his punch and shoot his punch from down low, from his waist. Most guys are taught to shoot their hands up at your chest, but he would come up from the bottom and it was hard to counter that because he was so strong. He would engulf you and tie you up, and it was a stalemate. If he got that low right hand on you, it was over."

Williams then added, "He had seasons where he hardly gave up any sacks. Then you look at the teams he was on and their rushing yards . . . he was a complete offensive lineman with his size, strength, footwork. . . . He was one of the best, and his track record speaks for himself. . . . It's hard to gauge offensive linemen because they don't get a lot of glory, but if anyone played against him, they'll tell you he was a great player."

And even though Randall McDaniel left Minnesota seven years before Hutchinson joined the Vikings, he said that he enjoyed watching him from afar, stating, "I loved his technique, his style . . . he was so sound fundamentally. I loved how he would finish blocks—there was no bouncing off a guy with Hutch. He finished his guy, which made me happy. I loved to see guys still play like he did."

McDaniel added, "There was no quit in Hutch. Win or lose, he had his man taken care of. You wouldn't hear much out of his guy in a game. His consistency is what set him apart. To play inside, you have to be consistent, and that's what running backs appreciate. They want to know you're going to handle your man. They want to know your guy isn't going to be hitting them, and Hutch always took care of that—at the point of attack or cutting a guy off, he always took care of his guy."

After starting every game for the Vikings in each of the previous four seasons, Hutchinson missed the final three contests of the 2010 campaign due to a broken thumb, ending his streak of 123 consecutive starts that dated back to his days in Seattle. Hutchinson missed another two games the following year, before being released by the Vikings on March 10, 2012.

Signed by the Titans five days later, Hutchinson spent one year in Tennessee, before announcing his retirement on March 11, 2013.

Singing the praises of Hutchinson upon learning of his retirement, Hall of Fame guard and Titans head coach Mike Munchak said, "Hutch obviously had a great career in this league. Over the past decade, he was the best guard in the league in my opinion. I've always enjoyed watching him on tape, how he dominated guys. It was great getting a chance to work with him this year and to know him as a player and a person. I wish him and his family the best in retirement."

Elected to the Pro Football Hall of Fame on February 1, 2020, Hutchinson returned to Seattle one month later, joining the Seahawks front office as a football consultant.

VIKINGS CAREER HIGHLIGHTS

Best Season

Hutchinson earned NFL Offensive Lineman of the Year honors in both 2006 and 2009, amazingly going the entire 2006 campaign without being called for a single penalty. But, while the Vikings finished near the bottom of the league rankings in total offense in 2006, scoring a total of just 282 points the entire year, they boasted one of the NFL's most potent offenses in 2009, finishing second in the league with 470 points scored. Furthermore, Hutchinson gained consensus First-Team All-Pro recognition in 2009, something he failed to do three years earlier. Factoring everything into the equation, the 2009 campaign would have to be considered Hutchinson's finest as a member of the Vikings.

Memorable Moments/Greatest Performances

Hutchinson helped the Vikings rush for 311 yards and amass 444 yards of total offense during a 34–31 win over the Bears on October 14, 2007.

Hutchinson and his line-mates controlled the line of scrimmage during a 35–17 victory over the San Diego Chargers on November 4, 2007, with the Vikings amassing 528 yards of total offense, 378 of which came on the ground.

Hutchinson's powerful blocking at the point of attack helped the Vikings rush for a season-high total of 239 yards during a 35–14 win over the Arizona Cardinals on December 14, 2008.

Hutchinson helped the Vikings amass 537 yards of total offense during a 36–10 win over the Bears on November 29, 2009.

Hutchinson and his line-mates turned in another dominant performance on November 7, 2010, with the Vikings amassing 507 yards of total offense during a 27–24 overtime win over Arizona.

Notable Achievements

- Two-time division champion (2008 and 2009).
- Two-time NFL Offensive Lineman of the Year (2006 and 2009).
- Four-time Pro Bowl selection (2006, 2007, 2008, and 2009).
- Three-time First-Team All-Pro selection (2007, 2008, and 2009).
- 2006 Second-Team All-Pro selection.
- Four-time First-Team All-NFC selection (2006, 2007, 2008, and 2009).
- Pro Football Reference All-2000s First Team.
- NFL 2000s All-Decade First Team.
- Elected to Pro Football Hall of Fame in 2020.

25

JEFF SIEMON

An intelligent player with strong intuitive abilities, Jeff Siemon spent his entire 11-year NFL career in Minnesota, proving to be one of the finest all-around middle linebackers in the game for much of the 1970s. Starting at that post for the Vikings from 1972 to 1979, Siemon recorded more than 100 tackles nine times, with his 1,382 career stops representing the third-highest total in franchise history. Appearing in 156 out of a possible 157 contests, Siemon helped the Vikings win seven division titles and three NFC championships, with his consistently excellent play in the middle earning him four Pro Bowl selections and five All-NFC nominations.

Born in Rochester, Minnesota, on June 2, 1950, Jeffrey Glenn Siemon grew up in Bakersfield, California, where he starred on the gridiron at multiple positions for Bakersfield High School, seeing action at quarterback, tight end, center, and linebacker. After accepting an athletic scholarship from Stanford University, Siemon spent his college career playing middle linebacker for the Cardinals, who he led to a pair of victories in the Rose Bowl. Earning numerous individual honors along the way, Siemon won the Butkus Award as the nation's best linebacker in his senior year, while also being named the winner of the Pop Warner Award as the top senior player on the West Coast.

Subsequently selected by the Vikings in the first round of the 1972 NFL Draft, with the 10th overall pick, Siemon spent the first few weeks of his rookie season backing up veteran middle linebacker Lonnie Warwick, before laying claim to the starting job in Week 7. Performing extremely well the rest of the way, Siemon ended up intercepting two passes, recovering two fumbles, and ranking among the team leaders in tackles.

Having adapted quickly to the pro game, Siemon established himself as one of the Vikings' defensive leaders the following year, beginning a string of five straight seasons in which he earned All-Conference honors. Also named to the Pro Bowl four times between 1973 and 1977, Siemon became the centerpiece of a talented but aging Minnesota defense that

Jeff Siemon recorded more than 100 tackles nine times for the Vikings.
Courtesy of FootballCardGallery.com

helped carry the team to six consecutive division titles and three conference championships.

Extremely smart and tough, Siemon took on the demeanor of his head coach, Bud Grant, doing his job in an efficient but understated manner. Known for his speed and quickness, the 6'2", 235-pound Siemon tracked down opposing ball-carriers from sideline to sideline, developing a reputation as one of the league's best tacklers. Outstanding in pass-coverage as well, Siemon did an excellent job of covering tight ends and backs coming out of the backfield, with his exceptional all-around play helping the Vikings rank among the league leaders in fewest points allowed four straight times from 1973 to 1976.

Siemon remained the Vikings' starting middle linebacker until 1980, when Scott Studwell displaced him as the starter at that position. However, with the team switching to a 3-4 defense the following year, Siemon rejoined the starting unit, starting all but one game at left-inside linebacker. Forced to assume a backup role once again in 1982 following the emergence of third-year linebacker Dennis Johnson, Siemon, dreading the Vikings' move to the Metrodome, asked to be traded to a Super Bowl–caliber team that played on natural turf. Subsequently dealt to the San Diego Chargers, Siemon failed to make much of an impression during training camp, prompting him to announce his retirement prior to the start of the 1983 regular season. In addition to his unofficial total of 1,382 tackles, Siemon ended his career with 11 interceptions and 11 fumble recoveries.

After retiring as an active player, Siemon, who grew up in a nominally Christian home where religion was "something you did" and was treated very matter-of-factly, embarked on a quest to develop a deeper relationship with God. Revealing that his thirst for knowledge truly began when a knee injury he sustained in college forced him to contemplate life without football, Siemon recalled, "I saw life through a different set of spectacles. Football had really served as the god of my life, so, when it was taken away from me, I really had to ponder the meaning of life." After earning a master's degree in Christian apologetics from the Simon Greenleaf School of Law in 1984, Siemon became the director for Minnesota Search Ministries, where he has spent more than three decades heading up the initiatives of an organization that works with churches and focuses on men's ministry.

CAREER HIGHLIGHTS

Best Season

Although Siemon failed to garner any postseason honors in 1978, he performed exceptionally well for the Vikings, setting a single-season franchise record by recording 170 solo combined tackles (i.e., defense + special teams). However, Siemon had his finest all-around season in 1975, gaining Pro Bowl and Second-Team All-NFC recognition by registering well over 100 tackles and recording a career-high three interceptions.

Memorable Moments/Greatest Performances

Siemon recorded the first two interceptions of his career during a 20–17 loss to the San Francisco 49ers in the 1972 regular-season finale.

In addition to anchoring a Vikings' defense that surrendered just 70 yards rushing and 45 yards of total offense to the Browns during a convincing 26–3 victory on November 4, 1973, Siemon intercepted a Mike Phipps pass, which he subsequently returned 21 yards.

Siemon recorded one of the four interceptions the Vikings registered against Roger Staubach during their 27–10 win over the Cowboys in the 1973 NFC championship game.

Siemon helped lead the Vikings to a lopsided 38–0 victory over Atlanta on November 9, 1975, by intercepting a pass and anchoring a defense that allowed just 60 yards of total offense.

Notable Achievements

- Missed just one game in 11 seasons, appearing in 156 out of 157 contests.
- Recorded more than 100 tackles nine times.
- Holds Vikings single-season franchise record for most solo tackles (170 in 1978).
- Ranks third in franchise history with 1,382 career tackles.
- Seven-time division champion (1973, 1974, 1975, 1976, 1977, 1978, and 1980).
- Three-time NFC champion (1973, 1974, and 1976).
- Four-time Pro Bowl selection (1973, 1975, 1976, and 1977).
- Five-time Second-Team All-NFC selection (1973, 1974, 1975, 1976, and 1977).

26

JARED ALLEN

Joining the Vikings in 2008 after spending the previous four seasons with the Kansas City Chiefs, Jared Allen arrived in Minnesota with a reputation as someone who flouted convention and defied authority. Although Allen subsequently remained very much a free spirit during his time in the Twin Cities, the talented defensive end, who previously ran into trouble with the law on numerous occasions, showed tremendous maturation and eventually became a solid citizen while wearing the Purple and Gold. Allen also continued to be a thorn in the side of opposing quarterbacks, averaging just over 14 sacks a season in his six years with the Vikings, after bringing down opposing signal-callers a total of 43 times while playing for the Chiefs. Ending his six-year stint in Minnesota as one of the franchise's all-time sack leaders, Allen helped the Vikings win two division titles, with his exceptional play earning him four trips to the Pro Bowl and three All-Pro nominations.

Born in Dallas, Texas, on April 3, 1982, Jared Scot Allen grew up on a horse ranch in Morgan Hill, California, where he attended Live Oak High School, before transferring to Los Gatos High School prior to the start of his senior year after school authorities accused him of stealing yearbooks. Seeking to make an impression on college scouts after losing most of his scholarship offers due to his off-field transgressions, Allen performed brilliantly in his one year at Los Gatos, earning First-Team All-League and First-Team All–Central Coast honors by recording 12 sacks and 96 tackles, forcing five fumbles, and recovering five others.

Subsequently offered a scholarship to Idaho State University, Allen spent four seasons starring for the Bengals at defensive end, earning First-Team All–Big Sky honors three times by registering 250 tackles, 38½ sacks, 73 tackles for loss, 13 forced fumbles, seven fumble recoveries, three interceptions, and three touchdowns. Performing especially well as a senior in 2003, Allen won the Buck Buchanan Award as the best lineman in small college football and gained First-Team Division I-AA All-America

Jared Allen's 22 sacks in 2011 represent a single-season franchise record.
Courtesy of Mike Morbeck

recognition by recording 17½ sacks, 102 tackles, and six forced fumbles. Allen also doubled as a long-snapper on offense, with former Vikings head coach Leslie Frazier once telling the *St. Paul Pioneer Press*, "He brags all the time about how he's the best [long-snapper] in the league, best in college when he came out."

Despite his outstanding play at Idaho State, Allen had several red flags surrounding him heading into the 2004 NFL Draft. In addition to his small-college background, Allen had a reputation as a barroom brawler, with Andrew Lawrence describing him in *Sports Illustrated* as "a keen bar fighter" at Idaho State who, in addition to being cited for DUI on multiple occasions, "had been arrested once for battery and twice for resisting arrest."

Ultimately selected by Kansas City in the fourth round, with the 126th overall pick, Allen began his pro career playing mostly on special teams and serving as a backup defensive end. But, before long, Allen joined the starting unit, eventually landing a spot on the 2004 NFL All-Rookie team by leading the Chiefs with nine sacks. Allen followed that up with two more strong seasons, recording 11 sacks and forcing six fumbles in 2005, before registering 7½ sacks, making a career-high 76 tackles, and leading the NFL with six fumble recoveries in 2006.

However, while Allen proved to be one of Kansas City's most effective players on defense, he also created headlines off the playing field in 2006 by being arrested twice within a span of five months for driving under the influence of alcohol, with his irresponsible behavior prompting the league office to suspend him for the first two games of the 2007 regular season. Revealing that those incidents forced him to take a good, hard look at himself, Allen later said, "I had to change my priorities. To me, it was a growing up process. I couldn't keep going out like I was in college. To take my game to the next level, I had to make some sacrifices. Drinking was the one thing I felt like I could sacrifice."

After eliminating alcohol and unhealthy foods from his diet during the offseason, Allen went on to have a banner year in 2007, earning Pro Bowl and First-Team All-Pro honors by leading the NFL with 15½ sacks and 19 tackles for loss. Nevertheless, with team management questioning Allen's overall commitment to the game, the Chiefs failed to offer him a contract extension, leading to both sides harboring ill feelings. Finally deciding to part ways with their talented but enigmatic defensive end, the Chiefs traded Allen to the Vikings for three high picks in the 2008 NFL Draft.

Expressing his thoughts on why the Chiefs elected to deal him to the Vikings, Allen subsequently told the Kansas City media, "His name was [Chiefs GM] Carl Peterson. You can write that in caps. . . . Obviously, I had a problem with (Chiefs owner) Clark Hunt, too, because he chose Carl over me, huh? When everything went down there, I didn't appreciate being lied to. I was told I'd get a contract extension and everything, and the way things played out, my biggest thing was, 'Listen, I don't lie to you guys. I show up and bust my tail for you. Don't lie to me.' . . . It's tough to go and give your all for someone like that."

After inking a long-term deal with the Vikings, Allen went on to have an outstanding first season in Minnesota, gaining Pro Bowl and First-Team All-Pro recognition for the second of three straight times by recording 14½ sacks, finishing second in the NFL with 20 tackles for loss, and leading the league with two safeties. Allen followed that up by placing near the top of the league rankings with 14½ sacks, 19 tackles for loss, and five fumble recoveries in 2009, before recording 11 sacks, 60 tackles, and two interceptions in 2010. Allen then reached the apex of his career the following year, setting a new single-season franchise record by recording a league-leading 22 sacks, with his extraordinary performance earning him Pro Bowl and First-Team All-Pro honors for the fourth time in five seasons.

An excellent all-around athlete who also played basketball in high school, the 6'6", 270-pound Allen combined size, speed, and strength to establish himself as one of the top pass-rushers of his era. Also blessed with good instincts and a motor that never stopped, Allen proved to be extremely effective against the run as well, displaying his relentless and aggressive approach to the game by pursuing ball-carriers all over the field. In addition to his exceptional play, Allen became known for his nonconformist nature and larger-than-life personality during his time in Minnesota. Sporting a lengthy mullet and rejoicing each time he or one of his teammates made a big play, Allen drew attention to himself with his wild hairstyles and calf-roping celebrations, with his unconventional behavior making him extremely popular with the hometown fans.

Allen spent two more years in Minnesota, recording another 23½ sacks, before signing with the Chicago Bears as a free agent on March 26, 2014. After one year in Chicago, Allen ended his playing career with the Carolina Panthers in 2015. Retiring with career totals of 136 sacks, 648 tackles, 171 tackles for loss, 32 forced fumbles, 19 fumble recoveries, four safeties, six interceptions, and four touchdowns, Allen currently ranks among the NFL's all-time leaders in sacks (12th), tackles for loss (tied-3rd), and safeties (tied-1st). In his six years with the Vikings, Allen recorded 85½ sacks, made 329 tackles, 104 of which resulted in a loss, forced 16 fumbles, recovered nine others, registered all four of his safeties, intercepted four passes, and scored two touchdowns.

On April 14, 2016, just two days after he announced his decision to leave the game, Allen signed a one-day contract with the Vikings that enabled him to officially retire as a member of the team. Making his feelings known at the time, Allen told the *Minneapolis Star Tribune*: "Minnesota was my heart. Six great years, not only with football, but I met my wife when I was there, I got married when I was there, I had my first child there. There are just so many life memories there that, from top to bottom in that organization, I feel a part of it. . . . I can say now that I'm a Viking for the remainder of my time on Earth."

Since retiring as an active player, Allen has continued his work with Jared Allen's Homes for Wounded Warriors, which he founded in 2009 to build and remodel homes for wounded war veterans. Allen also serves as an advocate for the Juvenile Diabetes Research Foundation and raises funds through his "Sack Diabetes" program. In his spare time, Allen enjoys hunting and competing in the sport of curling.

VIKINGS CAREER HIGHLIGHTS

Best Season

Allen performed exceptionally well for the Vikings in both 2008 and 2009, earning First-Team All-Pro honors each year by recording 14½ sacks and more than 50 tackles. However, he had the most dominant season of his career in 2011, once again gaining First-Team All-Pro recognition by forcing four fumbles, recovering four others, setting a single-season franchise record by recording a league-leading 22 sacks, registering 32 hits on opposing quarterbacks, and making 66 tackles, with his 21 solo stops placing him third in the league rankings.

Memorable Moments/Greatest Performances

Allen recorded the first of his NFL-record four career safeties when he sacked Dan Orlovsky in the end zone during a 12–10 win over the Lions on October 12, 2008.

Allen contributed to a 28–21 victory over the Houston Texans on November 2, 2008, by recording two sacks and forcing a fumble.

Allen tallied a critical two points for the Vikings when he sacked Aaron Rodgers in the end zone for a safety during a 28–27 win over the Packers on November 9, 2008.

Allen earned NFC Defensive Player of the Week honors by recording 2½ sacks and eight tackles during a 34–14 win over the Bears on November 30, 2008.

Allen turned in a tremendous all-around effort against the Packers on October 5, 2009, leading the Vikings to a 30–23 victory over their division rivals by recording 4½ sacks, seven tackles, and one forced fumble, with one of his sacks of Aaron Rodgers resulting in a safety.

Allen recovered two fumbles during a 38–10 win over the St. Louis Rams on October 11, 2009, returning one of them 52 yards for the first touchdown of his career.

Allen continued to be a thorn in the side of Aaron Rodgers on November 1, 2009, sacking the Green Bay quarterback three times during a 38–26 Vikings win.

Allen starred during a 36–10 victory over the Bears on November 29, 2009, recording two sacks and an interception.

Allen scored the only touchdown the Vikings managed during a 20–13 loss to the Lions in the final game of the 2010 regular season when he ran 36 yards to paydirt after intercepting a Shaun Hill pass.

Although the Vikings lost to the Lions once again on September 25, 2011, this time in overtime by a score of 26–23, Allen starred in defeat, recording three sacks and forcing one fumble.

Allen brought his season sack total to 22 by recording 3½ sacks during a 17–13 loss to the Bears in the final game of the 2011 regular season, establishing in the process a new single-season franchise record.

Notable Achievements

- Never missed a game in six seasons, starting 96 consecutive contests.
- Scored two defensive touchdowns.
- Finished in double digits in sacks six times.
- Led NFL with 22 sacks in 2011.
- Finished second in NFL in sacks once and tackles for loss twice.
- Finished third in NFL in tackles for loss once and forced fumbles once.
- Led Vikings in sacks six times.
- Holds Vikings single-season record for most sacks (22 in 2011).
- Holds Vikings career record for most safeties (4).
- Ranks among Vikings career leaders with 85½ sacks (6th) and 16 forced fumbles (4th).
- Holds share of NFL career record for most safeties (4).
- Two-time division champion (2008 and 2009).
- 2008 Week 13 NFC Defensive Player of the Week.
- October 2011 NFC Defensive Player of the Month.
- Four-time Pro Bowl selection (2008, 2009, 2011, and 2012).
- Three-time First-Team All-Pro selection (2008, 2009, and 2011).

27

CHAD GREENWAY

A n outstanding all-around linebacker who excelled in every aspect of the game, Chad Greenway spent his entire 10-year NFL career in Minnesota, serving as an integral part of Vikings teams that made four playoff appearances and won three division titles. A stout run-defender who also did an excellent job in pass coverage, Greenway led the Vikings in tackles six times, ending his career with the fourth-most stops in franchise history. Named the Vikings' most valuable player on defense three times, Greenway also gained Pro Bowl recognition twice and All-Pro honors once.

Born in Mount Vernon, South Dakota, on January 12, 1983, Chad Greenway grew up on his family farm, where he spent his mornings loading pigs before heading off to school. Looking back on his early years, Greenway said, "It was kind of a juggling act of trying to do a bunch of things we can on the farm, whether it be loading pigs with my sisters in the morning before you go to school, or what it might be you are doing. There was always a lot of activity and a lot of work to be done. It was a major way to grow up and definitely gave me an advantage when I went off to college to do my own thing in football. It was a definite advantage over a lot of other guys that I had that built-in ability to react to leadership, react to tasks, react to work ethic."

Excelling in multiple sports at Mount Vernon High School, Greenway lettered in baseball, basketball, football, and track and field, proving to be particularly proficient on the gridiron, where he starred at quarterback and free safety for the school's nine-man football team. Leading Mount Vernon to back-to-back state titles, Greenway compiled career totals of 2,572 yards passing, 3,118 yards rushing, 407 tackles, and 23 interceptions, earning in the process All-State honors three times. Also accorded Gatorade Football Player of the Year honors as a senior after he passed for 1,147 yards, gained another 1,320 yards on the ground, and recorded 132 tackles and four interceptions on defense, Greenway subsequently accepted a scholarship offer from the University of Iowa, where he began his college career as a 195-pound safety,

Chad Greenway led the Vikings in tackles six times.
Courtesy of Lance Cpl. Kevin Jones via Wikimedia Commons

before gradually transitioning into a 240-pound outside linebacker. Proving to be a natural at his new position, Greenway recorded a total of 416 tackles for the Hawkeyes, with his exceptional play gaining him All–Big Ten recognition three times and All-America honors as a senior in 2005.

Selected by the Vikings with the 17th overall pick of the 2006 NFL Draft, Greenway spent his first pro training camp competing with veteran linebackers E. J. Henderson and Ben Leber for a spot on the starting unit, before tearing the ACL in his left leg while covering a kickoff in Minnesota's first preseason game against the Oakland Raiders. After sitting out the entire year, Greenway began his career in earnest in 2007, when, after earning a starting job during the preseason, he ended up finishing second on the team with 105 tackles, beginning in the process a string of eight consecutive seasons in which he recorded at least 100 stops. Greenway followed that up by making a team-high 116 tackles in 2008, while also registering 5½ sacks and forcing three fumbles. After performing well once again in 2009, Greenway played the best ball of his career over the course of the next four seasons, earning two trips to the Pro Bowl, one All-Pro nomination, and team MVP honors on defense three times by registering more than 130 tackles each year.

Blessed with good size, above-average speed, and superb instincts, the 6'3", 240-pound Greenway played the run extremely well, doing an outstanding job of tracking opposing ball-carriers from sideline to sideline. Excellent in pass-coverage as well, Greenway recorded a total of 11 interceptions, which he returned for 222 yards and two touchdowns. Also capable of applying pressure to opposing quarterbacks when called upon to do so, Greenway registered 18 sacks in his 10 years in the league, with his 5½ sacks in 2008 representing his career-high mark.

In discussing the totality of Greenway's game, Hall of Fame linebacker Mike Singletary stated, "I think what he has that I really like is he has the ability to play the pass, play the run, he can blitz, and he can do so many things. He's not just a pass-rusher, and he's not just a run-stuffer. He is a guy that, when the ball is snapped, you can count that he's going to be around it, and he doesn't take plays off. That's really big."

Greenway spent three more seasons in Minnesota, recording just over 200 tackles during that time, before announcing his retirement on March 6, 2017. In addition to his 11 interceptions and 18 sacks, Greenway ended his playing career with 1,334 tackles, eight forced fumbles, and 11 fumble recoveries.

Upon learning of his former teammate's decision to retire, KFAN contributor and fellow South Dakota native Ben Leber said, "Congratulations to Chad and his family on a fantastic career. The Minnesota Vikings couldn't have had a better representative on and off the field. He played the game with a passion and enthusiasm that is becoming more and more rare. He always showed up to work with a smile and a work ethic that is among the best I've ever been around. He made the guys around him better players and, more importantly, better people. His positive energy and presence will forever be a part of the Minnesota Vikings."

Remaining in the Minneapolis area following his retirement, Greenway and his wife, Jennifer, give back to the community through the Chad Greenway Lead the Way Foundation, which they founded in 2008 to provide seriously ill and physically challenged children throughout the Twin Cities with daily support and life-changing experiences. Greenway also remains active in the state of Iowa, serving as a member of the University of Iowa and the Iowa Farm Bureau Federation to support the America Needs Farmers organization. In discussing his affiliation with the program, Greenway says, "For me, it is pretty easy to be part of it. It's a great program and promotes farming in so many ways. I think it does a good job of bringing recognition to people who deserve it, and, obviously, it is easy to promote one of the greatest professions in the world."

CAREER HIGHLIGHTS

Best Season

Greenway began to establish himself as one of the NFL's better all-around linebackers in 2008, when, in addition to recording more than 100 tackles for the second of eight straight times, he forced three fumbles and registered 5½ sacks. Greenway also performed extremely well in 2010 and 2013, finishing third in the NFL with 109 solo tackles in the first of those campaigns, while recording three sacks and three interceptions in the second. However, Greenway played his best ball for the Vikings in 2011 and 2012, gaining Pro Bowl recognition for the only two times in his career by making close to 150 tackles each year. Since Greenway earned his lone All-Pro nomination in 2012, we'll identify that as his finest all-around season.

Memorable Moments/Greatest Performances

Greenway excelled in his first game as a pro, recording 10 tackles and forcing a fumble during a 24–3 win over the Atlanta Falcons in the 2007 regular-season opener.

Greenway displayed his versatility during a 29–22 victory over the Oakland Raiders on November 18, 2007, recovering a fumble, making seven tackles, and recording the first interception of his career.

Greenway followed that up by returning his interception of an Eli Manning pass 37 yards for a touchdown during a 41–17 rout of the Giants on November 25, 2007.

Greenway contributed to a 20–10 win over the Carolina Panthers on September 21, 2008, by forcing a fumble and recording nine tackles and the first sack of his career.

Although the Vikings lost to Tampa Bay by a score of 19–13 on November 16, 2008, Greenway starred in defeat, recording one sack and 16 solo tackles.

Greenway earned NFC Defensive Player of the Week honors by recovering a fumble and intercepting two passes during a 27–13 win over the Lions on September 20, 2009.

Greenway recorded a season-high 16 combined tackles during a 33–26 victory over the Washington Redskins on December 24, 2011.

Greenway turned in a pair of outstanding all-around efforts in 2012, recording two sacks and 13 tackles during a 24–13 win over the 49ers on September 23, before recovering a fumble, recording a sack, and making 13 solo tackles during a 36–22 victory over the St. Louis Rams on December 16.

Greenway had another exceptional all-around game against the Steelers on September 29, 2013, contributing to a 34–27 Vikings win by recording an interception, a sack, and 10 solo tackles.

Greenway experienced one of the most memorable moments of his career during a 31–14 victory over the San Diego Chargers on September 27, 2015, when he returned his interception of a Philip Rivers pass 91 yards for a touchdown.

Notable Achievements

- Scored two defensive touchdowns.
- Recorded more than 100 tackles eight times, registering more than 140 stops three times.
- Finished second in NFL with 148 tackles in 2012.
- Finished third in NFL with 109 solo tackles in 2010.
- Led Vikings in tackles six times.
- Ranks fourth in franchise history with 1,334 career tackles.
- Three-time division champion (2008, 2009, and 2015).
- 2009 Week 2 NFC Defensive Player of the Week.
- Three-time Vikings Defensive MVP (2010, 2012, and 2013).
- Two-time Pro Bowl selection (2011 and 2012).
- 2012 Second-Team All-Pro selection.

28

ANTHONY CARTER

An outstanding wide receiver who excelled in big-game situations, Anthony Carter made huge contributions to Vikings teams that made five playoff appearances and won two division titles. Spending nine of his 11 NFL seasons in Minnesota, Carter surpassed 60 receptions four times and 1,000 receiving yards three times, leading the team in each of those categories on multiple occasions. A three-time Pro Bowler and two-time All-NFC selection, Carter continues to rank among the franchise's all-time leaders in virtually every offensive category more than a quarter of a century after he donned the Purple and Gold for the last time.

Born in Riviera Beach, Florida, on September 17, 1960, Anthony Carter attended Suncoast High School, where, in addition to starring on the gridiron, he played basketball and ran track. Offered an athletic scholarship to the University of Michigan, Carter spent his college career playing for legendary Wolverines head coach Bo Schembechler, who once called him "the greatest athlete I've ever coached."

Despite competing in a run-based offense at Michigan, Carter proved to be one of the school's most productive receivers ever, earning team MVP honors twice, while also gaining All-America recognition three times. Shattering virtually every Michigan pass-receiving, kick-return, and scoring record, Carter ended his four years at Ann Arbor with 161 receptions, 3,076 receiving yards, 5,802 all-purpose yards, 37 TD catches, 40 touchdowns, and 244 points scored. Performing exceptionally well in 1980 and 1981, Carter set a single-season school record by catching 14 touchdown passes in the first of those campaigns, before amassing 952 receiving yards, 1,019 yards from scrimmage, and 1,621 all-purpose yards in the second. Carter then earned a fourth-place finish in the Heisman Trophy balloting as a senior in 1982 by making 43 receptions for 844 yards, amassing 1,535 all-purpose yards, and scoring nine touchdowns, with his outstanding play also gaining him recognition as the Big Ten's Most Valuable Player.

Anthony Carter led the Vikings in receptions four times and receiving yards five times.
Courtesy of George A. Kitrinos

Commenting on his star wide receiver's extraordinary pass-receiving skills on one occasion, Bo Schembechler said, "He can adjust to the football like no one I've ever seen, that's what makes him great. Bad balls, balls over the wrong shoulder, balls that shouldn't be caught—it doesn't matter. He catches 'em."

Schembechler also expressed his admiration for Carter as a person when he stated, "After we won the Rose Bowl [at the end of 1980], Anthony was sitting in the training room on the traveling trunks. I said, 'Anthony, what are you doing here?' He told me if he went out, all the media would come to him and ignore the other guys. He didn't want the other guys ignored. That's why I like Anthony. He's solid. He left a legacy here that will be hard to equal."

Selected by the Miami Dolphins in the 12th round of the 1983 NFL Draft, with the 334th overall pick, Carter instead chose to sign with the Michigan Panthers of the United States Football League, who made him a territorial selection in that year's USFL Draft. Excelling in his first year as a pro, Carter caught 60 passes, finished second in the league with 1,081 receiving yards, and scored nine touchdowns. Carter subsequently missed much of the 1984 season after breaking his left arm in Week 6, before spending the following year with the Oakland Invaders, who merged with the Panthers. Starring in his one season in Oakland, Carter made 70 receptions for 1,323 yards and 14 touchdowns.

With the USFL folding after the 1985 season, Carter signed with the Dolphins, who still retained his NFL rights. However, Miami traded him to the Vikings for linebacker Robin Sendlein and a 1986 second-round draft pick prior to the start of the regular season.

Establishing himself as a major weapon in the Vikings' offense immediately upon his arrival in Minnesota, Carter made 43 receptions for 821 yards and eight touchdowns in 1985, with his average of 19.1 yards per catch placing him among the league leaders. Carter followed that up by catching 38 passes, amassing 686 receiving yards, and scoring seven touchdowns in 1986, before making another 38 receptions, accumulating 922 receiving yards, scoring seven touchdowns, and leading the league with an average of 24.3 yards per reception in 1987. Carter then had a postseason for the ages, making 23 receptions for 391 yards, amassing 642 all-purpose yards, and scoring two touchdowns in Minnesota's three playoff contests, which included upset victories over the New Orleans Saints and San Francisco 49ers.

Clearly the Vikings' most potent offensive weapon by 1988, Carter began an outstanding 3-year run during which he posted the following numbers:

YEAR	RECS	REC YDS	TD RECS
1988	72	1,225	6
1989	65	1,066	4
1990	70	1,008	8

Leading the Vikings in receptions and receiving yards all three years, Carter became the first player in franchise history to amass more than 1,000 yards through the air three straight times, with his exceptional play earning him Pro Bowl honors each season and Second-Team All-NFC recognition in 1988, when he finished fourth in the NFL with 1,225 receiving yards.

Carter performed at an elite level even though he jogged with an uneven, flat-footed gait and lacked the physique of a prototypical NFL wide receiver. Standing 5'11" and weighing somewhere close to 165 pounds, Carter had no legs to speak of, with Vikings head coach Jerry Burns once saying, "I've always said if the good Lord put anybody on earth to play football, it was AC. He just forgot to give him a body."

Carter, though, possessed many other qualities that enabled him to gradually emerge as one of the league's top wideouts. Although he walked somewhat awkwardly, Carter ran with a smooth, lengthy stride that allowed him to make quick cuts and beat his defender deep. Also blessed with exceptional hand-eye coordination, outstanding speed, excellent leaping ability, and tremendous route-running discipline, Carter proved to be a superb target on all types of pass patterns. Absolutely fearless going over the middle, Carter ran slant patterns extremely well, showing equal disdain for linebackers and safeties that patrolled the area. He also did an excellent job of running quick outs and curl patterns, using the threat of his great speed to keep his defender from crowding him at the line of scrimmage.

However, Carter's two greatest assets may well have been his superb body control and extraordinary ability to pick up the football. In discussing the first quality, Vikings quarterback Wade Wilson stated, "Against Detroit last season, we were just going for field goal position before the half. I throw him a little out, the cornerback comes up to make a good play, and AC just spins way up in midair, catches it, bounces off the defender, and goes for a 25-yard gain to set up the field goal."

Wilson added, "I've thrown him plenty of passes that weren't on rhythm, but nobody makes an adjustment on the in-flight pass like AC."

Meanwhile, Carter addressed his ability to gauge the flight of the football by saying, "I always watched Paul Warfield, and what I saw was how he picked up the ball early. He made a decision on the ball. Now, I seem to pick up the ball, see how fast it's coming, where it's going, and how I can reach it before the defensive back can stop me. I have the edge in the air."

Although the arrival of Cris Carter in 1991 forced his namesake to assume a somewhat diminished role, Anthony Carter remained a key contributor on offense the next three seasons, averaging 51 receptions, 636 receiving yards, and four touchdowns from 1991 to 1993, before signing with the Detroit Lions as a free agent. Leaving Minnesota with career totals of 478 receptions, 7,636 receiving yards, 7,925 yards from scrimmage, 8,106 all-purpose yards, 52 touchdown receptions, and 54 touchdowns, Carter continues to rank extremely high in team annals in each of those categories.

Hampered by injuries, Carter ended up spending just two seasons in Detroit, making only eight catches in seven games, before announcing his retirement at the end of 1995.

Unfortunately, Carter has experienced a significant amount of turmoil since retiring as an active player. Troubled by his son's poor health (his young son had cerebral palsy, which required constant and expensive medical care), Carter often exhibited violent behavior, causing him to be arrested twice on charges of domestic battery. Arrested a third time in October 2003, Carter pled guilty to aggravated assault with a deadly weapon in a case that stemmed from allegations made by his wife, Kimberly, that he struck her in the face, threw her to the ground repeatedly, and threatened her with a gun. Carter ended up serving three of his five years' probation, before having his sentence reduced.

VIKINGS CAREER HIGHLIGHTS

Best Season

Carter earned the first of his three straight trips to the Pro Bowl in 1987, when he amassed 922 receiving yards, caught seven touchdown passes, and averaged a league-leading 24.3 yards per reception. He also performed extremely well in 1989 and 1990, surpassing 65 receptions and 1,000 receiving yards in each of those campaigns. But Carter had his finest all-around season in 1988, when he gained All-Conference recognition for the second consecutive time by scoring six touchdowns and ranking among the league leaders with 72 receptions and 1,225 receiving yards, with each of the last two figures representing career-high marks.

Memorable Moments/Greatest Performances

Carter scored the first two touchdowns of his career during a 33–24 loss to the Bears on September 19, 1985, collaborating with Tommy Kramer on pass plays that covered 14 and 57 yards. He finished the game with four catches for 102 yards and those two TDs.

Carter helped the Vikings overcome a 23–0 fourth-quarter deficit to the Philadelphia Eagles on December 1, 1985, by gathering in a pair of late touchdown passes from Wade Wilson, with his 42-yard TD reception with just 1:11 remaining in regulation giving Minnesota a stunning 28–23 victory. Carter finished the day with five catches for 124 yards and those two touchdowns.

Carter starred during a 44–38 overtime win over the Dallas Cowboys on Thanksgiving Day 1987, making eight receptions for 184 yards and two touchdowns, which came on passes from Tommy Kramer that covered 11 and 37 yards.

Carter helped the Vikings record a 44–10 win over the Saints in the 1987 NFC wild card game by returning a punt 84 yards for a touchdown and catching six passes for 79 yards and one TD.

Carter subsequently led the Vikings to a shocking 36–24 upset win over the San Francisco 49ers in the divisional round of the postseason tournament by amassing 278 all-purpose yards. In easily the most memorable performance of his career, Carter made 10 receptions for 227 yards, carried the ball once for 30 yards, and gained another 21 yards on two punt returns. Commenting on Carter's brilliant effort after the game, then–49ers defensive coordinator George Seifert stated, "It was a beautifully graceful exhibition of athletic ability. Many times, we had great coverage. But Anthony had such timing, a superb sense of approaching the ball. He played above us. He was like (Babe) Ruth pointing to the stands that day."

Carter contributed to a 49–20 win over Tampa Bay on October 23, 1988, by catching six passes for 123 yards and one touchdown, which came on a 26-yard connection with Wade Wilson.

Carter had a big day against the Lions on November 6, 1988, making eight receptions for 188 yards during a convincing 44–17 Vikings win.

Carter helped the Vikings begin the 1989 campaign on a positive note by making seven receptions for 123 yards and one touchdown during a 38–7 victory over the Houston Oilers in the opening game of the regular season.

Carter earned NFC Offensive Player of the Week honors by carrying the ball twice for 41 yards and making three receptions for 71 yards and one touchdown during a 17–14 win over the 49ers on September 15, 1991, with his TD coming on a 46-yard pass from Wade Wilson.

Although the Vikings lost to the San Diego Chargers by a score of 30–17 on November 7, 1993, Carter had a huge game, making 10 receptions for 164 yards and one touchdown.

Notable Achievements

- Surpassed 60 receptions four times.
- Surpassed 1,000 receiving yards three times.
- Averaged more than 20 yards per reception once.
- Led NFL with average of 24.3 yards per reception in 1987.
- Finished fourth in NFL with 1,225 receiving yards in 1988.
- Led Vikings in receptions four times and receiving yards five times.
- Ranks among Vikings career leaders with 478 receptions (4th), 7,636 receiving yards (3rd), 52 touchdown receptions (3rd), 54 touchdowns (6th), 324 points scored (12th), 7,925 yards from scrimmage (7th), and 8,106 all-purpose yards (8th).
- Two-time division champion (1989 and 1992).
- 1991 Week 3 NFC Offensive Player of the Week.
- Three-time Pro Bowl selection (1987, 1988, and 1989).
- Two-time Second-Team All-NFC selection (1987 and 1988).

29

STEVE JORDAN

A n excellent receiver and solid run-blocker, Steve Jordan established himself as one of the NFL's finest all-around tight ends during his time in Minnesota. Starting at that position for the Vikings from 1984 to 1993, Jordan surpassed 50 receptions and 600 receiving yards five times each, earning in the process six Pro Bowl selections and four All-NFC nominations. A key contributor to Vikings teams that made six playoff appearances and won three division titles, Jordan proved to be particularly effective from 1986 to 1991, leading all NFL tight ends with 287 receptions and 3,885 receiving yards over that six-year stretch. Inducted into the Vikings Ring of Honor in 2019, Jordan trailed only Ozzie Newsome and Kellen Winslow in receptions by a tight end at the time of his retirement.

Born in Phoenix, Arizona, on January 10, 1961, Steven Russell Jordan attended South Mountain High School, where he performed well enough on the football field to draw a significant amount of interest from several college programs. Recalling the decision that he faced as he neared graduation, Jordan said, "At the age of 17, I wasn't quite sure which college I would attend. All I knew was that I wanted to study engineering, I wanted to play college football, and I wanted to be somewhere other than Arizona. My other criteria were that the institution had to have a good academic reputation, a solid athletic program with a track record of prioritizing academics over athletics for student athletes, and a vibrant undergraduate experience."

Eventually settling on Brown University in Providence, Rhode Island, Jordan remembered that it took him a while to discover his full potential as a football player at that Ivy League institution, stating during a 2002 interview, "I was kind of a late bloomer in high school. I was about 6-foot-3 and 195 pounds. I honed the concepts of tenacity and made the best of every opportunity. I was mostly a jay-vee player as a sophomore, but I became a full-time starter on the varsity as a junior. The coaching there

Steve Jordan led all NFL tight ends in receptions and receiving yards from 1986 to 1991.

was great. When I earned All-Ivy as a junior it was the first time that I got all-anything."

After finishing fifth in the League in receiving his junior year, Jordan earned First-Team All-Ivy and All-East honors as a senior by making 38 receptions for 693 yards. Although the Vikings subsequently selected him in the seventh round of the 1982 NFL Draft, with the 179th overall pick,

Jordan, who graduated with a degree in civil engineering, placed little hope in playing football professionally, recalling, "I had put in four grueling years studying and was all ready to get to work nine-to-five. I had my little engineering job all set up."

Nevertheless, Jordan revealed that his father gave him the inspiration he needed before he left for Vikings' training camp when he told him to "give it my best shot and leave no stone unturned." Arriving at Mankato State University in tremendous physical condition, Jordan remembered, "I did an intense workout regimen before camp, and I was in the best shape of my life to that point."

However, Jordan received a rude awakening at one of his first practice sessions, recalling, "On one of my first days there we're doing a 1-on-1 blocking drill, and I'm up against Matt Blair. . . . Blocking wasn't my forte. I was more of a receiving tight end coming out of college . . . I was in a 3-point stance, the whistle blows, and the next thing I know, I was looking up at the sky. Matt ran right through me like a revolving door. It was an eye-opening experience."

Despite his shaky start, Jordan ended up making the Vikings roster through much hard work and dedication, stating, "I wanted to make sure that I didn't get myself pushed out of training camp. There are certain things you can control and certain things you cannot control. You can't control the other person, like a Matt Blair, who was 6'5" and 250. I couldn't control his level of talent. One of the easiest ways to get bounced out of camp was by mental errors. I could control mental errors. There were some guys that would go out, but I went back in my room, studying and making sure I did not make the mental errors that were going to get me bounced out of camp."

Jordan added, "Bud Grant didn't keep many rookies back then, but I'd made enough of an impression on offense and special teams that I made the team." He subsequently spent his first two seasons in Minnesota playing mostly on special teams, starting just three games on offense, and making only 18 receptions for 254 yards and two touchdowns. Joining the starting unit in 1984, Jordan posted respectable numbers, finishing the season with 38 receptions, 414 receiving yards, and two touchdowns, before beginning an exceptional seven-year run during which he averaged 51 catches and 669 receiving yards. Performing especially well in 1985, 1986, and 1988, Jordan caught 68 passes and amassed 795 receiving yards in the first of those campaigns. He followed that up by making 58 receptions for 859 yards and six touchdowns in 1986, before catching 57 passes, amassing 756 receiving yards, and scoring five touchdowns in 1988. Jordan earned Pro Bowl honors six straight times from 1986 to 1991 and gained Second-Team All-NFC recognition each year from 1986 to 1989.

Blessed with good speed and soft hands, Jordan gradually emerged as a favorite target of Vikings quarterbacks Tommy Kramer, Wade Wilson, and Rich Gannon, all of whom greatly appreciated his ability to find holes in the defense and create separation between himself and his defender. And, once he got his hands on the football, the 6'3", 236-pound Jordan proved to be a powerful and elusive runner whose size and speed made him extremely difficult to bring down in the open field. Jordan also improved his blocking skills during his time in Minnesota, eventually developing into an above-average blocker in the running game.

Jordan had his last big year for the Vikings in 1991, earning his final Pro Bowl selection by making 57 receptions for 638 yards and two touchdowns, before injuries began to take their toll on him. Recalling how his performance began to fade during the early 1990s, Jordan said, "I could see the damage that artificial turf had done to me for 13 years. Still, I was fortunate to have no major injuries. There was no way I was going to take drugs to play. I was in a cycle of whirlpools, massages, tape jobs like a mummy, playing with a neck brace, a knee brace."

After making only 28 receptions for 394 yards and two touchdowns in 1992, Jordan rebounded somewhat the following year, catching 56 passes and amassing 542 receiving yards. However, injuries limited him to just four games in 1994, prompting him to announce his retirement at season's end. Retiring with career totals of 498 receptions, 6,307 receiving yards, 28 TD catches, and 29 touchdowns, Jordan continues to rank among the Vikings' all-time leaders in each of the first three categories.

After retiring as an active player, Jordan, who spent his summers working as an engineer for a construction firm in Minneapolis, returned to his home state of Arizona, where he assumed a similar position with Ryan Companies. Jordan also began to serve on Brown University's Board of Trustees, leading to his eventual involvement in campus race and diversity issues. Jordan further serves his community with his involvement with the Native Vision Sports & Life Skills Camp in the Southwest, which has as its goal providing Native American youth with healthy lifestyles, education, and leadership skills.

Upon announcing that the Vikings planned to induct Jordan into their Ring of Honor in 2019, team owner/president Mark Wilf said, "Steve Jordan's impact on the Vikings has carried on past his career on the field. As great a player as Steve was, he's just as great an ambassador for the Vikings and the game of football. He is a positive role model to young players about the value of education and using your platform as an NFL star for good."

CAREER HIGHLIGHTS

Best Season

Although Jordan failed to score a single touchdown in 1985, he made a career-high 68 receptions and amassed 795 receiving yards, which represents the second-highest total of his career. Jordan also posted excellent numbers in 1988, concluding the campaign with 57 receptions for 756 yards and five touchdowns. But Jordan had his finest all-around season in 1986, when he caught 58 passes and established career-high marks with 859 receiving yards and six touchdowns, earning in the process one of his four Second-Team All-NFC nominations.

Memorable Moments/Greatest Performances

Jordan scored the first touchdown of his career when he gathered in a 23-yard pass from Steve Dils during a 34–14 win over the Houston Oilers on October 16, 1983.

Jordan went over 100 receiving yards for the first time as a pro during a 42–7 rout of the Packers on September 28, 1986, finishing the game with six catches for 112 yards and two touchdowns, the longest of which came on a 23-yard pass from Tommy Kramer.

Jordan starred during a 44–38 OT loss to Washington on November 2, 1986, making six receptions for 179 yards and one TD, which came on a career-long 68-yard hookup with Kramer.

Jordan contributed to a 49–20 win over the Tampa Bay Buccaneers on October 23, 1988, by making six receptions for 79 yards and two touchdowns.

Jordan proved to be one of the few bright spots during a 41–13 loss to the 49ers in the divisional round of the 1989 playoffs, finishing the game with nine catches for 149 yards.

Although Jordan made just one reception during a 38–10 win over the Bears on November 2, 1992, it went for a 60-yard touchdown that represented the second longest gain of his career.

Notable Achievements

- Surpassed 50 receptions five times.
- Surpassed 800 receiving yards once.
- Led Vikings in receptions twice and receiving yards once.
- Ranks among Vikings career leaders with 498 receptions (3rd), 6,307 receiving yards (6th), 28 touchdown receptions (10th), and 6,311 yards from scrimmage (12th).
- Three-time division champion (1989, 1992, and 1994).
- Six-time Pro Bowl selection (1986, 1987, 1988, 1989, 1990, and 1991).
- Four-time Second-Team All-NFC selection (1986, 1987, 1988, and 1989).
- Inducted into Minnesota Vikings Ring of Honor in 2019.

30

AHMAD RASHAD

Although he is perhaps remembered more for his work as a sportscaster, Ahmad Rashad previously spent 10 years in the NFL excelling at wide receiver for three different teams. Having most of his finest seasons for the Purple and Gold, Rashad helped lead the Vikings to four division titles and one NFC championship by surpassing 50 receptions and 650 receiving yards six straight times from 1976 to 1981. The first Vikings player to amass more than 1,000 receiving yards in consecutive seasons, Rashad continues to rank among the franchise's all-time leaders in every major pass-receiving category, with his outstanding play earning him four Pro Bowl selections, four All-NFC nominations, and a place in the Vikings Ring of Honor.

Born Robert Earl Moore, in Portland, Oregon, on November 19, 1949, the man more commonly known as Ahmad Rashad grew up in Tacoma, Washington, where he attended a fundamentalist Pentecostal church, before converting to Islam years later. An outstanding all-around athlete, Moore played football and basketball at Mount Tahoma High School, with his excellence in both sports earning him an athletic scholarship to the University of Oregon in Eugene. Continuing to star on the gridiron under head coach Jerry Frei while at Oregon, Moore earned All-America honors at running back as a senior in 1971, after beginning his collegiate career as a wide receiver. Looking back fondly on his former Ducks teammate, Hall of Fame quarterback Dan Fouts says, "He was clearly the best player on our team, and one of the greatest players Oregon's ever had."

Subsequently selected by the St. Louis Cardinals with the fourth overall pick of the 1972 NFL Draft, Moore, who began studying Islam in college, converted to that religion shortly thereafter, legally changing his name to Ahmad Rashad, which means "admirable one led to truth" in Arabic. Moved back to his original position of wide receiver following his arrival in St. Louis, Rashad performed well for the Cardinals his first year in the

In 1980, Ahmad Rashad became the first Vikings player to surpass 1,000 receiving yards in consecutive seasons.
Courtesy of MearsOnlineAuctions.com

league, earning a spot on the United Press International NFL All-Rookie Team by making 29 receptions for 500 yards and three touchdowns, one of which came on a career-long 98-yard catch-and-run. Although Rashad posted solid numbers again in 1973, concluding the campaign with 30 catches, 409 receiving yards, and three touchdowns, the Cardinals elected to trade him to the Buffalo Bills for backup quarterback Dennis Shaw at season's end. Rashad then spent one season in Buffalo, serving primarily as a pass-receiving option in the Bills' offense to league-leading rusher O. J. Simpson, with whom he roomed on the road. Yet, even in that somewhat limited role, Rashad earned Second-Team All-AFC honors by making 36 receptions for 433 yards and four touchdowns.

After sitting out the entire 1975 season with a knee injury he sustained in the final preseason game, Rashad joined the Seattle Seahawks, who selected him in the 1976 expansion draft. However, Rashad never appeared in a single game with the Seahawks, who traded him to the Vikings for a future draft pick just days before the start of the 1976 regular season. Joining the Vikings' starting offensive unit in Week 4, Rashad had an outstanding first season in Minnesota, ranking among the league leaders with 53 receptions, while also amassing 671 receiving yards and scoring three touchdowns. Rashad followed that up by making 51 receptions for 681 yards and two touchdowns in 1977, before beginning an exceptional four-year run during which he posted the following numbers:

YEAR	RECS	REC YDS	TD RECS
1978	66	769	8
1979	80	1,156	9
1980	69	1,095	5
1981	58	884	7

Ranking among the NFL leaders in all three categories on multiple occasions, Rashad turned in perhaps the finest all-around performance of his career in 1979, when he finished second in the league in receptions, placed third in receiving yards, and finished fifth in TD catches. By surpassing 1,000 receiving yards in both 1979 and 1980, Rashad became the first Vikings player to reach that plateau in back-to-back seasons. Rashad gained Pro Bowl recognition all four years and earned four consecutive All-NFC nominations, being named to the first and second teams twice each. More importantly, the Vikings won the division title in two of those four seasons, finishing first in the NFC Central in both 1978 and 1980.

In addition to being one of the league's larger wide receivers, the 6'2", 205-pound Rashad possessed good speed, soft hands, and superior ball-skills. Although not a true "burner," Rashad had enough quickness to keep opposing defenses honest. Meanwhile, his size and strength enabled him to catch the ball well in traffic, making him particularly effective at using his body to ward off defenders. During his peak seasons in Minnesota, Rashad combined with speedster Sammy White to give the Vikings one of the better wide receiver tandems in the league, with Rashad playing the role of possession receiver to White's deep threat.

Rashad spent one more year in the Twin Cities, making just 23 receptions for 233 yards and no touchdowns during the strike-shortened 1982 campaign, before announcing his retirement at season's end. Retiring with career totals of 495 receptions, 6,831 receiving yards, 6,883 yards from scrimmage, 7,320 all-purpose yards, 44 touchdown receptions, and 46 touchdowns, Rashad ended his seven-year stint in Minnesota with 400 receptions, 5,489 receiving yards, and 34 TD catches.

After retiring as an active player, Rashad, who worked part-time at a Twin Cities TV station his last five years with the Vikings, began a lengthy career in broadcasting that saw him cover NFL, NBA, and MLB televised contests as a studio analyst and game reporter for NBC and ABC. He also hosted *NBA Inside Stuff* for 16 seasons, during which time he became known even more for his close personal relationship with Michael Jordan. Rashad gained an additional measure of fame when he proposed to *Cosby Show* actress Phylicia Ayers-Allen on national television during the pregame show of NBC's broadcast of the 1985 Thanksgiving Day football game between the Detroit Lions and New York Jets.

Extremely proud of his broadcasting career, Rashad says that he had job offers from all three major networks when he retired from football at age 33, adding, "I wanted to represent African-American athletes in a better way than what I saw when I grew up. Because every time I saw them, nobody could talk. They sounded like they never went to school. And I wanted to carry that torch, that you could be an African American athlete and you could be smart. You can have a personality. You can speak."

Now 71 years of age, Rashad currently spends most of his time working as a spokesman for companies, hosting special events for the NBA, and playing golf. Inducted into the Vikings Ring of Honor in 2017, Rashad said upon learning of his selection, "I've won Emmy Awards. I've won receiving titles, all of those things, but this is closer to my heart. I've always said that 'Once a Viking, always a Viking.' You don't ever get out of that, and [the Wilf Family ownership group] has shown that; that is a wonderful fraternity. We respect everybody."

VIKINGS CAREER HIGHLIGHTS

Best Season

Rashad posted outstanding numbers for the Vikings in 1980, concluding the campaign with 69 receptions, 1,095 receiving yards, and five TD catches. However, he performed even better the previous season, earning First-Team All-NFC honors for the first of two straight times in 1979 by establishing career-high marks with 80 receptions, 1,156 receiving yards, and nine touchdown catches.

Memorable Moments/Greatest Performances

Rashad topped 100 receiving yards for the first time as a member of the Vikings on October 10, 1976, when he made seven receptions for 109 yards during a 20–9 win over the Bears.

Rashad helped lead the Vikings to a 28–27 come-from-behind victory over the 49ers on December 4, 1977, by making seven receptions for 121 yards and one touchdown, which came on an 8-yard pass from Tommy Kramer early in the fourth quarter.

Rashad contributed to a 30–21 win over the Lions in the final game of the 1977 regular season by making eight receptions for 139 yards and one touchdown, with his TD coming on a 48-yard connection with Bob Lee late in the first half.

Rashad played a key role in Minnesota's 28–27 win over Philadelphia on December 3, 1978, making nine receptions for 107 yards and one touchdown, which came on a 20-yard fourth-quarter connection with Fran Tarkenton that provided the margin of victory.

Rashad proved to be the difference in a 28–22 win over the 49ers in the opening game of the 1979 regular season, making seven receptions for 152 yards, and scoring all four Vikings touchdowns on pass plays that covered 52, 32, 8, and 25 yards, with his 25-yard TD grab in the game's closing moments providing the winning margin.

Rashad gave the Vikings a dramatic 27–21 victory over the Packers on September 23, 1979, when he gathered in a 50-yard touchdown pass from Tommy Kramer in overtime. Rashad finished the game with nine receptions for 136 yards and two TDs.

Rashad helped the Vikings post a 24–23 victory over the Atlanta Falcons in the 1980 regular-season opener by making 11 receptions for 160 yards.

Although the Vikings lost to Atlanta by a score of 31–30 on November 23, 1981, Rashad torched the Falcons' defensive secondary once again, making nine receptions for 151 yards and two touchdowns, the longest of which came on a 42-yard connection with Tommy Kramer.

Rashad experienced the most memorable moment of his career on December 14, 1980, when he made a miraculous one-handed touchdown catch of a last-second "Hail Mary" pass thrown by Tommy Kramer that gave the Vikings a dramatic 28–23 win over the Cleveland Browns. Rashad's 46-yard TD reception, which later became known as the "Miracle at the Met," clinched the NFC Central Division title for the Vikings. Rashad finished the game with nine catches for 142 yards and two touchdowns.

Notable Achievements

- Surpassed 50 receptions six times.
- Surpassed 1,000 receiving yards twice.
- Finished second in NFL with 80 receptions in 1979.
- Finished third in NFL with 1,156 receiving yards in 1979.
- Led Vikings in receptions three times and receiving yards three times.
- Ranks among Vikings career leaders with 400 receptions (7th), 5,489 receiving yards (7th), and 34 touchdown receptions (7th).
- Four-time division champion (1976, 1977, 1978, and 1980).
- 1976 NFC champion.
- Four-time Pro Bowl selection (1978, 1979, 1980, and 1981).
- Two-time First-Team All-NFC selection (1979 and 1980).
- Two-time Second-Team All-NFC selection (1978 and 1981).
- Inducted into Minnesota Vikings Ring of Honor in 2017.

31

KEITH MILLARD

Although a devastating knee injury limited his period of dominance to just a few short seasons, Keith Millard established himself as one of the NFL's premier defensive tackles during his six-year stint in Minnesota. A feared pass-rusher known for his agility, strength, and tremendous intensity, Millard led the Vikings in sacks on three separate occasions, earning in the process two trips to the Pro Bowl, three All-Pro selections, and three All-NFC nominations. The 1989 NFL Defensive Player of the Year, Millard later received the additional distinction of being named to the NFL 1980s All-Decade Second Team.

Born in Pleasanton, California, on March 18, 1962, Keith Joseph Millard had the misfortune of watching his parents separate at the age of two. Greatly influenced by his parents' breakup, Millard developed an inner rage that he often exhibited later in life. Beginning his football career as a junior at Foothill High School, Millard spent one season playing tight end and linebacker, before being kicked off the team just three games into his senior year. Nevertheless, Millard performed so well in those three contests that he received an athletic scholarship to Washington State University, where he became one of the greatest players in that school's history. After spending his freshman year at WSU playing tight end, Millard found a home at defensive tackle the following year, eventually earning First-Team All–Pac-10 honors as a senior, while also winning the Morris Trophy as the conference's top defensive lineman.

Subsequently selected by the Vikings with the 13th overall pick of the 1984 NFL Draft, Millard chose instead to sign with the Arizona Wranglers of the United States Football League. However, when that league folded after just one season, Millard joined the Vikings prior to the start of the 1985 NFL campaign. Immediately establishing himself as a force-to-be-reckoned-with on the defensive side of the ball, Millard led the Vikings with 11 sacks, even though he started only six games for them at nose tackle. Shifted to right defensive tackle the following year, Millard recorded

Keith Millard earned NFL Defensive Player of the Year honors in 1989.
Courtesy of George A. Kitrinos

a team-leading 10½ sacks, with his strong play earning him Second-Team All-NFC honors. Yet, Millard also ran afoul of the law late in 1986, with police officers accusing him of making "terroristic threats" after he told them, "My arms are more powerful than your guns."

After recording just 3½ sacks during the strike-shortened 1987 campaign, Millard gained Pro Bowl and First-Team All-Pro recognition for the first of two straight times the following year by registering eight sacks and recovering two fumbles. Millard then had a season for the ages in 1989, earning NFL Defensive Player of the Year honors by recording 18 sacks for a Vikings team that captured its first division title in nine years.

The 6'6", 260-pound Millard developed into a terrific pass-rusher by studying film of the techniques used by some of the league's other top defensive linemen, including his two idols—Howie Long and Dan Hampton. By doing so, he learned to outmaneuver opposing linemen by mastering a variety of moves and changing his plan of attack from play to play. Serving as the prototype for defensive tackles of his era, Millard also possessed exceptional quickness, great strength, an explosive first step, and an uncanny ability to anticipate the snap from center.

In discussing Millard's ability to dominate his opponent at the line of scrimmage, Vikings defensive coordinator Floyd Peters stated, "Millard is as good an inside tackle as I have seen since I've been around football. I wouldn't trade him for Reggie White. Millard is a pure tackle who can whip two and three people. He is a real beauty to watch."

Green Bay Packers guard Rich Moran also had high praise for Millard, saying, "There's nobody else in football who plays the position the way he does. He can rip inside or outside. He's responsible for an area, but you don't know where he is going."

Millard's greatest asset, though, may well have been the tremendous intensity and inner rage that he brought with him to the playing field— both of which resulted from him being the product of a dysfunctional family. Millard, who denied ever using anabolic steroids or amphetamines, typically worked himself into a violent rage before kickoff, creating in his mind a hatred for his opponent that built up all week.

In addressing the manner with which he tended to conduct himself on game day, Millard said, "I used to get so fired up that I wore myself out before the end of the game. I was slapping my own guys around. My energy was ready to burst. By the fourth quarter, I had used up my tank. I'd lose my temper and play bad because I was out to beat up the other guy rather than do my job, and that hurt me."

Millard continued, "I have learned to better control my rage, make it work for me. My intensity has gotten me over the hump in rough times on the field. I don't give up. I'll play as hard in the fourth quarter as I do in the first. You can count on me from whistle to whistle and in overtime."

Even Millard's own teammates and coaches did not escape his anger at times, as he often screamed at them for making stupid mistakes, not playing hard enough, or installing ineffective game plans. In discussing his temperamental defensive tackle, Vikings head coach Jerry Burns suggested,

"Ninety percent of the time, Keith is one of the best people to be around. But the other 10 percent is like a total eclipse. You can almost see it coming. I usually let him blow off steam. Then the next day, he'll come back and apologize because he knows that wasn't the best thing to do."

The combination of Millard's extreme aggressiveness, outstanding athletic ability, and excellent technique made him extraordinarily difficult for opponents to contend with on game day, with Vikings guard Dave Huffman stating, "My best description of Keith Millard going for the quarterback is he's like a nuclear reactor. I'm sure that, if I ever got inside of Three Mile Island, I'd see little Keith Millards bouncing off the walls."

After facing Chicago's Dan Hampton in the 1988 NFC championship game just one week after he squared off against Millard in the divisional round of the playoffs, 49ers guard Jesse Sapolu said, "I don't mean any disrespect to Dan Hampton, but I was not worried about this matchup. He's a great player who does everything well. But last week I had to block Keith Millard. Do you think anything would bother me after going up against him? That guy's just a monster. He's not from this world. . . . He is strong, mean, and nasty. Every play was a war."

Unfortunately, Millard never again performed at an elite level after 1989, since he suffered a horrific knee injury just four games into the 1990 campaign. While trying to jump over a cut block by Tampa Bay center Randy Grimes during a 23–20 overtime loss to the Buccaneers on September 30, 1990, Millard tore his ACL, forcing him to miss the remainder of the year, and all of the following season as well. Although Millard eventually resumed his career with the Green Bay Packers in 1992, he ended up appearing in only 18 more games, splitting those between the Packers, Seattle Seahawks, and Philadelphia Eagles, before retiring at the end of 1993. Ending his career with 58 sacks, 10 fumble recoveries, two interceptions, and one touchdown, Millard recorded virtually all those numbers as a member of the Vikings, registering 53 sacks during his time in Minnesota.

Following his retirement, Millard began a career in coaching, serving on the staffs of several college teams, before coaching briefly for the Los Angeles Dragons of the Spring Football League and the San Francisco Demons of the XFL. Returning to the NFL in 2001, Millard became the assistant defensive line/pass rush specialist coach for the Denver Broncos, with whom he spent the next four seasons creating and implementing all pass rush techniques employed by the team. Millard then assumed a similar role with the Oakland Raiders from 2005 to 2007, before spending two seasons serving as defensive coordinator for the Merced College Blue

Devils. Millard later returned to the NFL once again, this time serving as an assistant on the coaching staffs of the Tampa Bay Buccaneers and Tennessee Titans.

VIKINGS CAREER HIGHLIGHTS

Best Season

Although Millard gained First-Team All-Pro recognition in both 1988 and 1989, he proved to be far more dominant in the second of those campaigns, earning NFL Defensive Player of the Year honors by finishing third in the league with 18 sacks, which established a new NFL record for defensive tackles (since broken).

Memorable Moments/Greatest Performances

Millard registered the first sack of his career in his first game as a pro when he brought down Joe Montana behind the line of scrimmage during a 28–21 win over the San Francisco 49ers in the opening game of the 1985 regular season.

Millard recorded multiple sacks for the first time in his career during a 27–20 victory over the Bills on September 29, 1985, getting to Buffalo quarterback Vince Ferragamo twice.

Millard contributed to a 31–7 win over the Pittsburgh Steelers on September 21, 1986, by recording the first of his two career interceptions, which he subsequently returned 17 yards.

Although the Vikings lost to Cleveland by a score of 23–20 on October 26, 1986, Millard sacked Browns quarterback Bernie Kosar three times during the contest.

Millard turned in an even more impressive performance against Philadelphia on September 25, 1988, making eight solo tackles, assisting on five others, and sacking Randall Cunningham four times during a 23–21 Vikings win. Commenting on his teammate's effort after the game, Vikings defensive tackle Henry Thomas said, "He was a dominating maniac." Fellow lineman Bubba Baker added, "He's always a maniac. Heck, he's a maniac at breakfast."

Millard recorded three of the seven sacks the Vikings registered against Warren Moon during a 38–7 manhandling of the Houston Oilers in the opening game of the 1989 regular season.

Millard earned NFC Defensive Player of the Week honors by recording three sacks and returning his interception of an Eric Hipple pass 48 yards during a 24–17 win over the Lions on October 8, 1989.

Millard equaled his career-high by registering four sacks during a 26–14 victory over the Packers on October 15, 1989.

Millard crossed the opponent's goal line for the only time in his career when he returned a fumble 31 yards for a touchdown during a lopsided 43–17 victory over the Atlanta Falcons on December 10, 1989.

Notable Achievements

- Scored one defensive touchdown.
- Finished in double digits in sacks three times.
- Finished third in NFL with 18 sacks in 1989.
- Led Vikings in sacks three times.
- Ranks 12th in franchise history with 53 career sacks.
- 1989 division champion.
- 1989 Week 5 NFC Defensive Player of the Week.
- October 1989 NFC Defensive Player of the Month.
- 1989 NFL Defensive Player of the Year.
- Two-time Pro Bowl selection (1988 and 1989).
- Two-time First-Team All-Pro selection (1988 and 1989).
- 1987 Second-Team All-Pro selection.
- Two-time First-Team All-NFC selection (1988 and 1989).
- 1986 Second-Team All-NFC selection.
- NFL 1980s All-Decade Second Team.

32

HARRISON SMITH

Known affectionately to his teammates as "Harry the Hitman" due to his ability to deliver jarring hits to the opposition, Harrison Smith has established himself as one of the finest all-around safeties in the game during his nine seasons in Minnesota. A sure tackler and outstanding pass-defender who has led the Vikings in interceptions five times, Smith ranks among the franchise's all-time leaders in interceptions and interception-return yards, with his career total of four pick-sixes placing him first in team annals. A member of Vikings teams that have made four playoff appearances and won two division titles, Smith has earned five Pro Bowl selections and two All-Pro nominations, being named to the First and Second Team once each.

Born in Knoxville, Tennessee, on February 2, 1989, Harrison J. Smith attended Knoxville Catholic High School, where he starred in basketball, football, and track. Competing primarily as a jumper in track, Smith won the state meet in the high jump his senior year by leaping 1.98 meters, while also winning the decathlon with a total of 6,230 points. Excelling in the long jump and triple jump as well, Smith posted personal-best marks of 6.54 meters in the first event and 14.15 meters in the second. Equally proficient on the gridiron, Smith starred on both sides of the ball, finishing his senior year with 1,340 yards rushing, 23 pass receptions, 453 receiving yards, 25 touchdowns, 61 tackles, two interceptions, and two forced fumbles, with his brilliant all-around play gaining him recognition as the Tennessee Gatorade Football Player of the Year.

Recruited by several major colleges, including Tennessee, Auburn, and Alabama, Smith ultimately chose to enroll at the University of Notre Dame, where he began his career as a linebacker, before transitioning to strong safety his junior year. Excelling at his new post, Smith went on to record seven interceptions and 250 tackles over the course of the next three seasons, with his acceptance into a graduate program at Notre Dame allowing him to spend an extra year playing for the Fighting Irish.

Harrison Smith has recorded more pick-sixes than anyone else in franchise history.
Courtesy of Jeffrey Beall

Selected by the Vikings in the first round of the 2012 NFL Draft, with the 29th overall pick, Smith started every game at free safety his first year in the league, earning a spot on the NFL All-Rookie Team by recording 104 tackles and a team-high three interceptions, two of which he returned for touchdowns. Smith subsequently missed half of the 2013 campaign with an injured left foot, limiting him to just 58 tackles and two picks. However, he rebounded the following year to register 92 tackles, three sacks, and five interceptions, which he returned for 150 yards and one TD. Smith then began a string of five straight seasons in which he gained Pro Bowl recognition, with the Associated Press also according him All-Pro honors in 2017 and 2018.

Although the 6'2", 214-pound Smith lacks elite speed, his outstanding instincts, superior ball-skills, and overall awareness allow him to excel in pass coverage, with Packers wide receiver Davante Adams commenting, "Harrison is one of the better players that I've played against since I've been in the league, just all-around. I don't know exactly what his measurables are, but it really doesn't matter because he's always there—he's gonna make the play."

An extremely hard hitter, Smith drew praise from former Viking Paul Krause for his tackling ability, with the Hall of Fame safety saying, "He's a very good player. He makes great plays. He's aggressive. He's a good team leader. I like his tackling ability, the way he goes to the ball. I like him a lot."

One of the league's most versatile defenders, Smith allows Mike Zimmer to use him in any number of ways, with the Vikings head coach stating, "He's a very instinctive player. I'm able to put him in positions where I can talk to him during the week. A couple weeks ago, I said, 'I want you to do this.' And he said, 'Well, that's usually where [fellow safety] Anthony [Harris] lines up.' I said, 'Not anymore, you're going to line up there.' He went in there and did it a couple of times and made some good plays. The guy is just really smart and disguises extremely well. He makes it tough for the quarterback."

Smith's Vikings teammates also greatly appreciate everything he brings to the defense, with Stefon Diggs saying, "It's crazy to watch Harry. Harry makes a lot of plays—plays that you don't think of much, you know, tackles for loss, gets fumbles, and he breaks up passes."

Adam Thielen noted, "He can play zone coverage, he can be the middle-of-the-field safety, he can be the down safety. I think that's what coaches love about him—especially in Coach Zimmer's defense—he can put him anywhere."

Danielle Hunter added, "This is just somebody that we look up to on the defense. He's a guy that can kind of do it all, you know, getting picks and covering guys."

Performing his job in a mostly understated manner, Smith prefers not to engage in elaborate on-field celebrations, saying, "I always liked to make plays, and I always liked being a playmaker. The spotlight comes from making plays. I don't hate the spotlight. I don't mind it, I just don't need to overly celebrate it, I guess. I want to be in the spotlight; if I'm not, it means I'm not making plays. I'm not necessarily going to be self-promotional. But I do like to make big plays. Naturally, that attention happens or comes with being in the NFL. I'm fine with that."

Providing further insight into Smith's persona, Vikings defensive backs coach Jerry Gray stated, "I think he internalizes a bunch of stuff. He understands it, and he absorbs it. He doesn't talk a lot, but he talks when he needs to. He's a guy where it's like, 'I'm a good football player, and I don't have to tell you I'm good.' He just goes out there and does his job."

Gray continued, "I think there's a lot of guys that do different things, but he's just a really good football player all-around. He can get the ball out of the air, he can make tackles, be close to the line of scrimmage, and he can be in the middle of the field. . . . He's the standard that way of being an all-around player. A lot of guys can't do that because they don't have the range or the ball skills or the smarts. They are good football players, but he's a guy that can separate himself. He's set a standard . . . young guys are looking up at the level he plays."

Although Smith failed to earn Pro Bowl honors in 2020, he had another fine year, picking off five passes and recording 89 tackles, giving him career totals of 28 interceptions and 747 stops. Smith has also amassed 430 interception-return yards, forced seven fumbles, recovered eight others, registered 13½ sacks, and scored four touchdowns.

A solid citizen off the playing field, Smith hosts the annual Kickin' It With Harrison dodgeball event at the team's headquarters that welcomes participants from Big Brothers Big Sisters of the Twin Cities, an organization he supports year-round. Smith also regularly visits the Hennepin County Juvenile Detention Center with teammates.

CAREER HIGHLIGHTS

Best Season

Smith played some of his best ball for the Vikings in 2014, when he ranked among the league leaders with five interceptions and 150 interception-return yards, recorded three sacks and 92 tackles, and scored one touchdown, earning in the process First-Team All-Pro honors from *Pro Football Focus*. But Smith's five picks, 42 interception-return yards, 12 passes defended, 1½ sacks, 78 tackles, seven tackles for loss, and consistently excellent play three years later prompted *Pro Football Focus (PFF)*, the Associated Press, the Pro Football Writers, and the *Sporting News* to all accord him First-Team All-Pro honors. Furthermore, *PFF* graded him as the third-best player in the NFL, with his mark of 98.8 representing the highest figure ever assigned to an NFL safety in the history of that website. That being the case, the 2017 campaign would have to be considered the finest of Smith's career.

Memorable Moments/Greatest Performances

Smith returned the first interception of his career 31 yards for a TD during a 21–14 win over the Arizona Cardinals on October 21, 2012.

Smith lit the scoreboard again when he returned his interception of a Jay Cutler pass 56 yards for a touchdown during a 21–14 win over the Bears on December 9, 2012.

Smith contributed to a lopsided 34–6 victory over the St. Louis Rams in the opening game of the 2014 regular season by recording a sack and picking off an Austin Davis pass, which he subsequently returned 81 yards for a touchdown.

The ever-opportunistic Smith victimized Eli Manning on December 27, 2015, returning his interception of an errant Manning pass 35 yards for a TD during a 49–17 win over the Giants.

Smith earned NFC Defensive Player of the Week honors by picking off two passes and recording eight tackles during a 16–0 win over the Packers on December 23, 2017.

Smith earned that distinction again by intercepting a pass, recovering a fumble, recording a sack, and registering seven tackles during a 24–16 win over the 49ers in the 2018 regular-season opener.

Notable Achievements

- Has scored four defensive touchdowns.
- Has recorded five interceptions three times.
- Has registered more than 100 tackles once.
- Finished second in NFL with 150 interception-return yards in 2014.
- Finished third in NFL with five interceptions in 2014.
- Has led Vikings in interceptions five times.
- Holds Vikings career record for most touchdown interceptions (4).
- Ranks among Vikings career leaders with 28 interceptions (7th), 430 interception-return yards (5th), and 747 tackles (12th).
- Two-time division champion (2015 and 2017).
- Two-time NFC Defensive Player of the Week.
- Member of 2012 NFL All-Rookie Team.
- 2017 Vikings Defensive Player of the Year.
- Five-time Pro Bowl selection (2015, 2016, 2017, 2018, and 2019).
- 2017 First-Team All-Pro selection.
- 2018 Second-Team All-Pro selection.

33

ED WHITE

powerful man who ranked among the NFL's strongest players throughout his career, Ed White proved to be a brute force in the middle of
Minnesota's offensive line for nine seasons. One of the league's most
complete guards, White excelled as both a run-blocker and pass-protector,
with his outstanding all-around play earning him three trips to the Pro
Bowl and four All-NFC selections. A key member of Vikings teams that
won eight division titles and appeared in four Super Bowls, White missed
a total of only four games during his nine years in Minnesota, appearing in
122 out of a possible 126 contests. And, after leaving the Vikings following
the conclusion of the 1977 campaign, White continued to perform at an
elite level, helping the San Diego Chargers advance to the playoffs in four
of the next eight seasons.

Born in San Diego, California, on April 4, 1947, Edward Alvin White
attended Helix High School in nearby La Mesa, before moving with his
family to Indio, California, where he earned his diploma from Indio High
School. After excelling on the gridiron as a two-way lineman in high school,
White received a scholarship offer from the University of California, Berke-
ley, where he spent three seasons starring at nose guard, gaining consensus
All-America recognition as a senior in 1968.

Subsequently selected by the Vikings in the second round of the 1969
NFL Draft, with the 39th overall pick, White spent his first season in
Minnesota learning the intricacies of offensive line play after being moved
to that side of the ball by the team's coaching staff. Explaining his thought
process at the time, longtime Vikings personnel guru Jerry Reichow said,
"We were looking for a guard. I had seen him play for a couple of years and
really liked him. Some scouts and I thought he could play guard. He had
brutal, unbelievable strength."

In discussing his change of positions years later, White told *Viking
Update* writer Tom Speicher, "Jerry Reichow just saw something in me that

Ed White excelled as both a run-blocker and pass-protector in Minnesota for nine seasons.

he thought would translate into a great offensive lineman. I enjoyed it. I begged them a bunch of years to also let me play defense."

Earning the starting left guard job midway through the 1970 campaign, White teamed up with future Hall of Famers Ron Yary and Mick Tingelhoff the next several years to give the Vikings one of the NFL's best offensive lines. The biggest and strongest member of the unit, White played at a listed height and weight of 6'1" and 269 pounds, although he later admitted to weighing anywhere from 265 to 300 pounds at different stages of his career. Described by longtime Vikings offensive line coach John Michels as a "huge elephant," White not only possessed great size and strength, but also excellent technique and outstanding quickness for a man of his proportions. Yet, White built his reputation primarily on his strength, gaining widespread recognition as the NFL's strongest man by winning the 1975 NFL Arm Wrestling Championship. In fact, White once stated that he hadn't lost an arm-wrestling match since a man some 200 pounds heavier than himself defeated him in high school.

Naturally amiable and good-natured, White had to learn to take full advantage of his great strength by developing a mean streak that he came to embrace, with Michels recalling, "Ed got meaner, and the elephant starting hurting people. I was very proud that the gigantic elephant turned into a mean hunter."

Looking back on the style of play he eventually adopted, White said, "I definitely played offensive line with a defensive mentality. It probably hurt me a lot of times too. I didn't always necessarily think things through. I approached it in more of an animalistic style rather than thoughtfulness. That's something that, as I got older, I became a little better at, but I always felt that getting into someone as quickly and aggressively as you could was one of the keys to success, and that mentality is how I played the game."

Considered one of the NFL's top guards by the mid-1970s, White earned Pro Bowl and All-NFC honors three straight times from 1975 to 1977, after being moved to the right side of Minnesota's offensive line in the first of those campaigns. But, with White expressing an interest in returning to his roots, the Vikings traded him to the San Diego Chargers for running back Rickey Young prior to the start of the 1978 season. White left Minnesota having played in all but one game in each of his last four seasons, starting 93 out of a possible 104 contests since he became a member of the starting unit in 1970.

Remaining one of the league's most durable players after he arrived in San Diego, White started all but three games for the Chargers over the course of the next eight seasons, with his consistently excellent play at right guard helping them earn four straight playoff berths and three division titles from 1979 to 1982. Praising White for his performance at one point during the 1983 campaign, Paul Zimmerman of *Sports Illustrated* wrote, "He has been taken for granted all these years, not watched closely enough. People have always raved about White's pass-blocking skills, but he has also been one of the NFL's best drive-blockers for years."

Named the Chargers Offensive Lineman of the Year in 1983, 1984, and 1985, White later received the additional distinction of being inducted into the team's Hall of Fame. And, with White gaining Pro Bowl recognition in 1979, he became one of the first players to appear in the game for both the NFC and AFC.

Yet, since announcing his retirement following the conclusion of the 1985 campaign, White has not come close to gaining induction into the Pro Football Hall of Fame, an oversight that Chargers Hall of Fame quarterback Dan Fouts addressed when he said, "No question about it [he belongs]. When he retired, nobody had played in more games (241) as an offensive lineman than Ed White. They don't have any statistics for offensive linemen other than Pro Bowls and Super Bowls, and those are things Ed has done. He was one of the most feared offensive linemen in the game. You talk to guys like Howie Long and Matt Millen who had to go against Big Ed. They hated it."

Following his playing days, White began a lengthy career in coaching offensive linemen that included stints with the Chargers (1986–1987 and 1989–1991), Los Angeles Rams (1988), San Diego State University Aztecs (1994–1997), St. Louis Rams (1998), and University of California Golden Bears (1999–2002). White also briefly served as president and general manager of the Arena Football League's San Diego Riptide and as a development officer at San Diego State. Since retiring to private life more than a decade ago, White has spent much of his time painting and sculpting. However, he received bad news early in 2018, when doctors informed him that he had Alzheimer's disease.

Revealing his condition to Nick Canepa of the *San Diego Union-Tribune* in June 2018, White said, "After all the head-knocking, I guess I shouldn't be surprised. . . . I was driving home after the MRI and the doctor called. He already knew what I had."

White continued, "I've had quite a few concussions. My mother had mild dementia, but in her 90s. My grandmother was 105 and sharp as a tack. My dad was sharp. So, I don't think it's a hereditary thing. Alzheimer's-related dementia is what I have. My hippocampus memory center is about half of what it should be."

White then added, "I get confused sometimes with dates . . . I feel like I walk like an old man . . . I'm 71 years old, but inside I feel like I'm 18. The brain is working differently. But I've never had a great memory . . . I'm doing a lot of brain games, trying to exercise my brain as much as I can. My art is helping. I'm mostly painting now, in the house. . . . It's such a weird deal. A lot of people think there's a solution. Nobody has a solution. There needs to be more investing to find a cure. There hasn't been enough research. Insurance covers a lot of things. But don't hurt your brain. They don't cover it."

VIKINGS CAREER HIGHLIGHTS

Best Season

White played his best ball for the Vikings in 1975 and 1976, earning his only two First-Team All-NFC selections. With the Newspaper Enterprise Association also according him First-Team All-Pro honors and Minnesota scoring more points (377 to 305), rushing for more yards (2,094 to 2,003), and averaging slightly more yards per carry (3.8 to 3.7) in the first of those campaigns, we'll identify the 1975 season as the finest of White's Vikings career.

Memorable Moments/Greatest Performances

White helped the Vikings gain 217 yards on the ground and amass 409 yards of total offense during a 28–21 win over the Philadelphia Eagles on October 21, 1973.

White's dominant blocking at the point of attack helped the Vikings rush for a season-high 220 yards during a 38–0 manhandling of the Atlanta Falcons on November 9, 1975.

White and his line-mates dominated the opposition at the line of scrimmage once again the following week, with the Vikings gaining 160 yards on the ground and accumulating a total of 470 yards on offense during a 20–7 win over the New Orleans Saints on November 16, 1975.

White's exceptional blocking helped the Vikings amass 491 yards of total offense during a 31–12 victory over the Eagles on October 24, 1976, with 242 of those yards coming on the ground.

Notable Achievements

- Missed just four games in nine seasons, appearing in 122 out of 126 contests.
- Eight-time division champion (1969, 1970, 1971, 1973, 1974, 1975, 1976, and 1977).

- 1969 NFL champion.
- Three-time NFC champion (1973, 1974, and 1976).
- Three-time Pro Bowl selection (1975, 1976, and 1977).
- Two-time First-Team All-NFC selection (1975 and 1976).
- Two-time Second-Team All-NFC selection (1974 and 1977).

34

HENRY THOMAS

One of the most overlooked and underappreciated players in franchise history, Henry Thomas spent eight seasons in Minnesota being overshadowed at different times by standout defensive linemen Chris Doleman, Keith Millard, and John Randle. Nevertheless, Thomas contributed greatly to the success of all three men with his ability to clog up the middle against the run and apply inside pressure to opposing quarterbacks. Despite spending most of his time battling in the trenches, Thomas managed to record at least eight sacks four times and 100 tackles twice, earning in the process two trips to the Pro Bowl, one All-Pro nomination, and two All-NFC selections. Continuing to perform at an elite level after he left Minnesota following the conclusion of the 1994 campaign, Thomas ended up registering more than 90 sacks and 1,000 tackles over the course of his 14-year NFL career, placing him among the league's all-time leaders in sacks by a defensive tackle.

Born in Houston, Texas, on January 12, 1965, Henry Lee Thomas Jr. first began competing in sports at the age of 10, recalling, "I started playing baseball when I was about 10 years old. I was a big kid and loved the game but, once I saw a few curveballs later on, I was out of there. No more of that sport for me."

Thomas continued, "My friends all thought I should get into football as a youngster, but my mom was against it. She did not want me to play. I had to forge a parent's signature on the signup document in order to play. I had to save my money in order to be on the team, and I remember it took me about four months to gather what I needed. . . . My mom eventually found out I was playing and came to one of my games but left after the first quarter. By the time I was playing in high school, she was into it. In high school, I was playing just about every position."

After excelling on the gridiron at Eisenhower High School, Thomas accepted an athletic scholarship to Louisiana State University, where he spent four seasons playing nose guard for the Tigers, before entering the

Henry Thomas spent eight seasons anchoring the Vikings' defensive line from his tackle position.
Courtesy of MearsOnlineAuctions.com

1987 NFL Draft. Selected by the Vikings in the third round, with the 72nd overall pick, Thomas earned the starting left tackle job immediately upon his arrival in Minnesota, later telling Tom Speicher of *Viking Update* how he managed to get an edge on the competition: "They gave us a playbook at mini-camp, and I took out all the pages and copied the defensive plays and brought them home with me. Between May and June, I was practicing in the driveway, and my mom would call out the plays and stunts. When camp started, I had it all down. So, while everybody else was second-guessing themselves, I was balls to the wall 100 miles per hour. I knew where I was going and what I was supposed to do."

Performing extremely well for the Vikings his first year in the league, Thomas landed a spot on the NFL All-Rookie Team by recording 81 tackles and 2½ sacks during the strike-shortened campaign. Thomas followed that up by registering 80 tackles, six sacks, and a league-leading four forced fumbles in 1988, before recording a team-high 94 solo tackles, registering nine sacks, forcing three fumbles, and recovering three others in 1989.

A veritable tackling machine, Thomas became known for his ability to defend against the run by dismantling the opposing offensive line at the point of attack. Extremely quick and strong, the 6'2", 277-pound Thomas spent much of his time in the offensive backfield, generating a tremendous amount of pressure from the interior of the Vikings' defense. Thomas also allowed the other players around him to make plays by constantly occupying multiple blockers, with Chris Doleman saying in *Vikings 50: All-Time Greatest Players in Franchise History*, "Henry was a very underrated player. He allowed others on the team to do well because of the way he played. Keith Millard, John Randle, and I were able to succeed because of Henry Thomas."

Yet even though Thomas's primary job was to diagnose, eat up blockers, and clean up in the run game, he also did an outstanding job of applying pressure to opposing quarterbacks, averaging seven sacks a season during his time in Minnesota.

Certainly, Thomas's natural athletic ability and aggressiveness at the line of scrimmage helped him excel in all phases of the game. But he also proved to be an avid studier of film who absorbed information well. Detailing how Thomas taught him how to study film in his book, *Alone in the Trenches: My Life as a Gay Man in the NFL*, Esera Tuaolo wrote:

> Minnesota played a four-man front with a nose guard—sometimes called a nose tackle—lined up across from the center and shaded to one side. The other inside lineman, the under tackle, lined up across from the guard. Henry Thomas was the Vikings' starting nose guard. He had played in the Pro Bowl in 1991 and 1992. He knew I was trying to take his job.
>
> During training camp, I would ask Henry how to do things. He would say, "If you make the team, I'll show you." He'd say it with a smirk. I'd ask him something else, and he'd say, "If you make the team." It became a joke between us.
>
> Henry was very smart, a great player. Once I made the team and proved myself to Henry, he taught me some of the tricks. I learned a lot from him, such as listening to the quarterback's cadence and what number a team liked to snap the ball on for each down.

For instance, about 80 percent of the time, an offense will go on "one"—the first "hut"—on first down. Some quarterbacks would try to throw off the defense with their rhythm; others would never stray from it. Henry taught me to study the quarterback on film. Some quarterbacks would look right and left, and as soon as they looked forward, you knew they were going to get the ball. I had never paid much attention to details like that.

Thomas had another outstanding season in 1990, leading the Vikings with 109 tackles and finishing second on the team with 8½ sacks. But he had to wait until the following year to make his first Pro Bowl appearance, earning a spot on the NFC squad by recording 100 tackles and eight sacks. Thomas gained that distinction again in 1992 by registering 69 tackles and six sacks, before earning his lone All-Pro selection in 1993 by recording 66 tackles and nine sacks, despite missing three games due to injury.

Thomas spent one more year in Minnesota, making 55 tackles and recording seven sacks in 1994, before signing with the Detroit Lions as a free agent after the Vikings asked him to take a pay cut due to salary-cap constraints. Performing well for the Lions over the course of the next two seasons, Thomas amassed 16½ sacks and 115 tackles, before signing with the New England Patriots, with whom he spent the last four years of his career. Announcing his retirement following the conclusion of the 2000 campaign, Thomas ended his career with 93½ sacks, 1,006 tackles, 19 forced fumbles, 14 fumble recoveries, four interceptions, and three touchdowns. During his time in Minnesota, he recorded 56 sacks and 654 tackles, forced 11 fumbles, recovered eight others, intercepted two passes, and scored two touchdowns.

Since retiring as an active player, Thomas has served as an intern on the coaching staffs of the Vikings and Indianapolis Colts.

VIKINGS CAREER HIGHLIGHTS

Best Season

Thomas gained All-Pro recognition for the only time in his career in 1993, when he sacked opposing quarterbacks nine times, made 66 tackles, and forced one fumble. But he performed even better in 1990, when, in addition to recording 8½ sacks, he forced one fumble, recovered another, and registered a career-high 109 tackles.

Memorable Moments/Greatest Performances

Thomas recorded the first sack of his career during a 44–38 overtime win over the Dallas Cowboys on Thanksgiving Day 1987.

Thomas also scored his first career touchdown against Dallas, returning a fumble two yards for a TD during a 43–3 rout of the Cowboys on November 13, 1988.

Thomas crossed the opponent's goal line again when he returned a fumble 27 yards for a touchdown during a 27–14 loss to the Pittsburgh Steelers on September 24, 1989.

Although the Vikings lost to New England in overtime by a score of 26–23 on October 20, 1991, Thomas had a huge game, sacking Patriots quarterback Hugh Millen three times.

Thomas proved to be a tremendous force in the middle the following week when the Vikings allowed just 36 yards rushing and 158 yards of total offense during a 28–0 shutout of the Phoenix Cardinals on October 27, 1991.

Thomas starred in defeat on October 3, 1993, sacking Steve Young three times during a 38–19 loss to the 49ers, with one of his sacks resulting in a safety.

Thomas recorded multiple sacks once again in the opening game of the 1996 regular season, getting to Scott Mitchell twice during a 17–13 win over the Lions.

Notable Achievements

- Scored two defensive touchdowns.
- Recorded at least eight sacks four times.
- Recorded at least 100 tackles twice.
- Led NFL with four forced fumbles in 1988.
- Led Vikings in tackles twice.
- Ranks among Vikings career leaders with 56 sacks (10th) and 11 forced fumbles (tied for 9th).
- Three-time division champion (1989, 1992, and 1994).
- Member of 1987 NFL All-Rookie Team.
- Two-time Pro Bowl selection (1991 and 1992).
- 1993 Second-Team All-Pro selection.
- 1992 First-Team All-NFC selection.
- 1994 Second-Team All-NFC selection.
- Pro Football Reference All-1990s Second Team.

35

DAUNTE CULPEPPER

Plagued by inconsistency and a serious knee injury that brought his time in Minnesota to a premature end, Daunte Culpepper never quite lived up to the enormous potential he displayed when he first joined the Vikings in 1999. Nevertheless, the huge quarterback posted excellent numbers in his five seasons as a full-time starter, ending his time in the Twin Cities with the third-most pass completions, passing yards, and touchdown passes in franchise history. The Vikings single-season record-holder for most passing yards and TD passes, Culpepper threw for more than 3,000 yards four times and completed more than 30 touchdown passes twice, earning in the process three trips to the Pro Bowl and two All-NFC nominations. Along the way, Culpepper helped lead the Vikings to two playoff appearances and one division title.

Born in Ocala, Florida, on January 28, 1977, Daunte Rachard Culpepper grew up barely knowing his biological mother and never even meeting his father. The son of a 16-year-old woman incarcerated for armed robbery, young Daunte was raised with 14 other children in the home of Emma Culpepper, a kindly woman who worked in the same correctional facility. Having already adopted three children and taken into her home 11 nieces and nephews, Culpepper found it impossible to turn away the infant boy, who later came to think of the family as his own. Recalling the manner with which Culpepper treated him, Daunte said, "She was loving and caring, but she was also very strict. She could lay down the law on me. She was both my mom and my dad."

Eventually developing into an outstanding all-around athlete, Culpepper starred in multiple sports at local Vanguard High School, excelling as a pitcher on the diamond, a guard on the hardwood, and a quarterback on the gridiron. Hoping to eventually pursue a career in football, Culpepper worked extremely hard year-round, spending endless hours in the weight room, while also improving his vertical leap to 36 inches and his speed in the 40-yard dash to 4.6 seconds.

Daunte Culpepper holds single-season franchise records for most passing yards and touchdown passes.
Courtesy of MearsOnlineAuctions.com

Unfortunately, Culpepper didn't prove to be nearly as conscientious in the classroom, allowing his grades to slip dangerously low. But, with Gene McDowell, the head football coach at the University of Central Florida in nearby Orlando, expressing an interest in offering him an athletic scholarship, Culpepper studied harder than ever before and gradually raised his GPA to a respectable level. Meanwhile, Culpepper performed brilliantly on the football field his senior year, gaining recognition as Florida's Mr. Football by throwing for 3,074 yards and 31 touchdowns, while also gaining 602 yards on the ground. Continuing to excel in basketball and baseball as well, Culpepper averaged 19.5 points, 11.3 rebounds, and 5.1 assists on the hardwood and performed so well on the diamond that the New York Yankees selected him in the 26th round of the MLB Draft.

But, with football remaining his first love, Culpepper chose to attend UCF, where he spent four seasons starring at quarterback for the Knights. Performing especially well in his final two seasons at Central Florida, Culpepper set 15 school records his junior year, before earning a sixth-place finish in the Heisman Trophy voting as a senior by passing for 3,690 yards, throwing 28 touchdown passes, and rushing for 463 yards and 12 TDs.

Despite his exceptional play at the collegiate level, Culpepper remained an uncertainty heading into the 1999 NFL Draft, with many pro scouts expressing concerns over the level of competition he faced at UCF and how much of a target his enormous 6'4", 255-pound frame might make him to opposing defenders. But, when Culpepper ran the 40-yard dash in 4.42 seconds, bench-pressed 405 pounds, and squatted more than 500 pounds at the scouting combine, the Vikings wasted little time in selecting him in the first round, with the 11th overall pick.

Culpepper subsequently spent his first season in Minnesota sitting on the bench, appearing in just one game, before replacing Jeff George behind center the following year. Taking the league by storm in 2000, Culpepper earned Pro Bowl and First-Team All-NFC honors by leading the NFL with 33 touchdown passes and finishing fourth in the circuit with 3,937 passing yards, a passer rating of 98.0, and a pass completion percentage of 62.7. Culpepper also ran for 470 yards and seven touchdowns, with his exceptional all-around play helping the Vikings capture the division title.

Commenting on the strong performance of his young signal-caller, Vikings head coach Dennis Green said, "I saw him on TV for the first time when he was a senior at Central Florida, playing Purdue. I loved everything about him. I loved his poise. I loved the fact that he's a classic drop-back passer, even though he can run. I loved how competitive he was and how he's got that spark, how he makes things happen. As I watched that game, it came to me that Daunte represents the new generation. Quarterbacks keep getting bigger and more athletic, and he is leading the way."

Green added, "As a quarterback, you're not ready to play as a rookie. When we drafted Daunte, we told him, 'This is the perfect situation for you. You are the only quarterback in this draft who's going to be given a chance to watch. They all think they're ready to play, but they're not.'"

Looking back on the one season he spent watching from the sidelines, Culpepper said, "I never doubted myself last year because I understood what my role was. If Coach Green said my role was to run scout squad every day and try to make our defense better, then that was what I was going to do. Don't get me wrong. It was definitely tough at times, but I always knew my day was coming."

However, Culpepper experienced more tough times in 2001, with the offseason retirement of star running back Robert Smith making the Vikings' offense far more one-dimensional. Frequently put in obvious passing situations, Culpepper threw 13 interceptions and only 14 touchdown passes in Minnesota's first 11 games, before missing the final five contests with an injured knee. Although Culpepper ranked among the league leaders with 3,853 yards passing and rushed for 609 yards and 10 touchdowns the following year, he continued to struggle somewhat, completing only 18 touchdown passes, posting a passer rating of just 75.3, and leading the NFL with 23 interceptions and 23 fumbles. Nevertheless, former Giants quarterback Phil Simms—then an analyst with CBS—remained convinced that Culpepper had a bright future ahead of him, stating, "If I were an NFL general manager, I would risk my reputation, my job, everything on betting Daunte is the guy. There's nothing he can't do physically, and he absolutely is a franchise quarterback."

After meeting regularly with offensive coordinator Scott Linehan during the subsequent offseason in an effort to improve his footwork, release, and ball-protection, Culpepper rebounded in a big way in 2003. Despite missing two games with a badly injured back, Culpepper passed for 3,479 yards and placed near the top of the league rankings with 25 touchdown passes, a pass-completion percentage of 65.0, and a passer rating of 96.4, earning in the process his second trip to the Pro Bowl. Culpepper followed that up by leading the NFL with 4,717 yards passing and ranking among the league leaders with 39 TD passes, a pass-completion percentage of 69.2, and a passer rating of 110.9 in 2004, with his brilliant performance gaining him Pro Bowl and First-Team All-NFC recognition.

Blessed with exceptional physical ability, Culpepper possessed a strong throwing arm, good speed, and surprising elusiveness for a man his size. Standing 6'4" and weighing somewhere between 255 and 260 pounds, Culpepper proved to be a handful for any would-be tackler, with Buffalo Bills linebacker Sam Rogers saying, "The guy is like a fullback. You have to make sure you get your head across his body when you try to tackle him. You can't come from the back side and expect to blow him up, because you'll bounce right off."

Recalling the first time he saw Culpepper closeup, Bubby Brister, who spent one season in Minnesota serving as his backup, stated, "I'm in the locker room, and this guy walks in. I didn't know Daunte, and I didn't recognize him. But I look at this big ol' guy, and I think, 'Holy smoke, if that's Daunte Culpepper, he's huge!'"

Brister then added, "I've been around awhile, and I can tell you: He's the biggest, strongest, fastest quarterback that ever was."

Extremely difficult to sack, Culpepper had the ability to deliver the ball with defenders draped all over him, although he also did an excellent job of avoiding the pass rush, with John Madden praising him for his pocket presence. Quite capable of gaining yardage with his legs and doling out punishment in the open field, Culpepper nevertheless considered himself a passer first, saying, "My first option is not to run. I am not a runner. I'm a quarterback."

An excellent thrower of the deep ball, Culpepper did an outstanding job of delivering the ball deep downfield to Randy Moss, often allowing the Hall of Fame receiver to use his height and leaping ability to his advantage. In discussing Culpepper's ability as a passer, Joe Namath stated, "He has the best throwing motion that I've ever seen since maybe Dan Marino."

In addition to his physical gifts, Culpepper possessed several intangible qualities that helped make him an elite signal-caller. Extremely confident in his own abilities, Culpepper enjoyed the pressure of playing in big games and being the player that his teammates looked to in the clutch, with his former college coach, Mike Kruczek, saying, "He's so confident. I bet he thinks he could beat Michael Jordan one-on-one."

Kruczek added, "He's the best I've ever seen, and I played with Terry Bradshaw. I saw Dan Marino in high school. . . . But, as great a player as Daunte Culpepper is, he's an even greater human being."

Dennis Green spoke of Culpepper's leadership skills when he stated, "He's a quarterback's quarterback, a true field general. He knows how to run a team."

And, Mike Tice, who replaced Green as head coach during the latter stages of the 2001 campaign, said of his quarterback, "I think he's phenomenal. He's very bright and has all kinds of class and charisma. I think he's a special player."

Unfortunately, Culpepper never again approached the same level of success he experienced in 2004 due to a devastating injury he sustained to his right knee during a 38–13 loss to the Carolina Panthers on October 30, 2005. Having suffered damage to his ACL, PCL, and MCL, Culpepper spent the remainder of the year on injured reserve, before being traded to the Miami Dolphins during the subsequent offseason after he refused management's request to rehabilitate his knee in Minnesota, rather than near his home in Florida.

Reporting on Culpepper's dissatisfaction with the team, the Associated Press quoted the disgruntled quarterback as saying, "Because of the fundamental differences I have with management regarding the approach to my personal and professional life, I think it is the best business decision for both parties to go our separate ways."

Ultimately dealt to the Dolphins for a second-round draft pick, Culpepper left Minnesota with career totals of 20,162 passing yards, 135 touchdown passes, 86 interceptions, 2,476 yards rushing, and 29 rushing touchdowns, a pass-completion percentage of 64.4, a passer rating of 91.5, and an overall record of 38-42 as a starter.

Continuing to experience problems with his knee following his arrival in Miami, Culpepper appeared in only four games in 2006, before being shut down for the remainder of the year. He then split the next three seasons between the Oakland Raiders and Detroit Lions, starting just 16 games during that time, before ending his playing career with the Sacramento Mountain Lions of the United Football League (UFL) in 2010. Since retiring as an active player, Culpepper has experienced financial problems that eventually forced him to sell his home in Florida.

VIKINGS CAREER HIGHLIGHTS

Best Season

Culpepper put up huge numbers for the Vikings in his first year as a starter, concluding the 2000 campaign with 3,937 yards passing, 470 yards rushing, seven rushing touchdowns, and a league-leading 33 TD passes. He also performed extremely well in 2003, finishing the year with 3,479 yards passing, 25 touchdown passes, and only 11 interceptions. But Culpepper reached the apex of his career in 2004, when, in addition to leading all NFL quarterbacks with 4,717 yards passing, he finished second in the league with 39 touchdown passes, a passer rating of 110.9, and a pass completion percentage of 69.2, setting in the process single-season franchise records for most passing yards and touchdown passes. Culpepper also ran for 406 yards, giving him 5,123 yards of total offense, which represented at the time a single-season NFL record for the most total yardage produced by a quarterback.

Memorable Moments/Greatest Performances

Culpepper excelled in his first start as a pro, throwing for 190 yards and running for 73 yards and three touchdowns during a 30–27 win over the Bears in the opening game of the 2000 regular season.

Culpepper led the Vikings to a 31–24 victory over the Lions on October 1, 2000, by throwing for 269 yards and three touchdowns, all of which went to Randy Moss.

Culpepper earned NFC Offensive Player of the Week honors for the first of eight times by running for one touchdown and passing for two others during a 30–23 win over Tampa Bay on October 9, 2000, with the longest of his TD passes going 42 yards to Randy Moss.

Culpepper turned in a similarly outstanding all-around effort against Arizona on November 12, 2000, running for one touchdown and completing 25 of 32 passes for 302 yards and three TDs during a 31–14 Vikings win.

Culpepper followed that up by throwing for 357 yards and three touchdowns during a 31–17 victory over the Carolina Panthers on November 19, 2000, with his exceptional play gaining him recognition as the NFC Offensive Player of the Week.

Culpepper performed extremely well in his first postseason appearance, passing for 302 yards and three touchdowns during a 34–16 win over the New Orleans Saints in the divisional round of the 2000 NFC playoffs.

Culpepper excelled during a 20–16 victory over Tampa Bay on September 30, 2001, throwing for 322 yards and scoring the game-winning touchdown on an 8-yard run with just 1:03 left in regulation.

Culpepper came up big for the Vikings again two weeks later, scoring a pair of touchdowns himself and passing for 244 yards and one TD during a 31–26 win over the Lions on October 14, 2001, with his touchdown pass to Cris Carter covering 47 yards.

Culpepper's stellar all-around play during a 32–31 win over the Saints on December 15, 2002, earned him NFC Offensive Player of the Week honors for the third time in his career. In addition to running for 73 yards and two scores, Culpepper threw for 312 yards and two touchdowns, with his 13-yard TD pass to Randy Moss and subsequent run up the middle for a two-point conversion with only five seconds remaining in regulation giving the Vikings the victory.

Culpepper enabled the Vikings to begin the 2004 campaign on a positive note by throwing five touchdown passes during a 35–17 win over the Cowboys in the regular-season opener, with his longest TD pass of the day being a 63-yard connection with Onterrio Smith.

Culpepper earned NFC Offensive Player of the Week honors by running for one score and passing for 360 yards and two TDs during a 27–22 win over the Bears on September 26, 2004.

Culpepper gave the Vikings a dramatic 34–28 overtime victory over the Houston Texans on October 10, 2004, by hitting Marcus Robinson with a 50-yard touchdown pass with 7:05 remaining in OT. He finished the game with 396 yards passing and five touchdown passes.

Culpepper followed that up by throwing for 425 yards and five touchdowns during a 38–31 win over the Saints on October 17, 2004, with his brilliant performance once again earning him NFC Offensive Player of the Week honors.

Although the Vikings lost to the Packers by a score of 34–31 on November 14, 2004, Culpepper starred in defeat, passing for 363 yards and four touchdowns.

Culpepper earned NFC Offensive Player of the Week honors for the fourth time in 2004 by throwing for 404 yards and three touchdowns during a 28–27 win over the Lions on December 19, with his longest TD pass of the day being an 82-yard connection with Randy Moss.

Culpepper continued his outstanding play in the postseason, leading the Vikings to a 31–17 victory over the Packers in the 2004 NFC wild card game by passing for 284 yards and four touchdowns, the longest of which came on a 68-yard hookup with Moe Williams.

Culpepper led the Vikings to a 23–20 come-from-behind win over the Packers on October 23, 2005, by rushing for 41 yards and throwing for 280 yards and two touchdowns in a game his team trailed at the half by a score of 17–0. With the Vikings winning the game on a 56-yard field goal by Paul Edinger as time expired in regulation, Culpepper ended up being named NFC Offensive Player of the Week for the final time in his career.

Notable Achievements

- Passed for more than 3,000 yards four times, topping 4,000 yards once.
- Threw more than 30 touchdown passes twice.
- Completed more than 65 percent of passes twice.
- Posted touchdown-to-interception ratio of better than 2–1 three times.
- Posted passer rating above 90.0 three times, topping 100.0 once.
- Ran for more than 400 yards five times, topping 600 yards once.
- Scored 10 touchdowns in 2002.
- Led NFL in pass completions once, passing yards once, and touchdown passes once.

- Finished second in NFL in touchdown passes once, pass completion percentage once, and passer rating once.
- Finished third in NFL in pass completion percentage twice and passer rating once.
- Holds Vikings single-season records for most passing yards (4,717 in 2004) and touchdown passes (39 in 2004).
- Ranks among Vikings career leaders with 2,607 pass attempts (3rd), 1,678 pass completions (3rd), 20,162 passing yards (3rd), 135 touchdown passes (3rd), and 29 rushing touchdowns (tied for 7th).
- 2000 division champion.
- Eight-time NFC Offensive Player of the Week.
- Two-time NFC Offensive Player of the Month (September 2003 and October 2004).
- Three-time Pro Bowl selection (2000, 2003, and 2004).
- Two-time First-Team All-NFC selection (2000 and 2004).

36

ADAM THIELEN

A classic case of "hometown boy made good," Adam Thielen defied the odds to establish himself as one of the NFL's most reliable wide receivers. After being bypassed by all 32 teams in the 2013 NFL Draft, Thielen, who grew up in Minnesota rooting for the Vikings, signed with the team of his youth as a free agent. Since that time, Thielen has recorded more than 100 receptions once and amassed more than 1,000 receiving yards twice, earning in the process two Pro Bowl selections and one All-Pro nomination. Along the way, Thielen who also earned the distinction of being named the Vikings Offensive Player of the Year in 2017, has contributed significantly to teams that have made three playoff appearances and won two division titles.

Born in Detroit Lakes, Minnesota, on August 22, 1990, Adam John Thielen spent his childhood rooting for the Vikings and his favorite receiver, Cris Carter, whose famous sideline catches he practiced in his own backyard. A four-sport star at Detroit Lakes High School, Thielen competed in baseball, basketball, football, and golf, serving as a member of a Detroit Lakes golf team that won the 2008 2A state championship, while also earning All-Conference and All-State honors for his performance on the gridiron his senior year.

Despite his outstanding play in high school, Thielen received no scholarship offers due to his lack of size and speed, prompting him to consider enrolling at Division III Concordia College in nearby Moorhead. However, Thielen quickly changed his mind after he received a call from Minnesota State University head football coach Todd Hoffner, whose assistant had raved about his pass receiving skills after watching him play in the state high school All-Star game. Offered a $500 scholarship to the more affordable public school with a Division II athletic program, Thielen jumped at the opportunity, after which he sat out his freshman year while adding some much-needed muscle onto his lean frame.

Adam Thielen has surpassed 100 receptions once and 1,000 receiving yards twice for the Vikings.
Courtesy of Keith Allison

Named a starter by the start of his sophomore year, Thielen went on to earn Minnesota State Offensive Player of the Year and Second-Team All-NSIC South Division honors by making 41 receptions for 686 yards and six touchdowns. Thielen followed that up with two more outstanding seasons, performing particularly well as a senior in 2012, when he made 74 receptions for 1,176 yards and eight touchdowns, earning in the process NSIC South Division All-NSIC First-Team and Don Hansen Super Region Second-Team honors.

Yet, with most pro scouts feeling that Thielen's small college background and lack of elite size and speed left him unprepared to compete at the professional level, he did not receive an invitation to the 2013 NFL Combine. Unbeknownst to them, though, Thielen had spent the previous few months working feverishly with former college teammate Tommy Langford on improving his measurables. Commenting on the determination that Thielen displayed throughout the process, Langford, who became his personal trainer, said, "You can't measure what's between the ears, what's in the chest, and what's in their guts."

After going undrafted by all 32 NFL teams, Thielen attended a Vikings rookie tryout and evaluation session at Winter Park, where, in addition to catching virtually every pass thrown in his direction, he posted a time of 4.45 seconds in the 40-yard dash, prompting Minnesota to sign him to a three-year, $1.48 million free agent contract. Although the Vikings waived Thielen on August 31, 2013, as part of their final roster cuts, they signed him to the practice squad the very next day.

Thielen subsequently spent the entire 2013 campaign watching from the sidelines as the Vikings stumbled to a 5-10-1 record. After earning a roster spot the following year, Thielen spent most of the next two seasons serving the Vikings on special teams and as a backup wide receiver, totaling just 20 receptions for 281 yards and one touchdown. Finally inserted into the starting lineup in 2016, Thielen emerged as a force on offense, making 69 receptions for 967 yards and five touchdowns. He followed that up by leading the Vikings in receptions and receiving yards in each of the next two seasons, catching 91 passes, amassing 1,276 receiving yards, and scoring four touchdowns in 2017, before making 113 receptions for 1,373 yards and nine touchdowns in 2018, when his eight consecutive games with more than 100 receiving yards tied Calvin Johnson's NFL record.

Thielen, who stands 6'2" and weighs 200 pounds, is somewhat unique in that he spends most of his time playing in the slot despite his rather lengthy frame. Yet, just like most of the smaller receivers in the league that man that post, Thielen possesses exceptional quickness, making him an extremely difficult matchup for the shorter cornerbacks he typically faces. In discussing the problems that Thielen presents to opposing defenses, Bill Belichick commented, "He's a problem wherever he is, but he's a problem inside. He has really good length, great hands, big catch radius, he's always open."

Hampered by a hamstring injury that lingered for weeks, Thielen appeared in only 10 games in 2019, limiting him to just 30 receptions, 418 receiving yards, and six touchdowns. Prior to his injury, though, Thielen made headlines when he criticized quarterback Kirk Cousins for failing to deliver the ball downfield during a 16–6 loss to the Chicago Bears in Week 4, saying after the game, "It's so frustrating, it's unbelievable." Claiming that, even though Cousins completed 75 percent of his passes, he missed several big opportunities downfield, Thielen found particularly frustrating his quarterback's inability to hit him on a deep pass, saying, "He made a great read of finding me open and just didn't complete the pass. It's as simple as that."

Thielen then added, "At some point, you're not going to be able to run the ball for 180 yards, even with the best running back in the NFL. That's when you have to be able to throw the ball. . . . You have to be able to hit the deep balls."

After publicly apologizing to Thielen, Cousins went on to lead the Vikings on a four-game winning streak, passing for more than 300 yards in each of the next three contests, while also completing a total of 10 touchdown passes.

Healthy again in 2020, Thielen made 74 receptions for 925 yards and 14 touchdowns, giving him career totals of 397 receptions, 5,240 receiving yards, and 39 TD catches. Thielen has also scored once on the ground and once on special teams.

In addition to his outstanding play on the field, Thielen contributes to the community through the Thielen Foundation, which he and his wife, Caitlin, launched in September of 2018 to help create programs that inspire individuals to reach their full potential. Thielen also hosts youth football camps in the Twin Cities and works extensively with the Humane Society.

CAREER HIGHLIGHTS

Best Season

Thielen performed exceptionally well in 2017, earning his lone All-Pro nomination by making 91 receptions for 1,276 receiving yards and four touchdowns. But he posted better overall numbers the following year, when, in addition to scoring nine touchdowns, he established career-high marks with 113 receptions and 1,373 receiving yards.

Memorable Moments/Greatest Performances

Thielen earned NFC Special Teams Player of the Week honors for his performance during a 31–13 win over the Carolina Panthers on November 30, 2014, when he blocked a punt, which he returned 30 yards for his first career TD.

Thielen made the first touchdown reception of his career during a 13–9 win over the Bears in the final game of the 2014 regular season when he collaborated with Teddy Bridgewater on a 44-yard scoring play, finishing the contest with three catches for 68 yards and that one TD.

Thielen helped the Vikings capture the division title with a 20–13 victory over the Packers in the 2015 regular-season finale by carrying the ball twice for 67 yards, 41 of which came on a fake punt on the game's opening drive.

Thielen topped 100 receiving yards for the first time as a pro by making seven receptions for 127 yards and one touchdown during a 31–13 victory over the Houston Texans on October 9, 2016.

Although the Vikings lost to the Packers by a score of 38–25 on December 24, 2016, Thielen performed brilliantly in defeat, making 12 receptions for 202 yards and two touchdowns, the longest of which came on a 71-yard pass from Sam Bradford.

Thielen helped the Vikings begin the 2017 campaign on a positive note by catching nine passes for 157 yards during a 29–19 win over the New Orleans Saints in the regular-season opener.

Thielen contributed to a 38–30 victory over the Washington Redskins on November 12, 2017, by making eight receptions for 166 yards and one touchdown.

Thielen gathered in six passes for 123 yards and one touchdown during a 24–7 win over the Los Angeles Rams on November 19, 2017, with his TD coming on a 65-yard connection with Case Keenum.

Thielen began a streak of eight straight games in which he amassed more than 100 receiving yards by making six receptions for 102 yards during a 24–16 victory over the San Francisco 49ers in the opening game of the 2018 regular season.

Thielen followed that up by making 12 receptions for 131 yards and one touchdown during a 29–29 tie with the Packers on September 16, with his TD coming on a 22-yard pass from Kirk Cousins that tied the score with just 31 seconds left in regulation.

Thielen topped 100 receiving yards for the sixth straight time during a 27–17 win over the Arizona Cardinals on October 14, 2018, finishing the game with 11 catches for 123 yards and one touchdown.

Thielen continued his streak by making nine receptions for 110 yards and one touchdown during a 37–17 victory over the Jets on October 21, 2018, with his TD coming on a 34-yard hookup with Kirk Cousins.

Although the Vikings lost to the Saints by a score of 30–20 on October 28, 2018, Thielen accumulated more than 100 receiving yards for the eighth consecutive time, concluding the contest with seven receptions for 103 yards and one touchdown.

Thielen starred during a 28–10 victory over the Giants on October 6, 2019, making seven receptions for 130 yards and two touchdowns.

Thielen proved to be a huge factor when the Vikings defeated New Orleans in overtime by a score of 26–20 in the wild card round of the 2019 NFC playoffs. After setting up a Vikings touchdown late in the third quarter by collaborating with Kirk Cousins on a 34-yard pass play, Thielen hooked up with Cousins for a 43-yard reception in overtime, making a brilliant over-the-shoulder catch at the New Orleans 2 yard line that led to Kyle Rudolph's game-winning TD grab moments later. Thielen finished the contest with seven receptions for 129 yards.

Notable Achievements

- Has surpassed 100 receptions once and 90 receptions another time.
- Has surpassed 1,000 receiving yards twice.
- Has surpassed 1,000 all-purpose yards three times.
- Finished third in NFL with 14 touchdown receptions in 2020.
- Finished fourth in NFL with 113 receptions in 2018.
- Has led Vikings in receptions twice and receiving yards twice.
- Ranks among Vikings career leaders with 397 receptions (8th), 5,240 receiving yards (8th), and 39 touchdown receptions (6th).
- Two-time division champion (2015 and 2017).
- 2014 Week 13 NFC Special Teams Player of the Week.
- 2015 Vikings Special Teams Player of the Year.
- 2017 Vikings Offensive Player of the Year.
- Two-time Pro Bowl selection (2017 and 2018).
- 2017 Second-Team All-Pro selection.

37

MATT BIRK

One of the few Ivy League school graduates to perform at an elite level in the NFL, Matt Birk spent 10 seasons in Minnesota anchoring the Vikings' offensive line from his center position. After earning a starting job his third year in the league, Birk went on to start every game for the Purple and Gold in seven of the next nine seasons, contributing to teams that made five playoff appearances and won three division titles. Along the way, Birk helped pave the way for four different running backs to rush for more than 1,000 yards, with his exceptional blocking earning him six trips to the Pro Bowl, one All-Pro nomination, and two All-NFC selections.

Born in St. Paul, Minnesota, on July 23, 1976, Matthew Robert Birk grew up hoping to one day play in the NFL, later describing himself as a chubby kid who daydreamed his way through school. Lettering in football, basketball, and track and field at Cretin-Derham Hall High School, Birk excelled on the gridiron as a two-way lineman, earning All–St. Paul Conference, Academic All-State, and All-State honors.

Gaining admission to Harvard University, Birk continued to perform well on the football field, although he found the transition to that Ivy League institution harder than expected, recalling years later, "Going away to college was quite a culture shock for me. I was homesick. I struggled in my classes. It was a tough experience. I was humbled a lot that first year, to the point where I thought I should leave and move back home."

However, after speaking with his father, Birk came to realize that going to Harvard offered him a wonderful opportunity to receive a fine education while continuing to pursue his dream of playing football professionally. Birk went on to graduate with a degree in economics, while also earning All–Ivy League, All–New England, and Division I-AA All-ECAC honors for his outstanding play at offensive tackle.

After being described by *Sports Illustrated* as "maybe the best Ivy League prospect to come along in several years" and as "someone who could be a nice developmental type pick," Birk found himself headed to Minnesota

Matt Birk earned six Pro Bowl nominations during his time in Minnesota.
Courtesy of Richard Lippenholz via Wikimedia Commons

when the Vikings selected him in the sixth round of the 1998 NFL Draft, with the 173rd overall pick. Birk subsequently spent his first two years in the league sitting on the bench behind starting center Jeff Christy, from whom he learned the intricacies of playing the position. Looking back at how those two seasons prepared him to perform more effectively once he eventually took the field, Birk said, "If you go out and play as a young player, you don't always get a second chance. I was grateful to have the time to develop. I understood the importance of being patient and waiting until I was good enough to start."

With Christy signing with Tampa Bay as a free agent following the conclusion of the 1999 campaign, Birk laid claim to the starting center job, which he retained for the next nine seasons, although he missed part of 2004 with a sports hernia and all of 2005 after undergoing surgery on his hip. After earning Pro Bowl and First-Team All-NFC honors in 2000 by helping Robert Smith rush for a career-high 1,521 yards, Birk gained Pro Bowl recognition in five of the next seven seasons as well, with Michael Bennett, Chester Taylor, and Adrian Peterson all gaining more than 1,000 yards on the ground during that time.

An excellent run-blocker, the 6'4", 310-pound Birk used his size, quickness, and athleticism to create holes through which Vikings running backs could maneuver. Yet, Birk proved to be even more effective in pass protection, rarely surrendering a sack to onrushing defensive linemen. In discussing his perennial Pro Bowl center, Mike Tice, who served as Birk's offensive line coach for two years before becoming head coach in 2002, said, "Matt was a star from the time he stepped on the field. He was so smart and athletic. He actually got better every day, and he still does. He's a special player."

A forceful presence in the locker room as well, Birk gained the respect and admiration of his teammates with his leadership ability, with his admonishment of Randy Moss for walking off the field during the latter stages of a looming defeat preventing the star wide receiver from ever again conducting himself in such an unprofessional manner during his time in Minnesota.

After starting all 16 games at center for the Vikings for the third straight time in 2008, Birk elected to sign with the Baltimore Ravens as a free agent during the subsequent offseason. Although Birk relished the opportunity to play for another team, he later admitted to leaving Minnesota with mixed emotions, recalling how he felt the first time he returned to his old stomping grounds when the Ravens played the Vikings at the Metrodome on October 18, 2009: "Being on the visitors' sidelines, it was weird. I would tell you, too, it was one of those games that I probably can't get over totally, because we were totally outplayed in the first half and then mounted a furious comeback, only to miss the field goal as time expired. . . . I was a little angry and, probably too pridefully, wanted to win for myself. It was interesting, and that's life in the NFL. I left because I thought greener pastures lay ahead, and then, here I am in the middle of October sitting on the visitors' sideline and watching this Vikings juggernaut with Brett Favre at quarterback."

Birk remained in Baltimore for four years, before announcing his retirement after the Ravens defeated San Francisco in Super Bowl XLVII. Expressing his appreciation for all Birk brought to the team during his four-year stint in Baltimore, Ravens general manager Ozzie Newsome said, "Matt's influence in his four years with the Ravens was evident to all. First, he played well and gave us stability on the offensive line. You can't underestimate the line calls he made to help a relatively young offense get set to run plays the right way. . . . Second, his leadership on and off the field was outstanding. We could go to young players and say, 'Do what Matt does, and you'll succeed. Watch him and follow him.' His work ethic was as good as any player we had."

Since retiring as an active player, Birk has continued his charitable work that he began during his playing career when he set up the HIKE Foundation in 2002 to help at-risk children through all stages of their education. Birk also launched the "Ready, Set, Read!" Foundation in 2010, which works with about 100,000 Baltimore students on improving their reading skills through an incentive-based system.

Holding a special place in his heart for children, Birk announced his retirement from football to the media before a class of 40 fifth-grade students at the Battle Grove Elementary School in Baltimore, saying at the time:

> The reason that I wanted to do it here today was because I have enjoyed playing football, but, as much as playing, I have enjoyed doing this [giving back to the community] as an NFL player. When I was a rookie . . . there are 53 guys on a team. I was like the 53rd guy. I was the worst player on the team, but I was on the team. That's all that mattered. I went out and did a visit my first week with the Vikings. I went to a school, and all the kids were going crazy. They didn't really know who I was. They just knew that I played for the Vikings, and I thought, "Wow. This is unbelievable." Like I said, this has been a big part of my career, and what I've enjoyed doing is coming to schools over the years and really being with young people like you guys. I get a lot of energy—get a lot of positive energy—from you guys and really enjoy it. I just thought that this would be a fitting place to do it.

Some 17 months later, on July 10, 2014, Birk returned to the NFL as the league's director of player development—a position he currently holds.

VIKINGS CAREER HIGHLIGHTS

Best Season

Birk had the finest season of his career in 2003, when he earned one of his two All-NFC selections and his lone All-Pro nomination by helping the Vikings finish first in the NFL in total yards gained, with Minnesota running backs averaging a robust 4.8 yards per carry.

Memorable Moments/Greatest Performances

Birk anchored an offensive line that enabled the Vikings to amass 468 yards of total offense during a 13–7 win over the Miami Dolphins on September 10, 2000.

Birk and his line-mates dominated the Tennessee Titans at the point of attack on December 9, 2001, with the Vikings amassing 496 yards of total offense during a 42–24 win.

Birk's superb blocking helped the Vikings amass 469 yards of total offense during a 45–20 victory over the Kansas City Chiefs on December 20, 2003, with 223 of those yards coming on the ground.

Birk helped the Vikings control the line of scrimmage during a 38–31 win over the New Orleans Saints on October 17, 2004, with the Minnesota offense amassing a total of 605 yards.

Notable Achievements

- Three-time division champion (1998, 2000, and 2008).
- Six-time Pro Bowl selection (2000, 2001, 2003, 2004, 2006, and 2007).
- 2003 Second-Team All-Pro selection.
- Two-time First-Team All-NFC selection (2000 and 2003).

38

SAMMY WHITE

An excellent all-around receiver who continues to rank among the Vikings' all-time leaders in every major pass-receiving category more than 35 years after he donned the Purple and Gold for the last time, Sammy White spent his entire 10-year NFL career in Minnesota, making significant contributions to teams that won four division titles and one NFC championship. Surpassing 50 receptions four times and 1,000 receiving yards once, White earned two Pro Bowl selections and three All-NFC nominations, before being awarded a spot on the Vikings' 50th Anniversary Team following his retirement. Yet, it is for the toughness that he exhibited on the playing field that White is remembered most.

Born in Winnsboro, Louisiana, on March 16, 1954, Samuel White grew up some 36 miles northwest, in the town of Richwood, where he attended Richwood High School. Excelling in football at Richwood High, White earned an athletic scholarship to Grambling State University, where he spent his college career playing for legendary head coach Eddie Robinson. Starring for Grambling at wingback, White helped lead the Tigers to three National Black College and three Southwestern Athletic Conference titles, with his outstanding play earning him a pair of All-SWAC First-Team selections. Performing especially well as a senior in 1975, White gained recognition as the conference's co–offensive player of the year by making 37 receptions for 802 yards and a school-record 17 touchdowns.

Despite White's exceptional play at Grambling, his small-college background left him feeling somewhat uncertain heading into the 1976 NFL Draft, as he later acknowledged when he said, "I wasn't sure what was going to happen on draft day. Someone had to actually come and find me on campus. I just didn't want to stay by the phone and wait for it to ring."

Ultimately selected by the Vikings in the second round, with the 54th overall pick, White made an immediate impact upon his arrival in Minnesota, earning Pro Bowl, All-Conference, and NFL Offensive Rookie of the Year honors by making 51 receptions and ranking among the league leaders

Sammy White earned NFL Offensive Rookie of the Year honors in 1976.
Courtesy of FootballCardGallery.com

with 906 receiving yards and 10 TD catches. Crediting Fran Tarkenton for much of his early success, White recalled, "Fran Tarkenton was a tremendous help to me. He took me under his wing from day one and really worked to teach me the professional game. I recall his throwing ball after ball to me. . . . He was one of the smartest players, and what he did for me I greatly appreciated."

White also revealed that he had to make some minor adjustments after he entered the NFL, saying, "Early on, I recall spending too much time worrying about what the defensive backs were doing and not concentrating on catching the football, but I got it straightened out eventually. For me, it was lessons well learned."

White followed up his exceptional rookie campaign with another outstanding year, earning his second consecutive trip to the Pro Bowl in 1977 by making 41 receptions, amassing 760 receiving yards, and finishing third in the league with nine touchdown catches, before compiling the following numbers over the course of the next four seasons:

YEAR	RECS	REC YDS	TD RECS
1978	53	741	9
1979	42	715	4
1980	53	887	5
1981	66	1,001	3

Combining with Ahmad Rashad during that time to give the Vikings one of the NFL's top wide receiver tandems, White ranked among the league leaders in touchdown receptions in two of those four seasons, earning in the process the last of his three All-NFC selections. A sure-handed receiver who possessed excellent moves and the ability to find the "soft spot" in the defense, White drew praise from former Vikings coach Jerry Burns, who said, "He had the ability to make all the plays. I always thought he ran routes as well as any receiver we've had here."

Although the 5'11", 190-pound White lacked elite size and speed, he had enough of both to keep the defense honest, excelling as both an intermediate and deep route-runner. Yet, White's greatest strength proved to be the courage and level of concentration he exhibited when crossing over the middle of the field, which he demonstrated in Super Bowl XI, when he held onto a Fran Tarkenton pass after absorbing a tremendous hit from Oakland Raiders defensive back Jack Tatum.

Eventually, though, White's lack of concern for his own safety began to catch up with him. After missing just one game his first six years in the league, White appeared in only 37 out of 73 contests from 1982 to 1986, missing most of 1985 with a groin pull, before sitting out the entire 1986 campaign after fracturing his finger during training camp. Choosing to announce his retirement during the subsequent offseason, White ended his playing career with 393 receptions, 6,400 receiving yards, 6,497 yards from scrimmage, 6,878 all-purpose yards, and 50 touchdowns—all of which continue to place him among the franchise's all-time leaders.

Following his playing days, White began a career in coaching, eventually returning to his alma mater, Grambling State University, where he has spent two decades serving as an assistant under former college teammate and longtime NFL quarterback Doug Williams. Coaching receivers at Grambling from 1998 to 2009, White contributed to teams that won six Western Division titles and five SWAC championships. After a brief one-year hiatus, White returned to Grambling for a second tour of duty in 2011, since which time he has continued to serve as a mentor for those fortunate enough to learn under him, saying, "I truly love to give back to these players. It means a lot to me to assist them and to be at Grambling."

Commenting on his longtime assistant, Doug Williams stated, "Sammy is Grambling football. He won championships here as a player and as a coach. He's dedicated to the program and willing to do what it takes to bring it back to the level where we want it to be. Like me, he wants that 'tradition of excellence' to return for Grambling football."

CAREER HIGHLIGHTS

Best Season

Although White scored just three touchdowns in 1981, he had one of his finest statistical seasons, establishing career-high marks with 66 receptions and 1,001 receiving yards. However, White made a greater overall impact in 1976, earning First-Team All-NFC and NFL Offensive Rookie of the Year honors by finishing third in the league with 10 TD catches, while also making 51 receptions and amassing 906 receiving yards and 1,114 all-purpose yards.

Memorable Moments/Greatest Performances

White scored the first touchdown of his career in his first game as a pro when he gathered in a 47-yard TD pass from Fran Tarkenton during a 40–9 blowout of the New Orleans Saints in the opening game of the 1976 regular season.

White followed that up by making nine catches for 139 yards and one touchdown during a 10–10 tie with the Los Angeles Rams in Week 2, with his TD coming on a 56-yard connection with Tarkenton.

White had the greatest day of his career on November 7, 1976, when he made seven receptions for a then-franchise-record 210 yards and two touchdowns during a 31–23 win over the Detroit Lions. Yet, the play that White remembers most vividly occurred when he fumbled away another potential score by celebrating too early. Recalling his gaffe, White says, "Over my whole career, that was my biggest celebration, holding the ball up—and it was one that cost me a touchdown. It didn't pay off at all."

White capped off his brilliant rookie campaign by making nine catches for 120 yards and three touchdowns during a 29–7 victory over the Miami Dolphins in the 1976 regular-season finale, with his longest TD of the day coming on a 36-yard hookup with Tarkenton.

White proved to be the difference in a 14–7 victory over the Lions on October 9, 1977, scoring both Vikings touchdowns on pass plays that covered 12 and 50 yards. He finished the game with four catches for 104 yards and those two TDs.

On December 4, 1977, White put the finishing touches on a memorable Vikings comeback against the 49ers when he hauled in a 69-yard TD pass from Tommy Kramer with just 1:38 remaining in the fourth quarter. White's TD grab gave the Vikings a 28–27 win in a game they once trailed by a score of 24–0.

White contributed to a 38–30 victory over the Tampa Bay Buccaneers on November 16, 1980, by making six receptions for 120 yards and one touchdown, which came on a 27-yard connection with Kramer.

White made a career-high 10 receptions for 177 yards and three touchdowns during a 35–7 win over the Bears on November 28, 1982, with his longest TD of the day coming on a 13-yard hookup with Kramer.

White is perhaps best remembered for the vicious hit he took from notorious Oakland Raiders headhunter Jack Tatum in Super Bowl XI. Crossing over the middle on a third-and-long play, White gathered in a pass from Fran Tarkenton, just before being hit so hard by Tatum that he lost his helmet and chin strap. Despite being shaken on the play, White amazingly held onto the football, with his 20-yard reception resulting in a first down for the Vikings. Although the Vikings ended up losing the game by a score of 32–14, White's catch remains the seminal moment of his career, displaying the toughness he exhibited during his 10 seasons in Minnesota. White finished the contest with five receptions for 77 yards and one touchdown, one carry for 7 yards, and 79 kickoff-return yards, giving him a total of 163 all-purpose yards that remains a Vikings Super Bowl record.

Notable Achievements

- Surpassed 50 receptions four times.
- Surpassed 1,000 receiving yards once.
- Amassed more than 1,000 all-purpose yards twice.
- Scored 10 touchdowns in 1976.
- Finished third in NFL in touchdown receptions twice.
- Led Vikings in receiving yards three times.
- Ranks among Vikings career leaders with 393 receptions (9th), 6,400 receiving yards (5th), 50 touchdown receptions (4th), 50 touchdowns (8th), 6,497 yards from scrimmage (9th), and 6,878 all-purpose yards (11th).
- Four-time division champion (1976, 1977, 1978, and 1980).
- 1976 NFC champion.
- Member of 1976 NFL All-Rookie Team.
- 1976 NFL Offensive Rookie of the Year.
- Two-time Pro Bowl selection (1976 and 1977).
- Two-time First-Team All-NFC selection (1976 and 1978).
- 1977 Second-Team All-NFC selection.

39

STEFON DIGGS

A big-play receiver with good speed and exceptional route-running ability, Stefon Diggs combined with Adam Thielen for five seasons to give the Vikings a premier pair of wideouts. Surpassing 100 receptions once and 1,000 receiving yards twice, Diggs led the team in catches three times and yards gained through the air twice, ending his relatively brief stay in Minnesota as one of the franchise's all-time leaders in both categories. Along the way, Diggs helped the Vikings make three playoff appearances and win two division titles, with his miraculous game-winning touchdown reception against New Orleans in the divisional round of the 2017 postseason tournament creating a permanent place for him in Vikings lore.

Born in Gaithersburg, Maryland, on November 29, 1993, Stefon Diggs had responsibility thrust upon him at an early age when he lost his father to congestive heart failure just two months after he turned 14. Serving as a father figure to his younger brothers throughout the remainder of his teenage years, Diggs had to assume numerous roles while attending Our Lady of Good Counsel High School, where he played football and ran track. Excelling on the gridiron on both sides of the ball, Diggs amassed 810 receiving yards and scored 23 touchdowns as a junior, earning in the process a runner-up finish in the Gatorade Maryland Player of the Year voting. Performing equally well his senior year, Diggs accumulated 1,047 yards from scrimmage, scored 11 touchdowns, and recorded 31½ tackles on defense, with his exceptional all-around play gaining him recognition from the *Washington Post* as a First-Team All-Metro selection. Starring in track as well, Diggs competed in both the 100-meter and 200-meter dashes, posting a personal-best time of 22.30 seconds in the latter event at the Darius Ray Invitational as a senior in 2012.

Subsequently offered athletic scholarships to several major colleges, including Florida, USC, Cal, Ohio State, and Auburn, Diggs elected to remain close to home and enroll at the University of Maryland, where he spent three seasons playing for head football coach Randy Edsall.

Stefon Diggs will always be remembered in Minnesota for the "Minneapolis Miracle."
Courtesy of Keith Allison

Performing brilliantly for the Terrapins his freshman year, Diggs earned a second-place finish to Duke's Jamison Crowder in the ACC Rookie of the Year balloting by amassing 1,896 all-purpose yards, gaining 848 of those on 54 receptions. After being limited the following year to 34 receptions and 587 receiving yards by a broken right fibula that forced him to miss the season's final six games, Diggs earned Second-Team All–Big Ten honors as a junior by making 62 receptions for 792 yards and five TDs, despite missing another three games due to injury.

Choosing to forgo his final year of college, Diggs declared himself eligible for the 2015 NFL Draft, where the Vikings selected him in the fifth round, with the 146th overall pick. After earning a starting job during the early stages of the 2015 campaign, Diggs acquitted himself extremely well his first year in the league, earning a spot on the NFL All-Rookie Team by leading the Vikings with 52 receptions and 720 receiving yards, while also finishing second on the team with four TD catches. Improving upon those numbers the following year, Diggs made 84 receptions for 903 yards, before catching 64 passes for 849 yards and eight touchdowns in 2017, in helping the Vikings compile a regular season record of 13-3 that tied them with the Philadelphia Eagles for the best mark in the NFC. Taking his game up a notch in the postseason, Diggs made six receptions for 137 yards and one touchdown during the Vikings' 29–24 win over New Orleans in the opening round of the playoffs, with his last-second 61-yard TD reception providing the margin of victory.

Diggs's game-winning TD grab against the Saints, which came on a play where he eluded New Orleans defensive back Marcus Williams after creating space for himself deep downfield, exhibited the 6-foot, 191-pound wide receiver's finest traits. An outstanding route-runner who excels at evading would-be tacklers in the open field, Diggs does a superb job of separating himself from his defender, making him extremely adept at running all kinds of pass patterns. And, even though Diggs lacks elite running speed, he possesses tremendous quickness that has enabled him to establish himself as one of the league's top big-play threats.

Diggs followed up his heroic playoff performance with an exceptional 2018 campaign, making 102 receptions for 1,021 yards and nine touchdowns, with the last figure placing him near the top of the league rankings. Although Diggs compiled excellent numbers once again in 2019, concluding the campaign with 63 receptions for 1,130 yards and six touchdowns, he became increasingly unhappy over the Vikings' reliance on their running game and his role in the offense as the season progressed, causing tensions to mount between him and the team. After the Vikings fined Diggs $200,000 for missing a practice following a Week 4 loss to the Chicago Bears, Ben Goessling of the *Star Tribune* wrote: "His absence stemmed from frustrations that had been building since the spring over the direction of the offense and his role in it. When asked whether he wished to be traded upon his return to the team, Diggs responded, 'I feel like there's truth to all rumors, no matter how you dress it up. I won't be saying nothing on it. I won't be speaking on it at all. But there is truth to all rumors, I guess.'"

Despite performing well the rest of the year, Diggs continued to express his dissatisfaction with the organization during the subsequent offseason, tweeting on separate occasions, "I don't forget or forgive . . . ," "I hate people that do you wrong then try to play the victim . . . ," "People don't appreciate things until they're gone . . . ," and "It's time for a new beginning."

Left with little choice, the Vikings worked out a trade with the Buffalo Bills on March 16, 2020, that sent the disgruntled receiver and a seventh-round pick in the 2020 NFL Draft to Buffalo for three picks in that year's draft (a first-, fifth-, and sixth-rounder) and a fourth-round selection in the 2021 draft.

Upon learning of the deal, Vikings running back Dalvin Cook told the *Pioneer Press*, "It hurt. That's my brother. You know how close me and Diggsie were. To see him leave, it hurts because you spend so much time with a guy. . . . It hurt a lot of guys in the locker room, but it's a part of the business. We've got to accept that Diggs wanted to be happy and be happy for him as a player."

Vikings quarterback Kirk Cousins told that same publication, "It became apparent that he wanted to play elsewhere, and I think it was smart of the Vikings to grant him that opportunity. I think it wasn't a mystery, and that's OK, and I wish him really well. I just so enjoyed playing with him. He's a special player, and we now have to find a way to move forward and replace that."

Adam Thielen added, "Obviously, it's a bummer that he's not here because it was such a fun duo to be able to work off one another and things like that, whether it be practice or games. So, I'm definitely going to miss that, but it will be fun to see him have success somewhere else."

Diggs, who left Minnesota with career totals of 365 receptions, 4,623 receiving yards, and 30 touchdowns, did indeed experience a tremendous amount of success in Buffalo in 2020, earning Pro Bowl and All-Pro honors for the first time in his career by leading the NFL with 127 receptions and 1,535 receiving yards, while also catching eight touchdown passes. Heading into the 2021 campaign, Diggs boasts career totals of 492 receptions, 6,158 receiving yards, and 38 touchdowns.

CAREER HIGHLIGHTS

Best Season

Although Diggs accumulated more receiving yards the following year, he had his finest all-around season for the Vikings in 2018, when, in addition to amassing 1,021 receiving yards and 1,083 yards from scrimmage, he made 102 receptions and scored 9 touchdowns.

Memorable Moments/Greatest Performances

Diggs went over 100 receiving yards for the first time as a pro during a 16–10 win over the Kansas City Chiefs on October 18, 2015, finishing the game with seven catches for 129 yards.

Diggs followed that up by making six receptions for 108 yards and one touchdown during a 28–19 win over the Lions on October 25, 2015, scoring his first career TD on a 36-yard pass from Teddy Bridgewater.

Diggs came up big in the clutch against the Bears the following week, hauling in a 40-yard touchdown pass from Bridgewater with just 1:49 remaining in the final period that tied the score at 20–20. The Vikings won the game shortly thereafter on a 36-yard field goal by Blair Walsh as time expired in regulation.

Diggs earned NFC Offensive Player of the Week honors by making nine receptions for 182 yards and one touchdown during a 17–14 win over the Packers on September 18, 2016, with his TD coming on a 25-yard connection with Sam Bradford.

Although the Vikings lost to the Washington Redskins by a score of 26–20 on November 13, 2016, Diggs starred in defeat, making a career-high 13 receptions for 164 yards.

Diggs contributed to a 34–17 victory over the Tampa Bay Buccaneers on September 24, 2017, by making eight receptions for 173 yards and two touchdowns, the longest of which came on a 59-yard pass from Case Keenum.

Diggs helped the Vikings forge a 29–29 tie with the Packers on September 16, 2018, by making nine receptions for 128 yards and two touchdowns, one of which came on a career-long 75-yard connection with Kirk Cousins.

Diggs had a huge game against Philadelphia on October 13, 2019, making seven receptions for 167 yards and three touchdowns during a 38–20 Vikings win, with his TDs coming on hookups of 62, 51, and 11 yards with Kirk Cousins.

Diggs followed that up with a pair of strong outings against Detroit and Washington, making seven receptions for 142 yards during a 42–30 win over the Lions, and catching seven passes for 143 yards during a 19–9 victory over the Redskins.

Diggs experienced the most seminal moment of his career against the New Orleans Saints in the divisional round of the 2017 NFC playoffs, when he gave the Vikings a dramatic 29–24 victory by collaborating with Case Keenum on a 61-yard touchdown as time expired in regulation. With the Vikings in possession of the ball at their own 39 yard line and trailing by one point with just 10 seconds remaining on the clock, Keenum threw a desperation pass to Diggs deep down the right sideline that gave the receiver an opportunity to step out of bounds with just enough time for the Vikings to attempt a long game-winning field goal. But, when Saints safety Marcus Williams missed his attempted tackle, Diggs, who had soared high in the air to make the reception, landed on his feet, quickly regained his balance, and raced down the sideline for the first walkoff game-winning touchdown in NFL playoff history, which has since become known as the "Minneapolis Miracle."

Notable Achievements

- Surpassed 100 receptions once and 80 receptions another time.
- Surpassed 1,000 receiving yards twice.
- Led Vikings in receptions three times and receiving yards twice.
- Ranks among Vikings career leaders with 365 receptions (10th), 4,623 receiving yards (9th), and 30 touchdown receptions (9th).
- Two-time division champion (2015 and 2017).
- 2016 Week 2 NFC Offensive Player of the Week.
- Member of 2015 NFL All-Rookie Team.

40

FRED COX

One of the longest-tenured players in franchise history, Fred Cox spent his entire 15-year NFL career in Minnesota, never missing a game during that time. Appearing in 210 consecutive contests for the Vikings, Cox scored more points, kicked more field goals, and converted more extra points than anyone else in team annals, retiring at the end of 1977 as the NFL's third-leading all-time scorer. A key member of Vikings teams that won nine division titles and made four Super Bowl appearances, Cox scored more than 100 points four times, earning in the process one All-Pro selection and two All-NFC nominations. Yet, it is for his invention of the Nerf Football that Cox is remembered most.

Born in Monongahela, Pennsylvania, on December 11, 1938, Frederick William Cox began playing football, baseball, and soccer at an early age largely because of his father, who insisted that his children assist him at the family grocery store unless they competed in sports. Developing into an outstanding running back while attending Monongahela High School, Cox received an athletic scholarship to the University of Pittsburgh, where he continued to excel on the gridiron at fullback.

Selected by the Cleveland Browns in the eighth round of the 1961 NFL Draft, with the 110th overall pick, and the New York Titans with the 221st overall pick of that year's AFL Draft, Cox chose to sign with the Browns, who planned to use him primarily as a blocker out of the backfield for Hall of Fame fullback Jim Brown. However, after Cox sustained an injury to his back that forced him to seek a less physically demanding position, he ended up spending his first pro training camp learning the placekicking trade under the tutelage of Hall of Famer Lou "The Toe" Groza. Dealt to the Vikings prior to the start of the 1962 regular season, Cox failed to earn a roster spot, prompting him to return to Pennsylvania, where he worked as a teacher until the Vikings invited him back for a tryout the following year.

After beating out holdover Jim Christopherson for the Vikings' place-kicking job during the 1963 preseason, Cox went on to score 75 points,

Fred Cox holds franchise records for most points scored and field goals made.

before tallying more than 100 points in each of the next two seasons, with his 113 points in 1965 placing him third in the league rankings. Cox also led all NFL kickers with 23 field goals and successfully converted 65.7 percent of his field goal attempts, which represented the second-highest mark in the league.

In addition to establishing himself as one of the NFL's most reliable kickers by the mid-1960s, the 5'11", 200-pound Cox contributed to the Vikings in many other ways, with head coach Bud Grant stating, "Fred was the ultimate team player for us. He took part in all our scout teams, playing running back or whatever we asked of him. He was a great asset to our team, a true credit to the team and his community. If you saw those games, he always stood right next to me on the sideline because he was such a big part of what we were doing with field position and knew the game so well."

Running back Chuck Foreman, who played with Cox during the latter stages of the placekicker's career, said, "He wasn't like your regular kicker. He was involved in all phases of our game, as far as getting ready for our opponent, because he came over and he, for instance, ran the offense. For example, we were playing Pittsburgh and he'd be the running back when we're running that offense, and he was a pretty shifty guy too."

But Cox made his greatest contributions to the Vikings with his sturdy right leg, consistently ranking among the NFL leaders in points scored, field goals made, and field goal percentage from 1964 to 1972. Performing particularly well in 1969 and 1970, Cox led the league in points scored and field goals made both years, scoring 121 points in the first of those campaigns, before tallying 125 points in the second.

Playing in an era before soccer-style placekicking became the norm, Cox used a square-toed shoe and kicked the football with the top of his foot after approaching it directly, rather than from an angle. Although he lacked great distance on his kicks, successfully converting just two of 24 field goal attempts from more than 50 yards out over the course of his career, Cox proved to be one of the most accurate kickers of his time, with his overall success rate of 62 percent being significantly higher than the league average, which typically ranged somewhere between 50 and 60 percent. And Cox stood out among his contemporaries even though he often faced severe weather conditions in Minnesota's cold and drafty Metropolitan Stadium, recalling years later, "You'd get up in the morning and hear the wind whistling outside the stadium and you'd cringe. Then, sometimes it was like kicking ice chunks. The ball would be as hard as a rock."

Cox remained the Vikings' placekicker until the end of the 1977 season, when he chose to announce his retirement, ending his career with 1,365 points scored, 282 field goals, and 519 extra points, all of which placed him among the NFL's all-time leaders, with only George Blanda and Lou Groza having scored more points, and only Blanda having kicked more field goals. Commenting on the level of trust that he placed in his longtime teammate during their years together, Fran Tarkenton said, "If I had one field goal or extra point that was needed to win a football game, I would want Fred Cox kicking it."

After retiring as an active player, Cox, who trained as a chiropractor during his playing days, set up a successful practice that thrived long after he left the game. However, Cox made an even greater name for himself as a business entrepreneur after he combined with Minneapolis-area football coach John Mattox to invent the Nerf Football, a squishy faux pigskin that sold in the millions after the two men introduced it to Parker Brothers in 1971. Looking back on how his creation helped revolutionize the toy football industry, Cox said, "They [Parker Brothers] were trying to make them the same way as their round balls, taking a block of foam and using a hot wire to cut balls out of the foam. Their footballs had holes in them. They had tried everything except for injection molding them."

Cox's invention and medical practice enabled him to live comfortably in retirement, until heart and kidney problems claimed his life on November 20, 2019, just three weeks prior to his 81st birthday. Cox, who had been in hospice care at his home in Monticello, Minnesota, discussed his failing health with a reporter from the *St. Paul Pioneer Press* just a few days earlier, saying, "I have kidneys that don't work and a heart that doesn't function, but, other than that, I'm great. . . . I'll be here until I'm gone, and I'm okay with that. Nobody's going to live forever, and nobody's going to live more than I did."

Upon learning of Cox's passing, Fran Tarkenton said, "He had a great brain and was a great thinker. He was an intellect that I spent every morning with before we played a game. I spent more time with him than any other player. Fred was a special, special human being who will be missed."

CAREER HIGHLIGHTS

Best Season

Cox had an outstanding year for the Vikings in 1970, earning team MVP honors by leading the NFL with a career-high 30 field goals and 125 points scored. However, he performed even better the previous season, earning his lone First-Team All-Pro nomination in 1969 by leading the league with 26 field goals made, 121 points scored, and a field goal percentage of 70.3.

Memorable Moments/Greatest Performances

Cox gave the Vikings a 24–23 win over the Packers on October 4, 1964, by successfully converting a 27-yard field goal attempt during the latter stages of the fourth quarter.

Cox helped the Vikings forge a 23–23 tie with the Lions on November 22, 1964, by kicking three field goals in one game for the first time in his career, successfully converting attempts of 20, 45, and 39 yards.

Although the Vikings lost to the Packers by a score of 24–19 on December 5, 1965, Cox kept them in the game by kicking four field goals, with one of those being a career-long 53-yarder.

Cox again kicked four field goals during a 19–7 win over the Packers on October 5, 1969, with the longest of his kicks traveling 41 yards.

Cox gave the Vikings a 9–7 victory over the Packers on November 16, 1969, by successfully converting all three of his field goal attempts.

Cox contributed to a 26–0 win over the New Orleans Saints on September 27, 1970, by kicking four field goals, the longest of which split the uprights from 47 yards out.

Cox proved to be the difference in a 19–10 win over the Washington Redskins on November 8, 1970, successfully converting all four of his field goal attempts, the longest of which traveled 44 yards.

Cox came up big for the Vikings in the opening game of the 1971 regular season, giving them a 16–13 victory over the Lions by kicking a pair of fourth-quarter field goals, one of which traveled 42 yards.

Cox scored the only points tallied by either team during a 3–0 win over the Packers on November 14, 1971, when he kicked a 25-yard field goal in the fourth quarter.

Cox kicked five field goals in one game for the only time in his career during a 22–13 win over the Bears on September 23, 1973, with the longest of his kicks traveling 41 yards.

The 36-year-old Cox showed that he still had something left in his aging right leg when he successfully converted field goal attempts of 52 and 46 yards during a 13–9 win over the Bears on October 27, 1975.

Notable Achievements

- Never missed a game in 15 seasons, appearing in 210 consecutive contests.
- Scored more than 100 points four times, topping 120 points twice.
- Converted more than 70 percent of field goal attempts twice.
- Led NFL in points scored twice, field goals made three times, and field goal percentage once.
- Finished second in NFL in field goals made once and field goal percentage once.
- Finished third in NFL in points scored once, field goals made once, and field goal percentage once.
- Holds Vikings career records for most points scored (1,365), field goals made (282), and extra points made (519).

- Ranks among Vikings career leaders with 15 seasons played (tied for 3rd) and 210 games played (3rd).
- Nine-time division champion (1968, 1969, 1970, 1971, 1973, 1974, 1975, 1976, and 1977).
- 1969 NFL champion.
- Three-time NFC champion (1973, 1974, and 1976).
- 1970 Vikings MVP.
- 1970 Pro Bowl selection.
- 1969 First-Team All-Pro selection.
- Two-time First-Team All-NFC selection (1970 and 1971).

41

ROY WINSTON

One of 11 men to play in all four Super Bowls in which the Vikings competed, Roy Winston served as an integral member of Minnesota's defense for 15 seasons—a period during which the Vikings won eight division titles, three NFC championships, and one NFL title. A tough, hard-nosed player who set the tone for the aggressive style of play Minnesota employed on that side of the ball, Winston started for the Vikings at left-outside linebacker for 13 years, combining with Lonnie Warwick and Wally Hilgenberg much of that time to form one of the most formidable linebacking corps in all of football. Although the presence of so many other outstanding players on Minnesota's Purple People Eaters defense likely prevented Winston from ever earning Pro Bowl or All-Pro honors, he nevertheless proved to be one of the team's most consistent and reliable performers, recording more than 100 tackles three times, while developing a reputation as one of the league's hardest hitters. And more than 40 years after he played his last game for the Vikings, Winston continues to rank among the franchise's all-time leaders in seasons and games played.

Born in Baton Rouge, Louisiana, on September 15, 1940, Roy Charles Winston began to display a desire to compete in sports at an early age, recalling, "I went to Hollywood Elementary School as a kid. It was a Catholic school, and I remember way back then how much I enjoyed competing. We would have 'Sport Day' and have all kinds of competitive events in track and so forth. We had running events and the shot put among other things—and I wanted to win. I was pretty good at most things, and I remember getting a reward once: a candy bar."

Winston continued, "Even at a very young age in elementary school, I was participating in football, basketball, and track. I carried those sports right into Hollywood Junior High and to Istrouma High School. I recall making the varsity team in the 10th grade, and, for a while, was a halfback, but then got switched into the line and played on both offense and defense as a defensive end and offensive tackle."

Roy Winston played in all four Super Bowls in which the Vikings competed.

Continuing to play on both sides of the ball at Louisiana State University, Winston starred for the Tigers at guard on offense and linebacker on defense, gaining unanimous All-America recognition as a senior in 1961. Subsequently selected by the Vikings in the fourth round of the 1962 NFL Draft, with the 45th overall pick, Winston had a difficult decision to make when the Buffalo Bills also tabbed him in the sixth round of that year's AFL Draft, with the 42nd overall pick. Ultimately choosing to sign with the Vikings, Winston recalled, "I signed with the Vikings for $12,000 per year, with a $4,000 signing bonus. I thought I was rich. I think my dad was making about $5,000 or $6,000 at the time. It was real good money."

After spending his first season in Minnesota backing up starting middle linebacker Rip Hawkins, Winston laid claim to the starting left-outside linebacker job in 1963, remembering, "When I first came to the Vikings, head coach Norm Van Brocklin had me playing the middle linebacker position, and I was playing initially behind Rip Hawkins. By the next season, I was starting at outside linebacker—and that's where I stayed."

Winston ended up remaining at that post for the rest of his career, appearing in all but six games for the Vikings from 1963 to 1974. Later joined by middle linebacker Lonnie Warwick and right-outside linebacker Wally Hilgenberg, Winston helped form one of the best linebacking units in the NFL, as Fran Tarkenton noted when he said, "Roy was one of a great and formidable trio of linebackers for the Minnesota Vikings, along with Lonnie Warwick and Wally Hilgenberg. He was an outstanding player."

Although somewhat undersized at 5'11" and 222 pounds, Winston did an exceptional job of defending against the run, bringing down opposing ball-carriers with great frequency. Unfortunately, the NFL did not begin recording tackles as an official statistic until well after Winston retired. Therefore, there is no way of knowing how many stops he made over the course of his career. Nevertheless, Winston excelled in that aspect of the game, with his ability to deliver bone-crunching hits making him one of the league's most feared tacklers. Called "quick, very fast, and a real tough guy" by teammate Mick Tingelhoff, Winston also provided outstanding pass coverage against tight ends and running backs coming out of the backfield, ending his career with 12 interceptions, 14 fumble recoveries, and three defensive touchdowns. An extremely intelligent player as well, Winston became known to his teammates as "the Computer" for his ability to quickly decipher the tendencies of opposing offenses and relay that information to the other players around him.

After sustaining an injury that limited him to just nine games in 1975, Winston lost his starting job to Matt Blair the following year, prompting him to announce his retirement at season's end. Winston ended his career having played in a total of 191 games, which places him second only to Scott Studwell in team annals among linebackers. After retiring as an active player, Winston became involved in the real estate business and worked in sporting goods, before spending 25 years working in sales for an oil service company. Still going strong at 80 years of age as of this writing, Winston now spends most of his time hunting and fishing.

CAREER HIGHLIGHTS

Best Season

Winston performed well for the Vikings in 1963, ranking among the league leaders with four fumble recoveries and scoring a touchdown in his first year as a full-time starter. He had another outstanding season in 1972, picking off three passes, which he returned for a total of 55 yards. However, the 1969 campaign would have to be considered the finest of Winston's career. In addition to intercepting three passes and recording more than 100 tackles, Winston helped the Vikings finish first in the NFL in points and total yards allowed, with his consistently excellent play earning him the highest single-season rating he ever received from Pro Football Reference.

Memorable Moments/Greatest Performances

Winston scored the first of his three career touchdowns during a 37–28 loss to the Packers on October 13, 1963, when he ran 26 yards into the end zone after recovering a fumble.

Although the Vikings lost to the Los Angeles Rams by a score of 27–24 on October 20, 1963, Winston recorded his first interception as a pro during the contest.

Winston helped lead the Vikings to a 27–22 victory over the 49ers on October 25, 1964, by picking off quarterback John Brodie three times.

Winston proved to be a thorn in the side of the 49ers once again on December 14, 1969, intercepting Steve Spurrier twice during a 10–7 Vikings win.

Winston contributed to the Vikings' 27–7 victory over Cleveland in the 1969 NFL championship game by recording one of the two sacks they registered against QB Bill Nelsen.

Winston helped the Vikings gain a measure of revenge against the Chiefs following their loss to them in Super Bowl IV by scoring a touchdown on a 36-yard fumble return during a 27–10 win in the opening game of the 1970 regular season.

Winston crossed the opponent's goal line again on December 11, 1971, when he returned an interception 29 yards for a touchdown during a 29–10 victory over the Lions.

Winston scored the final points of his career during an 11–3 win over the Packers on September 30, 1973, when he tackled running back MacArthur Lane in the end zone for a safety.

Yet, Winston is perhaps remembered most for a vicious hit he delivered to Miami running back Larry Csonka during a 16–14 loss to the Dolphins on October 1, 1972. With Csonka circling out of the backfield to catch a short swing pass, Winston arrived at virtually the same time as the football, hitting the 240-pound fullback so hard that he dropped the ball and rolled on the field in agony. Following the conclusion of the contest, Csonka, who literally crawled off the field after being driven to the turf by Winston, told reporters that he initially feared that the Minnesota linebacker had broken his back. Ironically, Csonka and Winston subsequently became close friends, with such a strong bond developing between the two men that Csonka invited Winston and his family to attend his Pro Football Hall of Fame induction ceremony.

Notable Achievements

- Scored three defensive touchdowns.
- Recorded more than 100 tackles three times.
- Ranks among Vikings career leaders with 15 seasons played (tied for 3rd) and 191 games played (8th).
- Eight-time division champion (1968, 1969, 1970, 1971, 1973, 1974, 1975, and 1976).
- 1969 NFL champion.
- Three-time NFC champion (1973, 1974, and 1976).

42

JOHN GILLIAM

Although largely forgotten by Vikings fans, John Gilliam proved to be one of the NFL's top deep threats for much of his career, with his ability to stretch the field making him Fran Tarkenton's favorite target during his four seasons in Minnesota. Blessed with exceptional speed and quickness, Gilliam amassed more receiving yards than any other player in the league from 1972 to 1975, with only Cincinnati's Isaac Curtis averaging more yards per catch. A member of Vikings teams that won three division titles and two NFC championships, Gilliam earned four consecutive Pro Bowl selections and three All-NFC nominations during his time in Minnesota, while also gaining All-Pro recognition once. Yet, Gilliam is mostly remembered today for scoring the first points in New Orleans Saints history when he returned the opening kickoff of their inaugural game 94 yards for a touchdown.

Born in Greenwood, South Carolina, on August 7, 1945, John Rally Gilliam attended Brewer High School, where he starred in multiple sports, excelling in football, basketball, and track and field. Beginning his career on the gridiron in his senior year after the school's head football coach challenged him to try out for the squad, Gilliam earned All-State and All-America honors, setting off a recruiting frenzy that ended with him accepting a scholarship to South Carolina State University. Continuing to develop his pass-receiving skills while in college, Gilliam gained All-America recognition in each of his last two seasons. Also lettering in track at South Carolina State, Gilliam posted a personal-best time of 9.5 seconds in the 100-yard dash, which put him four-tenths of a second off the world record at the time.

Selected by the expansion New Orleans Saints in the second round of the 1967 NFL Draft, with the 52nd overall pick, Gilliam became the first football player from SCSU to be drafted by an NFL team. He subsequently saw a limited amount of action on offense as a rookie, catching just 22 passes for 264 yards and one touchdown. Making much more of an impact

John Gilliam led the NFL in receiving yards from 1972 to 1975.

on special teams, Gilliam amassed a total of 481 yards returning kickoffs, with his 94-yard kickoff return for a touchdown the very first time he touched the football as a pro putting him in the record books.

Gilliam assumed a backup role on offense once again in 1968, before being dealt to the St. Louis Cardinals at season's end. After earning a starting job upon his arrival in St. Louis, Gilliam developed into one of the NFL's most dangerous wideouts, ranking among the league leaders in receiving yards and yards per reception in each of the next three seasons, with his average of 21.2 yards per catch in 1971 placing him second only to Bob Hayes in the NFC. Performing especially well in 1969, Gilliam made 52 receptions for 997 yards, scored 10 touchdowns, and amassed 1,332 all-purpose yards. Yet, despite the success that Gilliam experienced in St. Louis, he found himself headed to Minnesota when the reacquisition of Fran Tarkenton on January 27, 1972, prompted the Vikings to trade quarterback Gary Cuozzo to the Cardinals for Gilliam and a pair of future draft picks.

Developing an exceptional rapport with Tarkenton before long, Gilliam had an outstanding first season in Minnesota, earning Second-Team All-NFC honors and the first of his four straight trips to the Pro Bowl in 1972 by making 47 receptions, finishing second in the NFL with 1,035 receiving yards, catching seven touchdown passes, and leading the league with an average of 22 yards per reception. Amassing another 369 yards returning kickoffs, Gilliam also placed near the top of the league rankings with 1,431 all-purpose yards. Continuing his excellent play in 1973, Gilliam earned First-Team All-NFC and Second-Team All-Pro honors by making 42 receptions, finishing second in the NFL with 907 receiving yards, and ranking among the league leaders with eight touchdown catches and an average of 21.6 yards per reception. After averaging a career-high 22.2 yards per catch in 1974, Gilliam jumped to the Chicago Winds of the World Football League prior to the start of the ensuing campaign. However, when the Winds folded at the end of August after only five games, Gilliam returned to the Vikings, with whom he gained First-Team All-NFC recognition in 1975 by making 50 receptions for 777 yards and seven touchdowns.

In addition to his great speed, the 6'1", 195-pound Gilliam possessed good size, excellent moves, and sure hands, with his outstanding skill set forcing opposing teams to typically cover him with multiple defenders. Capable of going the distance any time he touched the football, Gilliam caught a total of 27 touchdown passes from 1972 to 1975, a figure that placed him third in the league rankings, behind only Harold Jackson and San Francisco's Gene Washington. Meanwhile, Gilliam's 3,297 receiving yards over that same period led all NFL receivers.

Nevertheless, with both Ahmad Rashad and Sammy White arriving in Minnesota early in 1976, the Vikings decided to trade Gilliam to the Atlanta Falcons. In addition to his 27 TD receptions and 3,297 receiving yards, Gilliam ended his four-year stint in Minnesota with 165 catches, 3,433 yards from scrimmage, 629 kickoff-return yards, 4,075 all-purpose yards, and one rushing touchdown. And, nearly half a century after he played his last game for the Vikings, Gilliam continues to hold the franchise record for most yards per reception (20.0).

Commenting on the overall impact that Gilliam made during his relatively brief stay in Minnesota, longtime Vikings fan Ted Glover of the *Daily Norseman* suggested, "He was Sammy White before Sammy White. He was only around for a few seasons, and the Vikings offense was pretty much built around [Chuck] Foreman, but Gilliam was a guy that really stretched the field, and he was one of the bigger deep threats in the game at that time. I could be remembering through purple-colored glasses, but he was really fast, had good hands, and it seemed like all of his catches were for 15 yards, minimum, sort of the prototypical home run/big play threat guy for the Vikings offense back then."

Experiencing a precipitous decline in production after he left the Twin Cities, Gilliam ended up spending just one year in Atlanta, making only 21 receptions for 292 yards and two touchdowns in 1976, before splitting the next season between the Chicago Bears and New Orleans Saints. Choosing to announce his retirement following the conclusion of the 1977 campaign, Gilliam ended his playing career with 382 receptions, 7,056 receiving yards, 7,349 yards from scrimmage, 9,340 all-purpose yards, 48 TD catches, and 52 touchdowns. Since retiring as an active player, Gilliam has spent most of his time serving as a motivational speaker and child advocate. He is currently the president and CEO of John Gilliam Enterprises, Inc., which raises money for several philanthropic causes.

VIKINGS CAREER HIGHLIGHTS

Best Season

Gilliam had an outstanding season for the Vikings in 1973, earning his lone All-Pro nomination by making 42 receptions, placing near the top of the league rankings with 907 receiving yards, eight TD catches, and an average of 21.6 yards per reception, and amassing 1,152 all-purpose yards. But he performed even better the previous year, concluding the 1972 campaign with 47 receptions, a career-high 1,035 receiving yards, seven touchdown catches, 1,431 all-purpose yards, and a league-leading average of 22 yards per reception.

Memorable Moments/Greatest Performances

Gilliam scored his first touchdown with the Vikings in his first game as a member of the team, hauling in an 11-yard TD pass from Fran Tarkenton during a 24–21 loss to Washington in the opening game of the 1972 regular season.

Gilliam followed that up in Week 2 by making four receptions for 109 yards and one touchdown during a 34–10 win over the Lions, with his TD coming on a 40-yard hookup with Tarkenton.

Gilliam contributed to a 45–41 victory over the Los Angeles Rams on November 19, 1972, by making four receptions for 105 yards and one touchdown, which came on a 66-yard pass from Tarkenton.

Gilliam displayed his versatility during a 28–21 win over the Eagles on October 21, 1973, by running 44 yards for one score and catching six passes for 116 yards and one TD, which came on a 24-yard connection with Tarkenton.

Gilliam helped lead the Vikings to a 31–13 win over the Bears on November 25, 1973, by making five receptions for 139 yards and two touchdowns, hooking up with Tarkenton on a 54-yard scoring play and collaborating with backup QB Bob Berry on a TD pass that covered 30 yards.

Gilliam played a huge role in Minnesota's 27–20 victory over Washington in the divisional round of the 1973 playoffs, making a pair of fourth-quarter touchdown receptions that put the Vikings ahead to stay.

Once again proving to be a major factor in the 1973 NFC championship game, Gilliam collaborated with Fran Tarkenton on a 54-yard scoring play that contributed to the Vikings' 27–10 win over the Dallas Cowboys.

Gilliam helped set the tone for a 51–10 rout of the Houston Oilers on October 13, 1974, by hauling in an 80-yard touchdown pass from Tarkenton on the game's opening possession.

Gilliam had his last big game as a member of the Vikings on November 16, 1975, when he made six receptions for 139 yards and two touchdowns during a 20–7 win over the New Orleans Saints.

Notable Achievements

- Surpassed 50 receptions once.
- Surpassed 1,000 receiving yards once.
- Amassed more than 1,000 all-purpose yards twice.
- Averaged more than 20 yards per reception three times.
- Led NFL with average of 22 yards per reception in 1972.
- Finished second in NFL in receiving yards twice.
- Finished third in NFL with average of 21.6 yards per reception in 1973.
- Led Vikings in receptions twice and receiving yards three times.

- Holds Vikings career record for most yards per reception (20.0).
- Three-time division champion (1973, 1974, and 1975).
- Two-time NFC champion (1973 and 1974).
- Four-time Pro Bowl selection (1972, 1973, 1974, and 1975).
- 1973 Second-Team All-Pro selection.
- Two-time First-Team All-NFC selection (1973 and 1975).
- 1972 Second-Team All-NFC selection.

43

ANTHONY BARR

The first player drafted by the Vikings after Mike Zimmer assumed head coaching duties in 2014, Anthony Barr has proven to be one of the NFL's most complete linebackers during his time in Minnesota. Equally effective in pass coverage, rushing the quarterback, or defending against the run, Barr brings a tremendous amount of versatility to the Vikings' defense, which has consistently ranked among the best in the league since he arrived in the Twin Cities. A member of Vikings teams that have made three playoff appearances and won two division titles, Barr has earned four Pro Bowl selections, which ties him with Jeff Siemon for the second most nominations of any linebacker in franchise history.

Born in South Bend, Indiana, on March 18, 1992, Anthony Barr grew up rooting for the Notre Dame Fighting Irish, even though he moved with his mother to her hometown of Los Angeles as a young child. The son of Tony Brooks and the nephew of Reggie Brooks, both of whom played running back at Notre Dame before entering the NFL, Barr spent much of his youth hoping to pursue a career as a running back himself, before changing his mind shortly after he graduated from Loyola High School.

Lettering in football and track at Loyola, Barr earned All-State honors his junior year by rushing for 1,890 yards and 20 touchdowns, before missing most of the ensuing campaign after breaking his ankle in September. Excelling in track as well, Barr competed in the 100-meter and 200-meter dashes, earning a silver medal in the latter event at the 2009 Mission League Championships by posting a personal-best time of 21.86 seconds.

Subsequently recruited by Notre Dame and USC, Barr eventually decided to accept an athletic scholarship to UCLA instead when he learned that the Irish intended to use him as a wide receiver. Recalling the choice that faced him at the time, Barr said, "I had a Notre Dame family and USC was frowned upon in the house, to say the least. I wasn't a big UCLA fan growing up, but, if I had to choose the lesser of the two evils, USC wasn't the choice."

Anthony Barr has earned four trips to the Pro Bowl since joining the Vikings in 2014.
Courtesy of Jeffrey Beall

Looking back at the impression that Barr made on him during his time at Loyola, Seattle Seahawks head coach Pete Carroll, who headed the USC program in those days, stated, "I go all the way back to when we recruited him in college. He'd have been a tailback if he had been on my team. . . . He was a terror in high school."

Far less effective at UCLA, Barr struggled his first two seasons at Westwood, gaining just 54 yards on 15 carries in a backup role, with former Bruins and current Vikings teammate Eric Kendricks recalling, "I thought, 'How's this tall dude playing running back, playing this skill position where it requires leverage?' You have to be low and things. But he always showed the athleticism. He was always very strong in the weight room. You put him on the field, and he could run as fast as anybody."

Prior to the start of his junior year, though, Barr had a meeting with new UCLA head coach Jim Mora and his coaching staff that ended up reaping huge benefits for all parties concerned, with Barr remembering, "I was looking to either change schools or change positions or something just because I wasn't really doing much my first couple of years. I was looking for something new, and we all came together, and I switched to defense, and things just started clicking."

Claiming that Barr initially came up with the idea of moving to the defensive side of the ball, then UCLA assistant coach Scott White said, "We knew that he could be a good linebacker because of his size, athleticism, and skill set, but we didn't envision he would be so good so quick. He was a natural. Not only is he a big, strong, physical athlete, he is really intelligent. He was great in the meeting room, and it translated right to the field."

Barr, who ended up earning First-Team All–Pac 12 and Second-Team All-America honors his junior year by recording 12½ sacks and 83 tackles, later drew praise from Eric Kendricks, who said, "I'm not going to sit here and say I'm not surprised. But obviously I knew what kind of athlete he is. It didn't really hit me until we played that first game against Rice, and I saw his motor during the game. I was like, 'OK, this is going to work.'"

Barr performed exceptionally well once again as a senior, gaining First-Team All–Pac 12 and consensus First-Team All-America recognition by registering 10 sacks, forcing five fumbles, and recovering four others. With Barr also earning consideration for the Butkus, Lombardi, and Bednarik Awards, the Vikings subsequently made him the ninth overall pick of the 2014 NFL Draft when they selected him during the early stages of the first round.

Named the starting right-outside linebacker immediately upon his arrival in Minnesota, Barr had a solid first season for the Vikings, recording four sacks, 70 tackles, two forced fumbles, and three fumble recoveries, one of which he returned for a touchdown, before missing the final four games with a knee injury. Continuing his strong play in each of the next four seasons, Barr earned four consecutive trips to the Pro Bowl and one First-Team All-Pro nomination from *Pro Football Focus* by averaging 67 tackles and 2½ sacks for Vikings teams that won two division titles.

An exceptional all-around athlete, the 6'5", 255-pound Barr brings size, speed, and versatility to the Vikings' defense, with San Diego Chargers head coach Anthony Lynn stating, "He's one of the best in the game. I mean, he's big, he's fast, he's instinctive. He can play the run, he can play the pass, he can rush the passer. I don't know if there's anything he can't do."

Vikings head coach Mike Zimmer expressed his appreciation for all Barr brings to the team when he said, "He's a good leader on the defense. He does his job. We ask him to do a lot of different things. We ask him to do a lot of communication type of things with the front guys and the back-end guys. I think he's played very well. He plays hard. He's a good tackler. He's physical, he's a good rusher."

Vikings teammate Linval Joseph added, "He's a special player. He can rush. He can play coverage. He's really good at tackling."

Barr has also developed a reputation as a solid citizen during his time in Minnesota, giving his time, effort, and monetary support to The Jeremiah Program, which provides financial assistance for higher education and childcare to single mothers. He also established the Raise the Barr Foundation, which has a similar goal.

Nevertheless, Barr drew a considerable amount of criticism for a hit he delivered to Aaron Rodgers during a 23–10 victory over the Packers on October 15, 2017, that injured the Green Bay quarterback's collarbone, knocking him out of the game. In discussing the incident in a television interview with Conan O'Brien, Rodgers claimed that Barr gave him "the finger" and told him to "suck it." Meanwhile, Packers head coach Mike McCarthy called Barr's hit "illegal." In response, Barr tweeted that Rodgers trash-talked him during the contest and suggested that he "needs to get over it." Barr also stated that he doesn't consider himself to be a dirty player and that he did not intend to injure Rodgers.

A free agent at the end of 2018, Barr appeared to be on the verge of leaving Minnesota when he reportedly signed a multiyear deal with the New York Jets that would have paid him more than $15 million a season. But Barr changed his mind shortly thereafter, later revealing, "Talking to my agent, within minutes, it was like, 'I think we should maybe revisit it.' An epiphany happened."

Following a night of negotiations, the Vikings came up with a number acceptable to Barr, who stated, "I didn't know if Minnesota was going to get to a number that I was comfortable with, and fortunately they were able to, and I always said that, if that happened, I could come back here."

Although Barr ultimately signed with the Vikings for less money, agreeing to a new five-year, $67.5 million contract, he has never regretted making that decision, saying, "Happiness, peace of mind, being somewhere you want, I think that's all priceless. It's all invaluable. You can't put a number on being in the place you want to be."

Expressing his satisfaction with Barr's decision to re-sign with the team, Vikings linebackers coach Adam Zimmer said, "I was fired up and excited and glad to have him back. There are few linebackers that do the physical things that he does. A lot of it gets unnoticed because they don't throw to his guy when he's covering them because he's covering them so well."

Continuing to perform at an elite level after re-signing with the Vikings, Barr recorded a career-high 79 tackles in 2019. However, he subsequently missed all but two games this past season after suffering a torn pectoral muscle during a 28–11 loss to the Indianapolis Colts on September 20, 2020. Still only 29 years old as of this writing, Barr will enter the 2021 campaign with career totals of 423 tackles, 15 sacks, two interceptions, eight forced fumbles, five fumble recoveries, and one touchdown.

CAREER HIGHLIGHTS

Best Season

Although Barr established career-high marks with four sacks in 2014 and 79 tackles in 2019, he turned in his finest all-around performance in 2015, when, in addition to earning Pro Bowl honors for the first of four straight times, he gained First-Team All-Pro recognition from *Pro Football Focus* by registering 3½ sacks, 68 tackles, one interception, and three forced fumbles.

Memorable Moments/Greatest Performances

Barr earned NFC Defensive Player of the Week honors for his outstanding all-around play during a 19–13 overtime victory over the Tampa Bay Buccaneers on October 26, 2014. In addition to recording a sack and eight solo tackles, Barr forced a fumble on the first play from scrimmage in overtime that he subsequently recovered and returned 27 yards for the game-winning touchdown.

Although the Vikings lost to the Broncos by a score of 23–20 on October 4, 2015, Barr recorded the first interception of his career when he picked off a Peyton Manning pass, which he subsequently returned 32 yards to the Denver 27 yard line to help set up a Minnesota touchdown.

Barr contributed to a 20–10 victory over the Atlanta Falcons on November 29, 2015, by recording a sack, eight tackles, and two forced fumbles.

Barr helped lead the Vikings to a 24–16 win over the Baltimore Ravens on October 22, 2017, by registering a sack and a season-high 11 tackles, three of which resulted in a loss.

Barr made a key play during the Vikings' 29–24 win over the Saints in the divisional round of the 2017 NFC playoffs when he ended a New Orleans scoring threat late in the first half by picking off a Drew Brees pass at the Minnesota 10 yard line.

Barr recorded two sacks in one game for the only time in his career during a 41–17 rout of Miami on December 16, 2018.

Barr contributed to a 28–10 win over the Giants on October 6, 2019, by intercepting a Daniel Jones pass and recording a safety when he tackled running back Jonathan Hillman in the end zone.

Notable Achievements

- Has scored one defensive touchdown.
- Two-time division champion (2015 and 2017).
- 2014 Week 8 Defensive Player of the Week.
- Four-time Pro Bowl selection (2015, 2016, 2017, and 2018).

44

CARL LEE

An outstanding cover corner who became known for his intelligence and relatively mistake-free style of play, Carl Lee spent 11 seasons in Minnesota, earning Pro Bowl honors at both cornerback positions. One of the Vikings' best all-around players during his time in the Twin Cities, Lee did an exceptional job of defending against both the run and the pass, with his consistently excellent play earning him three trips to the Pro Bowl, three All-NFC nominations, and one All-Pro selection. A member of Vikings teams that won two division titles and made five playoff appearances, Lee also proved to be extremely durable, appearing in 169 out of 172 contests while wearing the Purple and Gold.

Born in Vandalia, West Virginia, on February 6, 1961, Carl Lee III grew up some 110 miles southwest, in the town of Spring Hill, where he realized at an early age that he wished to pursue a career in football. Looking back on his childhood, Lee said, "I was born in Vandalia, but we moved when I was very young to Spring Hill. I absolutely loved sports, football specifically, and the Cleveland Browns. I remember watching the Browns with my dad and knowing I wanted to do that. Everybody got that I was literally crazy over football. . . . I used to play Midget league by myself. I would throw the ball, catch it, and tackle myself. As I got older, we played sandlot football. It was about who you wanted to be. I always wanted to be Paul Warfield. No. 42 was the first number I loved."

Lee continued, "The first year I played, I was about seven. I only had a helmet, no uniform, so I quit. The next year, I was able to play, but I wasn't a star. I played quite a bit in eighth and ninth grades. Homer Criddle was my coach at South Charleston. . . . I didn't make varsity my 10th-grade year. From my dad, it wasn't like, 'Oh, the coach made a mistake.' It was, 'Well, what are you going to do about it? You need to work harder.' And I worked harder and started as an 11th-grader."

Lee subsequently earned First-Team All-State honors in his senior year at South Charleston High School, prompting West Virginia University

Carl Lee earned Pro Bowl honors at both cornerback positions during his time in Minnesota.
Courtesy of MearsOnlineAuctions.com

to pay him a visit. But they never made him a scholarship offer, with Lee recalling, "WVU came down but they thought I was too small. I weighed 155."

Scouts from Marshall University in Huntington, West Virginia, felt differently, though, allowing Lee to remain relatively close to home. Lee ended up starring at defensive back for the Thundering Herd for four years, adding a considerable amount of bulk onto his lanky frame during that time, as he later noted when he said, "By the time I got to Marshall, I was 165, and I gained 10 pounds every year I was there."

And, with Lee performing so well on the football field, he began to generate interest among pro teams, recalling, "By the time I was a junior, I had tons of people coming in. The first letter I got was from Dallas. My senior year, they started coming and working me out. That's when I thought it might be a possibility. I got invited to the combine in Seattle. The letter talked about only the top 100 players in the country. Could I be one of those? . . . I didn't do real well, which is why I probably ended up going in the seventh round to the Vikings."

Ultimately selected by the Vikings with the 186th overall pick of the 1983 NFL Draft, Lee vividly remembers the events that transpired on draft day, saying, "During the draft, I was in Huntington with my now-wife. The call came the second day, near the end of the draft. I had fallen asleep. The phone rang, and I picked it up without even thinking. It was the Minnesota Vikings. I'm thinking, 'Did this really happen?' Before I knew it, everybody came over and it was a crazy night."

Although Lee started just three games as a rookie in 1983, he performed well while assuming various roles in the secondary, recording one interception and 49 tackles. Named the Vikings' starting free safety in 1984, Lee registered a career-high 100 tackles, before being moved to right cornerback the following year. Manning that post for the next five seasons, Lee established himself as one of the NFL's top cover corners by picking off 19 passes and recording 370 tackles, en route to earning Pro Bowl and All-NFC honors twice each. Particularly effective in 1988, Lee gained First-Team All-Pro recognition by finishing second in the NFL with eight interceptions, which he returned for a total of 118 yards and two touchdowns.

Crediting current Seattle Seahawks head coach and former Vikings defensive backs coach Pete Carroll for much of the success he experienced at the cornerback position, Lee stated, "Pete Carroll is the coach who took me to the next level. He brought in the bump-and-run, and it fit me perfectly."

A physical player who enjoyed engaging opposing wide receivers at the line of scrimmage, the 5'11", 190-pound Lee possessed good size, speed, and strength. He also had excellent ball-skills and a strong work ethic, with longtime teammate Scott Studwell saying, "Carl Lee was very fast and had extremely good cover skills. He worked hard at the game and was a self-made player."

Keith Millard also praised Lee, calling him "one of the best cover corners of his time," and adding, "He shut down Jerry Rice in the playoffs; never seen anybody do that to Jerry in my time."

Continuing to excel after the Vikings shifted him to left cornerback in 1990, Lee spent his final four seasons in Minnesota at that spot, earning one more Pro Bowl selection and his last All-NFC nomination, before a clash of personalities with new defensive backs coach Richard Solomon led to his release in 1994. Recalling his abrupt dismissal, Lee said, "Richard Solomon was my coach. At a minicamp in April, he told me I backpedaled too high and that was a sign of getting old and not getting in shape. I had never been to camp out of shape. We just didn't click. . . . About two weeks before camp, my phone rings, the Vikings office. On a Saturday morning, it wasn't going to be good news. They said they were letting me go."

Lee, who left Minnesota with career totals of 29 interceptions, 349 interception-return yards, 771 tackles, six fumble recoveries, and two touchdowns, subsequently signed with the New Orleans Saints, with whom he spent one final season, before announcing his retirement. Looking back on his playing career, Lee said, "I played 11 years with the Vikings and one year with the Saints. In the beginning, there was the innocence of it. I didn't know much about the money. I didn't do it for the money. I did it because it was what I loved. We get hurled into this NFL world with no clue about what it is like."

After retiring as an active player, Lee spent 10 seasons serving as head football coach at West Virginia State University, before resigning his post at the end of 2005. He subsequently remained with the school in other capacities for another seven years, before ending his association with the institution. Lee currently holds the position of project director for youth football at the South Charleston Recreation Center.

VIKINGS CAREER HIGHLIGHTS

Best Season

Although Lee also earned Pro Bowl honors in 1989 and 1990, he had easily the finest season of his career in 1988, when, in addition to being named to the Pro Bowl roster for the first of three straight times, he earned his lone All-Pro nomination by scoring two touchdowns and finishing among the league leaders with eight interceptions and 118 interception-return yards.

Memorable Moments/Greatest Performances

Lee contributed to a 20–17 win over the Lions on September 25, 1983, by recording the first interception of his career, which he subsequently returned 31 yards.

Lee picked off two passes in one game for the first time as a pro during a 33–17 win over the New Orleans Saints in the final game of the 1986 regular season.

Although the Vikings lost to the Miami Dolphins by a score of 24–7 on October 2, 1988, Lee intercepted Dan Marino twice, returning one of his picks 48 yards for Minnesota's only touchdown of the game.

Lee recorded another pair of interceptions during a 12–3 win over the Indianapolis Colts on November 20, 1988, picking off Chris Chandler and Gary Hogeboom once each.

Lee earned NFC Defensive Player of the Week honors by returning his interception of a Bobby Hebert pass 58 yards for a touchdown during a 45–3 rout of the New Orleans Saints on December 4, 1988.

Lee turned in one of his finest all-around performances in the divisional round of the 1987 playoffs, intercepting a Steve Young pass and holding Jerry Rice to just three receptions for 28 yards during a 36–24 win over the San Francisco 49ers.

Notable Achievements

- Missed just three non-strike games in 11 seasons, appearing in 169 out of 172 contests.
- Scored two defensive touchdowns.
- Amassed more than 100 interception-return yards once.
- Recorded more than 100 tackles once.
- Finished second in NFL with eight interceptions in 1988.
- Ranks among Vikings career leaders with 29 interceptions (6th), 349 interception-return yards (7th), and 771 tackles (10th).
- Two-time division champion (1989 and 1992).
- 1988 Week 14 NFC Defensive Player of the Week.
- Three-time Pro Bowl selection (1988, 1989, and 1990).
- 1988 First-Team All-Pro selection.
- 1988 First-Team All-NFC selection.
- Two-time Second-Team All-NFC selection (1989 and 1992).

45

ED MCDANIEL

The Vikings' emotional leader on defense for nearly a decade, Ed McDaniel spent his entire nine-year NFL career in Minnesota, serving as the driving force behind teams that won four division titles and made seven playoff appearances. Possessing a larger-than-life personality, McDaniel inspired his teammates with his vocal leadership and aggressive style of play, making him one of the most popular players in franchise history. Excelling at all three linebacker positions at different times, McDaniel recorded more than 100 tackles on five separate occasions, ending his career as one of the franchise's all-time leading tacklers. An effective pass-rusher as well, McDaniel registered 19½ sacks and forced 15 fumbles, with the last figure also placing him extremely high in team annals.

Born in Batesburg, South Carolina, on February 23, 1969, Edward McDaniel attended Batesburg-Leesville High School, where he starred in football, prompting Clemson University to offer him an athletic scholarship. Continuing to excel on the gridiron in college, McDaniel started at linebacker for four years, during which time he recorded a total of 389 tackles. Leading the Tigers in stops in three of his four seasons, McDaniel performed especially well as a senior in 1991, earning First-Team All-America honors and being named a semifinalist for the Butkus Award, presented annually to the nation's top linebacker.

Yet, despite his exceptional play at the collegiate level, McDaniel's smallish 5'11", 230-pound frame scared off many pro scouts, forcing him to wait until the fifth round of the 1992 NFL Draft to hear his name called. Finally selected by the Vikings with the 125th overall pick, McDaniel subsequently spent his first two seasons in Minnesota playing mostly on special teams, while assuming a backup role on defense behind starting linebackers Jack Del Rio, Carlos Jenkins, and Fred Strickland.

Laying claim to the starting right-outside linebacker job in 2004, McDaniel quickly established himself as one of the Vikings' most impactful players on the defensive side of the ball, finishing second on the team with

Ed McDaniel excelled at all three linebacker positions for the Vikings.
Courtesy of MearsOnlineAuctions.com

119 tackles, including 89 of the solo variety. McDaniel followed that up
by recording 4½ sacks, a league-leading six forced fumbles, and a team-
high 117 tackles in 1995, before missing the entire 1996 campaign after
undergoing reconstructive surgery on his left knee during the offseason.
Returning to action in 1997, McDaniel moved to the left side of Minnesota's defense, where he ended up recording 90 tackles, before once again

undergoing reconstructive surgery during the subsequent offseason, this time on his right knee.

Despite his relatively small stature, McDaniel excelled wherever the Vikings put him largely because of his ability to read opposing offenses and break quickly on the snap from center. Displaying a nose for the football throughout his career, McDaniel also took good angles, never gave up on plays, and delivered huge hits that helped set the tone for the rest of Minnesota's defense.

However, McDaniel perhaps made his greatest impact with the vocal leadership he provided to his teammates, which made him, in many ways, the heart and soul of the Vikings' defense. Although surrounded by other "Type-A" personalities such as John Randle, Jack Del Rio, and Robert Griffith during his time in Minnesota, McDaniel took a backseat to no one in terms of his leadership ability, which, combined with his outstanding play, made him a huge contributor to any success the Vikings experienced as a team.

Moved inside to middle linebacker in 1998, McDaniel had one of his most productive seasons, earning his lone Pro Bowl selection by recording 128 tackles (93 solo) and seven sacks. He followed that up with another outstanding year, registering 121 tackles in 1999, before moving back to the outside for his final two seasons, during which time he recorded a total of 191 tackles. Released by the Vikings in February 2002 due to salary-cap constraints, McDaniel subsequently announced his retirement, ending his career with 796 tackles (575 solo), 19½ sacks, 15 forced fumbles, five fumble recoveries, and four interceptions.

After retiring as an active player, McDaniel became a successful businessman, co-owning D1 Sports Training in Greenville, South Carolina. McDaniel, who resides in a suburb of the Twin Cities in Minnesota, also owns several apartment buildings in Minneapolis and St. Paul.

CAREER HIGHLIGHTS

Best Season

McDaniel performed extremely well for the Vikings in 1995, leading the NFL with six forced fumbles, while also recording 4.5 sacks and 117 combined tackles. However, he had his finest all-around season in 1998, earning Pro Bowl honors by forcing three fumbles, recovering two others, and establishing career-high marks with seven sacks and 128 tackles.

Memorable Moments/Greatest Performances

McDaniel recorded the first sack of his career during a 17–7 loss to the Arizona Cardinals on October 2, 1994.

McDaniel recorded his first interception as a pro when he picked off a Jim Everett pass during a 21–20 win over the New Orleans Saints on November 6, 1994.

McDaniel turned in an outstanding all-around effort when the Vikings defeated the Lions by a score of 29–6 on September 20, 1998. In addition to helping limit Barry Sanders to just 69 yards on 22 carries, McDaniel registered 1½ sacks and forced a fumble, which he recovered himself.

McDaniel contributed to a 24–3 victory over the Cincinnati Bengals on November 15, 1998, by recording a sack and 10 tackles, including nine of the solo variety.

McDaniel helped lead the Vikings to a 40–16 win over the San Francisco 49ers on October 24, 1999, by recording two sacks and 14 tackles, including 12 solo stops.

McDaniel starred during a 30–27 victory over the Bears in the opening game of the 2000 regular season, registering a sack, making 13 tackles, and forcing a fumble.

Notable Achievements

- Recorded more than 100 tackles five times.
- Led NFL with six forced fumbles in 1995.
- Led Vikings in tackles three times.
- Ranks among Vikings career leaders with 796 tackles (9th) and 15 forced fumbles (5th).
- Four-time division champion (1992, 1994, 1998, and 2000).
- 1998 Pro Bowl selection.

46

JAKE REED

One of the better number two receivers ever to play the game, Jake Reed spent his first few seasons in Minnesota playing second fiddle to Hall of Fame wideout Cris Carter. Then, after Randy Moss joined the Vikings in 1998, Reed became part of one of the most productive receiving trios in NFL history. Yet even though he never had the spotlight to himself, Reed carved out an extremely successful career in the Twin Cities, surpassing 60 receptions and 1,000 receiving yards four times each. A member of Vikings teams that made seven playoff appearances and won three division titles, Reed continues to rank among the franchise's all-time leaders in every major pass-receiving category nearly two decades after he played his last game as a member of the team.

Born in Covington, Georgia, on September 28, 1967, Willie Jake Reed began his football career at local Newton High School, where he spent much of his time trying to prove his doubters wrong. Although Reed excelled on the gridiron at wide receiver, earning High School All-America honors, he received little encouragement from his teachers, coaches, and counselors, recalling, "In high school, I never got into trouble. I did my schoolwork and was about a C student—though I admit I could have done better. . . . I went to see my counselor about going to college. She said, 'I don't think you should think about college. You'd probably be better off going into the service.'"

Revealing that his basketball coach also failed to be a source of inspiration to him when he predicted that he wouldn't amount to anything, Reed stated during a 1995 interview, "What makes me happy is knowing all the obstacles I've overcome, the people telling me I couldn't do it, at a time when I was so vulnerable. Kids listen to their coaches and counselors. We have so many people throwing kids off, taking the easy way out instead of saying to them, 'You can make it.'"

Ultimately offered an athletic scholarship to Grambling State University, Reed spent his college career playing for legendary head coach Eddie

Jake Reed amassed more than 1,000 receiving yards four times for
the Vikings.
Courtesy of MearsOnlineAuctions.com

Robinson. Continuing his development under Robinson's watchful eye,
Reed finished his senior year with 47 receptions and 954 receiving yards,
prompting the Vikings to select him in the third round of the 1991 NFL
Draft, with the 68th overall pick—one they acquired in the Herschel
Walker trade.

After suiting up for just one game as a rookie in 1991, Reed spent the
next two seasons serving the Vikings primarily on special teams, making
just 11 receptions for 207 yards, and failing to score a touchdown. Hampered by injuries and a lack of self-confidence, Reed appeared to be headed

nowhere until Cris Carter took him under his wing prior to the start of the 1994 season. Looking back on how Carter helped alter his mindset, Reed said, "Cris was the guy who ultimately built me up in my career. There were a couple of times when I was still questioning myself. . . . Cris taught me a lot of the ropes about being an NFL wide receiver."

Warren Moon also proved to be a positive influence on Reed, with Moon recalling, "When I came here in 1994, I saw this big, strong, tall, fast, fluid man who had been injured a lot, so nobody really knew how good he could be. I sensed that he didn't have the confidence that he could be a prime-time, go-to receiver on a consistent basis. That's what I had to get across to him."

His confidence buoyed by his two veteran teammates, Reed subsequently began an outstanding four-year run during which he posted the following numbers:

YEAR	RECS	REC YDS	TD RECS
1994	85	1,175	4
1995	72	1,167	9
1996	72	1,320	7
1997	68	1,138	6

In addition to leading the Vikings in receiving yards in two of those four seasons, Reed finished second in the league in that category in 1996. Two years earlier, Reed combined with Carter to set a new NFL record (since broken) for most catches by a receiving tandem (207). Reed and Carter also became the first wide receiver duo to each surpass 1,000 receiving yards in four straight seasons.

The 6'3", 217-pound Reed offered the Vikings a powerful alternative to Carter in the passing game. Absolutely fearless going over the middle, Reed excelled at running routes of the short and intermediate variety, making good use of his size and strength to ward off opposing defensive backs. Blessed with outstanding speed as well, Reed also possessed the ability to beat his man deep, ranking among the league leaders in yards per catch on three separate occasions.

Following the arrival of Randy Moss in 1998, Reed assumed a somewhat less prominent role in the Minnesota offense, being relegated to the position of third wideout. Nevertheless, he remained extremely productive over the course of the next two seasons, with the Vikings' exceptional receiving corps becoming known to fans of the team as "Three Deep." Despite missing the final five games of the 1998 campaign after undergoing surgery on his back, Reed made 34 receptions for 474 yards and four touchdowns. He then caught 44 passes for 643 yards and two touchdowns in 1999, before signing with the New Orleans Saints as a free agent at season's end. After one year in New Orleans, Reed returned to Minnesota, where he made 27 receptions for 309 yards and one touchdown in 2001. Reed then rejoined the Saints in 2002, spending one final season in "The Big Easy," before announcing his retirement. Ending his career with 450 receptions, 6,999 receiving yards, and 36 touchdown receptions, Reed caught 413 passes, amassed 6,433 receiving yards, and scored 33 TDs during his time in Minnesota.

Following his playing days, Reed moved his family to Frisco, Texas, saying during a 2015 interview, "I loved being in Minnesota and enjoyed all of the lakes. Randy Moss, Cris Carter, and me would go out fishing all the time. I really enjoyed that. I would have stayed in Minnesota, but it was just too cold."

After spending the early years of his retirement owning an Arena Football team and a pizzeria, Reed decided to adopt a less stressful lifestyle. He now spends most of his time serving as a mentor to high school boys and being with his family.

VIKINGS CAREER HIGHLIGHTS

Best Season

Reed played his best ball for the Vikings from 1994 to 1997, surpassing 1,000 receiving yards four straight times during that period. After making a career-high 85 receptions in 1994, Reed caught 72 passes and scored a career-best nine touchdowns the following year. However, Reed had his finest all-around season in 1996, when, in addition to making 72 receptions and scoring seven touchdowns, he placed near the top of the league rankings with 1,320 receiving yards and an average of 18.3 yards per reception.

Memorable Moments/Greatest Performances

Reed scored the first touchdown of his career when he hauled in an 18-yard pass from Warren Moon during a 42–14 win over the Bears on September 18, 1994. He finished the game with seven catches for 90 yards and that one TD.

Reed topped 100 receiving yards for the first time as a pro during a 38–35 victory over the Miami Dolphins on September 25, 1994, concluding the contest with nine catches for 127 yards.

Reed helped lead the Vikings to a 21–20 win over the Saints on November 6, 1994, by making eight receptions for 157 yards and one TD, which came on a 13-yard pass from Warren Moon.

Reed contributed to a 30–21 victory over the Packers on September 22, 1996, by making seven receptions for 129 yards and one touchdown, which came on a 26-yard hookup with Moon.

Reed collaborated with Brad Johnson on a career-long 82-yard touchdown reception during a 16–13 overtime win over the Oakland Raiders on November 17, 1996, finishing the game with four catches for 134 yards and that one TD.

Reed proved to be a major factor when the Vikings defeated the Bears by a score of 27–24 on September 7, 1997, making a career-high 12 catches for 118 yards and one touchdown, which came on a 21-yard connection with Brad Johnson early in the fourth quarter.

Reed helped set the tone for a 28–19 victory over the Philadelphia Eagles on September 28, 1997, when he collaborated with Johnson on a 48-yard scoring play on the Vikings' first possession of the game. He finished the contest with six catches for 134 yards and that one TD.

Although the Vikings lost to the Jets by a score of 23–21 on November 23, 1997, Reed starred in defeat, making eight receptions for 150 yards and two touchdowns.

Reed experienced the most memorable moment of his career against the Giants in the wild card round of the 1997 NFC playoffs when he helped the Vikings record a stunning come-from-behind victory by making a critical TD catch during the latter stages of the contest. With the Vikings trailing New York by a score of 22–13 late in the fourth quarter, Reed gathered in a 30-yard touchdown pass from Randall Cunningham that reduced the deficit to just two points with 90 seconds remaining in regulation. The Vikings subsequently recovered an onside kick by Eddie Murray, who completed the comeback with a 24-yard field goal with just 10 ticks left on the clock. Looking back on his key touchdown reception, Reed, who injured his leg earlier in the contest, said, "I remember that game like it was yesterday. I was hurting so bad, but I knew we needed it. Randall Cunningham threw it to me, and I made that catch in the back of the end zone." Reed finished the game with five catches for 89 yards and that one TD.

Notable Achievements

- Surpassed 60 receptions four times.
- Surpassed 1,000 receiving yards four times.
- Scored nine touchdowns in 1995.
- Finished second in NFL with 1,320 receiving yards in 1996.
- Finished third in NFL with average of 18.3 yards per reception in 1996.
- Led Vikings in receiving yards twice.
- Ranks among Vikings career leaders with 413 receptions (6th), 6,433 receiving yards (4th), 33 touchdown receptions (8th), and 6,433 yards from scrimmage (tied for 10th).
- Three-time division champion (1992, 1994, and 1998).
- September 1997 NFC Offensive Player of the Month.

47

GARY LARSEN

The fourth and final member of the Purple People Eaters to make our list, Gary Larsen spent most of his 10 seasons in Minnesota being overshadowed by his more flamboyant line-mates. Yet, Larsen's steady play on the interior of the Vikings' defensive line enabled Alan Page, Carl Eller, and Jim Marshall to freelance as much as they did, making him vital to the success the unit experienced as a whole. Primarily responsible for stopping the run, Larsen performed his role brilliantly, earning in the process two trips to the Pro Bowl. Meanwhile, the Vikings won six division titles, two NFC championships, and one NFL title with Larsen starting for them at left defensive tackle.

Born in Fargo, North Dakota, on March 13, 1940, Gary Lee Larsen grew up on a wheat farm just outside the small town of Moorhead, in northern Minnesota, where he received his introduction to organized sports while attending Moorhead High School. Participating in baseball, basketball, eight-man football, and the shotput at Moorhead High, Larsen recalled, "In my playing days, I was considered big as a football player, but small by comparison to today's players. I grew pretty fast. In the eighth grade, I was 5'8" and weighed 160 pounds, and by the time I was a senior in high school, I was 6'5" and weighed 260 pounds."

Enrolling at Concordia College following his graduation, Larsen spent one year furthering his education before he decided to join the US Marines, with whom he spent the next three years playing on base football teams while fulfilling his military commitment. Returning to Concordia following his discharge in 1961, Larsen played football and basketball for the next three years, proving to be particularly outstanding on the gridiron, where he starred at defensive tackle. Yet, despite the success he experienced at the collegiate level, Larsen never dreamed of turning pro, revealing years later, "I never gave a thought to professional football. My plan was to be a teacher. I wanted to get an education and become a physical education teacher. Then one day, a scout from the Los Angeles Rams came to Concordia and looked

Gary Larsen played for Vikings teams that won six division titles, two NFC championships, and one NFL title.

at some of our game film and became very interested in my potential as a football player in the National Football League."

After garnering interest from the Baltimore Colts as well, Larsen headed to Los Angeles when the Rams selected him in the 10th round of the 1964 NFL Draft, with the 133rd overall pick. Signing with the Rams when they offered him $9,500, plus a $500 signing bonus, Larsen recalled, "I didn't have an agent. Nobody had an agent. I talked with my wife. She said sign. So, I signed."

Larsen ended up spending just one season in Los Angeles, filling in as a reserve for the original Fearsome Foursome of Merlin Olsen, Deacon Jones, Lamar Lundy, and Rosey Grier. Looking back on his one year with the Rams, Larsen said, "I'd play Merlin Olsen's left tackle spot. Merlin would move over to Lamar's left end spot. The front four and me was all we had. In those days, there were only 40 players on the team."

Claiming that he saw his greatest amount of action with the Rams when they met the Green Bay Packers in the final game of the 1964 regular season, Larsen recalled, "I played the whole game. Kickoffs, kickoff returns, punts, punt returns, and the whole game on defense against [Forrest] Gregg in the L.A. Coliseum. I was whipped. That was probably the hardest game I ever played."

With the Vikings subsequently selecting All-America wide receiver Jack Snow in the first round of the 1965 NFL Draft, head coach Norm Van Brocklin worked out a trade with the Rams when Snow indicated that he had no desire to play in Minnesota. Revealing that the Vikings wanted more than just former All-Pro receiver Jimmy "Red" Phillips in return, Larsen said, "Of course, they needed something else thrown in. So, Norm said he'd make the trade if they threw in that Larsen kid. That's how I got to Minnesota."

Laying claim to the starting left tackle job shortly after he joined the Vikings, Larsen spent his first two seasons in Minnesota starting alongside right tackle Paul Dickson and ends Jim Marshall and Carl Eller. But Larsen assumed a backup role following the arrival of Alan Page in 1967, before regaining his starting job when the Vikings shifted Page to the right side of their defensive front in 1968.

Larsen spent the next seven years playing alongside Marshall, Eller, and Page, with the quartet eventually being dubbed the Purple People Eaters due to the havoc they wreaked on opposing offenses. While his line-mates specialized in applying pressure to opposing quarterbacks, Larsen typically "stayed at home" to defend against the run. Big and strong at 6'5" and 260 pounds, Larsen did an excellent job of clogging up the middle, gradually acquiring the nickname the "policeman" for the sense of order he created up front. More than just a run-stopper, though, Larsen proved to be a capable pass-rusher as well, recording an unofficial total of 38½ sacks as a member of the Vikings.

Recognizing the degree to which Larsen contributed to the success of the unit, longtime Vikings offensive line coach John Michels stated, "Gary did a lot of cleaning up for those guys. They'd start the play, and he'd help finish it up. Gary never let anything get past him. He was like a giant vacuum cleaner. He picked up the pieces."

Known for his tremendous heart, Larsen started every game for the Vikings from 1968 to 1973, a period during which they won five division titles and appeared in two Super Bowls. In discussing his motivation for giving so much of himself to the team, Larsen said, "With the Vikings, I always had the feeling that we worked our way up to the top. We all knew where we had come from—as part of an early expansion team—and we never wanted to go back to the tough times we had gone through. . . . You just didn't want to miss a game."

After being overlooked for postseason honors his first few years in Minnesota, Larsen finally received his just due in 1969, when he joined Page, Eller, and Marshall at the Pro Bowl. Larsen received his second Pro Bowl nomination the following year, before injuries gradually began to take their toll on him. Although Larsen started every game for the Vikings in each of the next three seasons, he lost his starting job to Doug Sutherland in 1974, contributing to his decision to announce his retirement at season's end. Recalling his thought process at the time, Larsen said, "I was 35 years old. I had a foot injury. My knee was bothering me. There were four of us that went out the same year."

Following his playing days, Larsen moved his family to Bellevue, in Morrison County, Minnesota, where he worked as a manager of a Ford dealership. Retiring to private life many years later, Larsen now spends much of his time doing autograph shows and playing in golf tournaments with former teammates.

Although Larsen spent much of his career being overlooked in favor of his more colorful line-mates, Bob Lurtsema, who served as a backup defensive lineman in Minnesota for six seasons during the 1970s, had this to say about his former teammate: "Gary belonged with the greatness of the Purple People Eaters. He truly belonged."

VIKINGS CAREER HIGHLIGHTS

Best Season

Larsen had the finest season of his career in 1969, earning one of his two Pro Bowl nominations by recording eight sacks. With Larsen joining line-mates Alan Page, Carl Eller, and Jim Marshall on the Pro Bowl roster, it marked the first time that four defensive linemen from the same team had been accorded that honor.

Memorable Moments/Greatest Performances

Larsen helped anchor a Vikings' defense that allowed just 34 yards rushing and 167 yards of total offense during a 27–17 win over the Browns on October 31, 1965, with the great Jim Brown gaining only 39 yards on 18 carries.

Larsen and his line-mates turned in another dominant performance later that year, limiting the Detroit Lions to just 29 yards rushing and 135 yards of total offense during a 29–7 victory on December 12, 1965.

Larsen proved to be a force in the middle when the Vikings surrendered just 49 yards rushing and 154 yards of total offense during a 28–3 manhandling of the 49ers on October 30, 1966.

Larsen had a huge impact on the Vikings' 27–10 victory over the Cowboys in the 1973 NFC championship game, recording a sack and recovering two fumbles.

Notable Achievements

- Six-time division champion (1968, 1969, 1970, 1971, 1973, and 1974).
- 1969 NFL champion.
- Two-time NFC champion (1973 and 1974).
- Two-time Pro Bowl selection (1969 and 1970).

48

GENE WASHINGTON

The first in a long line of outstanding wide receivers to don the Purple and Gold, Gene Washington established himself as one of the NFL's most dangerous wideouts during his six seasons in Minnesota. An excellent route-runner who possessed size, speed, soft hands, good moves, and outstanding athleticism, Washington recorded 10 touchdown receptions of more than 40 yards as a member of the Vikings, two of which covered more than 80 yards. Despite playing for Vikings teams that depended primarily on the run to wear down their opponents, Washington surpassed 40 receptions twice and 800 receiving yards once, leading the team in each of those categories three times. A member of Minnesota's first four division championship teams, Washington earned two Pro Bowl selections and one All-Pro nomination, before being dealt to the Denver Broncos following the conclusion of the 1972 campaign.

Born in La Porte, Texas, on January 25, 1944, Eugene Washington grew up in the segregated South, where he starred in football, baseball, basketball, and track while attending George Washington Carver, an all-Black high school. Not permitted to compete with or against anyone of a different ethnicity, Washington recalled, "I competed in an all-black league because whites and blacks couldn't compete against each other or play on the same teams."

Things being as they were at the time, Washington had no hope of playing for any of the football powerhouses in his home state, with schools such as Texas A&M, Texas Tech, and the University of Houston remaining open to whites only. But Washington suddenly found his horizons expanding when he received a visit from Michigan State University head football coach Duffy Daugherty, who learned about the talented receiver from Willie Ray Smith Sr., the head coach of Pollard High School, an opponent of George Washington Carver. Reflecting back on his meeting with Daugherty, Washington said, "Duffy was talking to me and my parents about going to Michigan State, and, at the time, I had no clue where Michigan State was. After

Gene Washington proved to be one of the NFL's most dangerous wideouts from 1968 to 1970.

spending all those years down in Texas . . . back in those days, in terms of taking a trip, 15 or 20 miles was a long distance. The whole idea of getting on an airplane, flying through Chicago, and then going on to East Lansing, I could never have imagined that happening."

Offered an athletic scholarship to MSU, Washington soon found himself playing on one of the first fully integrated teams in the history of college football, with the school also having recruited other standout performers from segregated southern schools such as Bubba Smith, George Webster, and Clint Jones. Looking back on how he and his Black teammates adapted to life at Michigan State, Washington said, "We were all embraced by the university. We didn't have the racial concerns, but we all came from segregated situations. It really worked out great that we were all able to experience that."

Contributing greatly to Spartan teams that went undefeated for two straight seasons, Washington ended his college career with 106 receptions, 1,938 receiving yards, and 16 touchdowns, making 44 receptions for 719 yards in his junior year, before earning All-America honors as a senior by amassing 677 receiving yards and scoring seven TDs. Also excelling in track at Michigan State, Washington recorded a personal-best time of 9.6 seconds in the 100-yard dash, won the Big Ten hurdles championship three times, and captured the 1965 NCAA Indoor Championship in the 60-yard hurdles.

Impressed with Washington's pass-receiving skills and exceptional athletic ability, the Vikings selected him with the eighth overall pick of the 1967 NFL Draft, making him the fourth Spartans player to come off the board (Smith, Jones, and Webster had previously been selected). Washington subsequently saw a limited amount of action his first year in the league, making just 13 receptions for 384 yards and two touchdowns, although one of those went for 85 yards. Posting far more impressive numbers after he joined the starting unit in 1968, Washington helped the Vikings capture the division title for the first of four straight times by leading the team with 46 receptions, 756 receiving yards, and six TD catches. He followed that up by making 39 receptions for 821 yards and nine touchdowns in 1969, earning in the process Pro Bowl and First-Team All-Pro honors. Washington gained Pro Bowl recognition again in 1970 by recording a team-high 44 receptions and 702 receiving yards.

A well-rounded receiver to whom Vikings signal-caller Joe Kapp once referred as "a quarterback's dream," the 6'3", 208-pound Washington had the ability to catch the short pass, go over the middle, or beat his man deep, with the last quality making him one of the most feared receivers in the league. In discussing the man who became his "go-to" receiver, Joe Kapp said, "When I don't see that double coverage on Gene, I forget about all the other receivers and I go for him. There's no way anyone can cover him man-to-man."

With Washington often being compared to his namesake, fellow wideout Gene Washington of the San Francisco 49ers, Vikings offensive coordinator Jerry Burns weighed in on the debate, suggesting, "Their Gene Washington is probably quicker. He probably catches the ball a little better on the inside. But our Washington has better deep speed, and our Washington can go up higher for the ball. They are both outstanding—good soft hands and quick."

Hampered by an old foot injury he sustained in college, Washington totaled just 30 receptions and 424 receiving yards from 1971 to 1972, undergoing bone spur surgery at the end of each season. Believing that Washington had already seen his best days, the Vikings traded him to the Denver Broncos for wide receiver Rod Sherman and a draft pick prior to the start of the 1973 campaign. Washington left Minnesota with career totals of 172 receptions, 3,087 receiving yards, and 23 touchdowns.

Washington ended up spending just one year in Denver, making only 10 receptions in 1973, before announcing his retirement at season's end. He subsequently continued his work in college student personnel administration that he began during his playing days, making trips back to Michigan State, during which he advised students and supported them in their career searches. Washington also communicated with employers and encouraged them to hire MSU students. Washington eventually became a manager for diversity hiring at 3M, spending 22 years serving in that capacity before retiring to private life. Now 77 years of age, Washington takes great pride in his three daughters, who are all college graduates with postgraduate degrees.

VIKINGS CAREER HIGHLIGHTS

Best Season

Although Washington caught more passes in both 1968 and 1970, he made his greatest overall impact in 1969, when he earned All-Pro honors for the only time by making 39 receptions for a career-high 821 yards and nine touchdowns, with the last figure placing him fourth in the league rankings.

Memorable Moments/Greatest Performances

Washington scored his first career TD on an 85-yard pass from Joe Kapp during a 34–24 loss to the St. Louis Cardinals on October 8, 1967.

Washington went over 100 receiving yards for the first time as a pro on October 27, 1968, when he made six receptions for 133 yards and two touchdowns during a 26–24 loss to the Bears, with his TDs coming on connections of 54 and 25 yards with Joe Kapp.

Although the Vikings lost the opening game of the 1969 regular season to the Giants by a score of 24–23, Washington starred in defeat, finishing the contest with seven catches for 152 yards and one touchdown, which came on a 48-yard pass from Gary Cuozzo.

Washington followed that up by making six receptions for 172 yards and two touchdowns during a 52–14 rout of the Baltimore Colts, scoring his TDs on pass plays that covered 83 and 42 yards.

Washington helped lead the Vikings to a 51–3 thrashing of the Browns on November 9, 1969, by catching seven passes for 119 yards and three TDs, the longest of which covered 16 yards.

Although Washington made just one reception during a 10–7 victory over the San Francisco 49ers on December 14, 1969, it proved to be a big one, with his 52-yard fourth-quarter hookup with Joe Kapp resulting in the game-winning touchdown.

Washington made three receptions for 120 yards and one touchdown during the Vikings' 27–7 win over Cleveland in the 1969 NFL championship game, scoring his TD on a 75-yard connection with Joe Kapp in the first quarter.

Washington contributed to a 24–0 victory over the Bears on October 11, 1970, by making eight receptions for 122 yards and one TD, which came on a 49-yard connection with Gary Cuozzo.

Washington topped 100 receiving yards for the final time in his career on December 13, 1970, catching seven passes for 101 yards and one touchdown during a 35–14 win over the Boston Patriots, with his TD coming on a 21-yard pass from Bob Lee.

Notable Achievements

- Surpassed 40 receptions twice.
- Surpassed 800 receiving yards once.
- Averaged more than 20 yards per reception twice.
- Finished second in NFL with average of 21.1 yards per reception in 1969.
- Finished fourth in NFL with nine touchdown receptions in 1969.
- Led Vikings in receptions and receiving yards three times each.
- Ranks second in franchise history with average of 17.9 yards per reception.
- Four-time division champion (1968, 1969, 1970, and 1971).
- 1969 NFL champion.
- Two-time Pro Bowl selection (1969 and 1970).
- 1969 First-Team All-Pro selection.

49

TOMMY KRAMER

Originally drafted by the Vikings as the heir apparent to Fran Tarkenton, Tommy Kramer eventually acquired the nickname "Two-Minute Tommy" for his ability to excel in the closing moments of contests, with his late-game heroics providing the hometown fans many thrills through the years. The first quarterback in NFL history to throw for more than 450 yards in two different games, Kramer proved to be one of the league's better signal-callers for much of his career, passing for more than 3,000 yards five times and throwing more than 20 touchdown passes on three separate occasions, en route to leading the Vikings to four division titles. And, despite being plagued by injuries that forced him to miss a significant amount of playing time in five of his 13 seasons in Minnesota, Kramer continues to rank second in franchise history in pass attempts, pass completions, passing yards, and touchdown passes.

Born in Seguin, Texas, on March 7, 1955, Thomas Francis Kramer moved with his parents and 10 siblings some 70 miles east at the age of 10, to the town of Hallettsville, before relocating once again three years later, this time to the city of San Antonio. Developing a love for football shortly after he arrived in San Antonio, Kramer recalled, "It started in the seventh grade in the backyard with my dad. He hung up a bicycle tire and made me throw passes through that tire four or five days a week. I'd say to myself, 'If I make this throw, we win the district championship.' Then, when we got into those games in high school, I felt no pressure because I'd already done it right there in my backyard."

Beginning his career on the gridiron at Robert E. Lee High School, Kramer guided the Volunteers to a state title in 1971 and then to the state semi-finals the following year, all the while retaining inside of him a strong desire to eventually play in the NFL. Looking back at his thought process at the time, Kramer said, "My hero was Johnny Unitas early on, and then Joe Namath after that. So, being a pro quarterback was my goal. . . . It was something that, in my mind, that was the only thing that was driving me."

Tommy Kramer ranks second in franchise history only to Fran
Tarkenton in most passing categories.
Courtesy of George A. Kitrinos

Having gained Texas High School Player of the Year recognition as
a senior in 1972, Kramer received several scholarship offers, recalling, "I
could've gone anywhere I wanted to go coming out of high school." Eventually settling on Rice University, Kramer said, "I didn't really want to go out
of state. I wanted my parents to be able to see me play. But the main thing
was I wanted to go to a team that was putting the ball in the air because I
wanted to play pro football. The quickest way to do that is to go to a school
that's putting the ball in the air all the time, and, at that time, Rice was
doing that as much as anybody. Plus, it's a great educational school."

A four-year starter at Rice, Kramer set every school passing record, ending his college career with 6,197 passing yards, 37 touchdown passes, and 48 total touchdowns. Performing especially well as a senior in 1976, Kramer set then-single-season school records for most pass completions (269), passing yards (3,317), and touchdown passes (21), prompting the Vikings to select him in the first round of the 1977 NFL Draft, with the 27th overall pick.

Kramer subsequently spent his first two seasons in Minnesota sitting on the bench, starting just one game and throwing a total of only 73 passes. However, with Fran Tarkenton retiring at the end of 1978, Kramer laid claim to the starting quarterback job the following year, finishing his first season behind center with 3,397 passing yards, 23 touchdown passes, 24 interceptions, a pass-completion percentage of 55.7, and a quarterback rating of 69.3, with the first two figures placing him near the top of the league rankings.

Kramer put up solid numbers once again in 1980, completing 57.3 percent of his passes, posting a QBR of 72.2, and ranking among the league leaders with 3,582 passing yards and 19 touchdown passes. Also finishing first in the NFL with four game-winning drives, Kramer began to earn his aforementioned moniker when he gave the Vikings a miraculous 28–23 win over the Cleveland Browns in the final home game of the regular season by completing a 46-yard touchdown pass to Ahmad Rashad with just six seconds remaining in regulation.

After missing the first two games of the 1981 season with a sprained knee, Kramer went on to have one of his finest statistical seasons, finishing second in the league with 3,912 passing yards and placing fourth in the circuit with 24 TD passes. He followed that up with another strong year, throwing for 2,037 yards and 15 touchdowns during the strike-shortened 1982 campaign, before missing much of the next two seasons due to injury. Appearing in a total of only 12 games during that time, Kramer spent much of the 1984 season recuperating from a torn ligament in his right knee.

Healthy again in 1985, Kramer passed for 3,522 yards and 19 touchdowns, although he also led the league with 26 interceptions. Kramer then reached the apex of his career in 1986, when, despite missing three games, he passed for 3,000 yards, ranked among the league leaders with 24 touchdown passes, and topped the circuit with a quarterback rating of 92.6, with his exceptional performance earning him Pro Bowl, Second-Team All-Pro, and NFL Comeback Player of the Year honors.

Standing 6'2" and weighing 200 pounds, Kramer possessed average size for a quarterback of his day. Known for his quick release, Kramer had a strong arm and delivered the ball well deep downfield. Although he rarely ran with the football, Kramer moved well in the pocket, with Philadelphia Eagles defensive tackle Ken Clarke commenting, "I think he's the best quarterback we play against. He does everything, and he's always mixing it up. He's hard to get to, like Fran Tarkenton. I guess he learned from Tarkenton. You don't know what he's going to do."

Kramer spent three more years in Minnesota, never again performing at the same lofty level. Starting only 15 games during that time, Kramer missed several contests each season due to injury, before being released by the Vikings following the conclusion of the 1989 campaign. In addition to throwing for 24,775 yards and tossing 159 touchdown passes and 157 interceptions in his 13 seasons with the Vikings, Kramer completed 55.1 percent of his passes and posted a QBR of 72.9.

Subsequently signed by the New Orleans Saints, Kramer appeared in only one game in 1990, before announcing his retirement at season's end. Since leaving the game, Kramer has spent most of his post-playing career working in San Antonio at United Laboratories as an industrial-strength chemical salesman.

Commenting on how much the game has changed since he retired some 30 years ago, Kramer, who estimates that he suffered 20 concussions during his professional career, says, "Cornerbacks could literally maul receivers trying to come off the line of scrimmage. Now, they have rules to protect the players and allow them to put on a show. I'm fine with that."

VIKINGS CAREER HIGHLIGHTS

Best Season

Kramer posted an impressive stat-line for the Vikings in 1981, when he threw for a career-high 3,912 yards and 26 touchdowns. Nevertheless, he had easily the finest season of his career in 1986, earning NFL Comeback Player of the Year honors, his only trip to the Pro Bowl, and his lone All-Pro nomination by passing for 3,000 yards, completing 55.9 percent of his passes, leading the NFL with a quarterback rating of 92.6, finishing third in the league with 24 touchdown passes, and throwing only 10 interceptions.

Memorable Moments/Greatest Performances

Kramer threw the first touchdown pass of his career when he hooked up with Brent McClanahan on a 6-yard scoring play during a 42–10 rout of the Cincinnati Bengals on November 13, 1977.

After replacing starting quarterback Bob Lee behind center late in the third quarter on December 4, 1977, Kramer led the Vikings on a furious fourth-quarter comeback that enabled them to overcome a 24–7 deficit to the 49ers and defeat their stunned opponents by a score of 28–27. Completing 9 of 13 pass attempts for 188 yards and three touchdowns, Kramer completed the comeback by throwing a 69-yard TD pass to Sammy White with just 1:38 remaining in regulation. Looking back years later at the events that transpired at the time, Kramer recalled, "I didn't get to warm up or anything. I had a big old overcoat on, and I had some sauna rocks I'd taken out of the sauna at halftime to keep my hands warm. So, I dropped that thing, and those sauna rocks fall out of the pockets. I tried to run out there, and I could hardly bend my ankles, but then, once the adrenaline got started, it was a different story. I threw three touchdown passes in the last eight minutes and we beat Frisco, 28–27, to get us into the playoffs."

Kramer provided further heroics when he gave the Vikings a 28–22 win over the 49ers in the 1979 regular-season opener by completing a 25-yard TD pass to Ahmad Rashad in the closing moments of the fourth quarter. Kramer finished the game with 297 yards passing and four touchdown passes, all of which went to Rashad.

Kramer also began the 1980 campaign in fine fashion, throwing for 395 yards and three touchdowns during a 24–23 win over Atlanta in the opening game of the regular season.

Kramer led the Vikings to a 38–30 victory over the Tampa Bay Buccaneers on November 16, 1980, by passing for 324 yards and two touchdowns, the longest of which went 27 yards to Sammy White.

Kramer turned in one of his finest performances against Cleveland on December 14, 1980, giving the Vikings the division title by completing 38 of 49 pass attempts for 456 yards and four touchdowns during a 28–23 victory over the Browns that Minnesota won on a 46-yard "Hail Mary" pass to Ahmad Rashad on the game's final play.

Kramer had another huge game against San Diego on October 11, 1981, leading the Vikings to a 33–31 win over the Chargers by throwing for 444 yards and four touchdowns, the longest of which went 43 yards to Terry LeCount in the final period.

Kramer followed that up by throwing another four touchdown passes during a 35–23 win over the Philadelphia Eagles on October 18, 1981. Following the conclusion of the contest, Philadelphia head coach Dick Vermeil praised Kramer for his excellent play, saying, "He was outstanding. He has the ability to keep a defense off balance, as he did ours. We knew we were going to have trouble with him."

Kramer led the Vikings to a lopsided 35–7 victory over the Bears on November 28, 1982, by passing for 342 yards and five touchdowns, three of which went to Sammy White.

Kramer led the Vikings to a pair of late come-from-behind wins during the latter stages of the 1982 campaign, first enabling them to advance to the playoffs as a wild card by hitting Rickey Young with a game-winning 14-yard touchdown pass in the closing moments of a 31–27 victory over the Dallas Cowboys in the regular-season finale, before directing them to two fourth-quarter TDs during a 30–24 win over the Atlanta Falcons in the opening round of the postseason tournament.

Kramer earned NFC Offensive Player of the Week honors by throwing for 241 yards and six touchdowns during a 42–7 rout of the Packers on September 28, 1986.

Although the Vikings lost to the Washington Redskins in overtime by a score of 44–38 on November 2, 1986, Kramer had arguably the greatest day of his career, throwing four touchdown passes and setting a single-game franchise record that still stands by passing for 490 yards. Contributing to Kramer's record-setting performance were TD connections of 67 and 76 yards with Leo Lewis, and another with Steve Jordan that covered 68 yards.

Notable Achievements

- Passed for more than 3,000 yards five times.
- Threw more than 20 touchdown passes three times.
- Completed more than 60 percent of passes once.
- Posted touchdown-to-interception ratio of better than 2–1 once.
- Led NFL with passer rating of 92.6 in 1986.
- Finished second in NFL in pass completions once and passing yards once.
- Finished third in NFL in pass completions once and touchdown passes once.
- Ranks second in Vikings history in pass attempts (3,648), pass completions (2,011), passing yards (24,775), and touchdown passes (159).

- Four-time division champion (1977, 1978, 1980, and 1989).
- Member of 1977 NFL All-Rookie Team.
- 1986 Week 4 NFC Offensive Player of the Week.
- 1986 NFL Comeback Player of the Year.
- 1986 Pro Bowl selection.
- 1986 Second-Team All-Pro selection.
- 1986 First-Team All-NFC selection.

50

WALLY HILGENBERG

One of the most impactful waiver wire pickups in NFL history, Wally Hilgenberg arrived in Minnesota in 1968 after earlier spending three mostly uneventful seasons in Detroit. A starter at right-outside linebacker for the Vikings for the next nine years, Hilgenberg ended up making huge contributions to Minnesota teams that won 10 division titles and appeared in four Super Bowls over the course of the next 12 seasons, combining with Roy Winston to form one of the most devastating outside linebacker tandems in the league. Excelling against both the run and the pass, Hilgenberg proved to be a key member of Minnesota's dominant defense, recording 748 regular-season tackles and 123 postseason stops for the Vikings, with the last figure representing the second-highest mark in franchise history.

Born in Marshalltown, Iowa, on September 19, 1942, Walter William Hilgenberg grew up some 130 miles southeast, in the city of Wilton, where his older brother, Jerry, a former All-America football player at the University of Iowa, played a huge role in his athletic development. Looking back at his early years, the younger Hilgenberg recalled, "I always looked up to my big brother. My memories are of the awesome sight of that stadium and the Hawkeyes playing."

Hoping to follow in his brother's footsteps, Wally played baseball, football, and basketball at Wilton High School, spending most of his time on the gridiron at the fullback position. After being recruited by Northwestern University and a few small state colleges, Hilgenberg ultimately accepted a combined athletic-academic scholarship from the University of Iowa, where he received a rude awakening at freshman football tryouts, recalling, "I remember the first day of practice. [Freshman coach] Bill Happel had all the players introduce themselves. When I stood up and said, 'I'm Wally Hilgenberg of Wilton Junction, Iowa, and I'm going to play quarterback,' I was the 14th guy to say I was going to be the quarterback. It scared me to death. I was ready to come home."

Wally Hilgenberg played for Vikings teams that won 10 division titles and appeared in four Super Bowls.

After struggling behind center as a freshman, Hilgenberg moved to guard and linebacker in his sophomore year, when his brother, Jerry, became his coach on defense. Reflecting back on what it was like playing for his older sibling, Hilgenberg said, "Having my brother be my coach made it tougher. He made me run more wind sprints, and he was on my back more. I had to pay my dues, but it was worth it."

Developing into a standout linebacker under his brother's tutelage, Hilgenberg earned All-America and United Press International First-Team All–Big Ten honors as a senior in 1963, prompting the Detroit Lions to select him in the fourth round of the 1964 NFL Draft, with the 48th overall pick. Also selected by the Denver Broncos in the eighth round of that year's AFL Draft, Hilgenberg chose to sign with the Lions, with whom he spent his first three NFL seasons serving primarily as a backup. After Hilgenberg missed the entire 1967 campaign with a knee injury, the Lions traded him to the Pittsburgh Steelers, who released him shortly thereafter. Subsequently claimed by the Vikings for the $100 waiver fee, Hilgenberg arrived in Minnesota in 1968 ready to begin his career in earnest.

Breaking into the starting lineup midway through the 1968 season, Hilgenberg began an outstanding nine-year run during which he missed just two games, starting 117 out of 126 contests. And, over the course of those nine seasons, the Vikings won eight division titles, three NFC championships, and one NFL title.

Contributing to the success of the team with his consistently excellent play, Hilgenberg proved to be stout against the run and extremely effective in pass coverage, with his ability to blanket tight ends and running backs coming out of the backfield often forcing opposing quarterbacks to look elsewhere for pass completions. A hard-hitter and sure tackler, Hilgenberg became known for his aggressive style of play, which he discussed on one occasion, saying, "I like to hit. That's where it's at. If you can put the sights on that guy and drill him . . . those good sticks are what makes it fun."

Gradually emerging as one of the Vikings' most respected players, Hilgenberg nevertheless never considered himself to be anything special, saying years after he left the game, "Even after I played 16 years of pro football, I would think, 'Gee, I've fooled them for 16 years. I'm not really that good.'"

Hilgenberg's days as a starter came to an end in 1977, when he lost his starting job to Fred McNeill. Yet even though he saw less playing time, Hilgenberg remained one of the Vikings' team leaders, with longtime teammate and close friend Stu Voigt claiming years later that Hilgenberg not only made the other members of the team better football players, but that his strong religious faith and community involvement also made them better people. In speaking of Hilgenberg, Voigt said, "We were back in the era when athletes were role models. He was a role model for me and a lot of other guys."

Hilgenberg spent three more years in Minnesota before announcing his retirement following the conclusion of the 1979 campaign. In addition to his 748 tackles, he recorded eight interceptions, recovered 13 fumbles, and scored two touchdowns as a member of the Vikings. Reflecting back on his playing career, Hilgenberg once said, "The fact that I played 16 years of pro football against Gale Sayers and O. J. Simpson and Walter Payton and those kinds of guys was thrilling to me. I look back now at what kind of great athletes they were, and the fact that I was competitive against them amazes me."

After retiring as an active player, Hilgenberg, who spent his offseasons working as a manufacturer's representative, began a career in financial planning, eventually branching out into the banking and real estate businesses. He also began working with youngsters after making a personal commitment to Christ, becoming very active in the Fellowship of Christian Athletes.

Unfortunately, Hilgenberg was diagnosed with amyotrophic lateral sclerosis, more commonly known as Lou Gehrig's disease, in November 2006. He lived another 22 months, spending much of that time in a wheelchair, before finally losing his battle with the dreaded disease on September 23, 2008, passing away just four days after he turned 66 years of age. In discussing the effect that the disease had on his longtime friend, Stu Voigt said, "It takes away your body. But I could tell the mind was there, and the twinkle in his eye. . . . He was really quite a guy."

Voigt then added, "He'd say, 'It's not when you go, it's where you go.' He handled these last six months with a lot of dignity."

Expressing his sadness over his former teammate's passing, Jim Marshall said, "We lined up together for every game, and for every practice, for all those years. We relied on each other on the field, but it was in our personal lives where we were close. . . . I'm always linked with Alan [Page] and Carl [Eller], as it should be, but Wally was as close a friend as I had with the Vikings. Our lives were intertwined. Those Vikings teams . . . our families grew up together."

VIKINGS CAREER HIGHLIGHTS

Best Season

Although Hilgenberg earned All-Conference honors for the only time in his career in 1973, he had his finest all-around season in 1971, when, in addition to picking off two passes and recovering three fumbles, he led the Vikings with a career-high 110 tackles.

Memorable Moments/Greatest Performances

Hilgenberg contributed to Minnesota's 27–7 win over Cleveland in the 1969 NFL championship game by intercepting a Bill Nelsen pass.

Although the Vikings lost their October 23, 1972, meeting with the Bears by a score of 13–10, Hilgenberg recorded a career-high 13 solo tackles during the contest.

Hilgenberg clinched a 27–13 win over the Packers one week later by returning his fourth-quarter interception of a Scott Hunter pass 14 yards for a touchdown.

Hilgenberg lit the scoreboard again during a 28–7 victory over the Lions on November 11, 1973, when he recovered a fumble on special teams, which he subsequently returned two yards for a touchdown.

Hilgenberg scored again on special teams when he tackled Chicago punter Bob Parsons in the end zone for a safety during an 11–7 win on September 29, 1974.

Hilgenberg made a key play during the Vikings' 14–10 victory over the Rams in the 1974 NFC championship game when he snuffed out a Los Angeles scoring drive late in the third quarter by intercepting a James Harris pass in the end zone for a touchback.

Notable Achievements

- Scored two defensive touchdowns.
- Led Vikings with 110 tackles in 1971.
- Ranks 15th in franchise history with 748 career tackles.
- 10-time division champion (1968, 1969, 1970, 1971, 1973, 1974, 1975, 1976, 1977, and 1978).
- 1969 NFL champion.
- Three-time NFC champion (1973, 1974, and 1976).
- 1973 Second-Team All-NFC selection.

SUMMARY
AND HONORABLE MENTIONS
(THE NEXT 30)

Having identified the 50 greatest players in Minnesota Vikings history, the time has come to select the best of the best. Based on the rankings contained in this book, the members of the Vikings' all-time offensive and defensive teams are listed below. Our squads include the top player at each position, with the offense featuring the best quarterback, tight end, and center, and the two best wide receivers. Meanwhile, the defense features two ends, two tackles, two outside linebackers, one middle linebacker, two cornerbacks, and a pair of safeties. Special teams have been accounted for as well, with a place-kicker, punter, kickoff returner, and punt returner also being included, some of whom were taken from the list of honorable mentions that will soon follow.

OFFENSE		DEFENSE	
PLAYER	POSITION	PLAYER	POSITION
Fran Tarkenton	QB	Carl Eller	LE
Adrian Peterson	RB	John Randle	LT
Chuck Foreman	RB	Alan Page	RT
Steve Jordan	TE	Chris Doleman	RE
Cris Carter	WR	Matt Blair	LOLB
Randy Moss	WR	Scott Studwell	MLB
Grady Alderman	LT	Chad Greenway	ROLB
Randall McDaniel	LG	Carl Lee	LCB
Mick Tingelhoff	C	Paul Krause	FS
Ed White	RG	Joey Browner	SS
Ron Yary	RT	Bobby Bryant	RCB
Fred Cox	PK	Chris Kluwe	P
Darrin Nelson	KR	Anthony Carter	PR

Although I limited my earlier rankings to the top 50 players in Vikings history, many other fine players have worn a Minnesota uniform through the years, some of whom narrowly missed making the final cut. Following is a list of those players deserving of an honorable mention. These are the men I deemed worthy of being slotted into positions 51 to 80 in the overall rankings. Where applicable and available, the statistics they compiled during their time in Minnesota are included, along with their most notable achievements while playing for the Vikings.

51—DARRIN NELSON
(RB, KR, PR; 1982–1989, 1991–1992)

Courtesy of MearsOnlineAuctions.com

Vikings Numbers: 4,231 Yards Rushing, 251 Receptions, 2,202 Receiving Yards, 6,433 Yards from Scrimmage, 313 Punt-Return Yards, 3,623 Kickoff-Return Yards, 10,377 All-Purpose Yards, 23 Touchdowns, 4.3 Rushing Average.

Notable Achievements

- Rushed for more than 800 yards once.
- Surpassed 50 receptions and 500 receiving yards twice each.
- Amassed more than 1,000 yards from scrimmage three times.

- Amassed more than 1,000 all-purpose yards five times, topping 1,500 yards twice.
- Averaged more than 5 yards per carry twice.
- Led NFL with rushing average of 4.9 yards per carry in 1987.
- Finished second in NFL with 891 kickoff-return yards in 1984.
- Led Vikings in rushing four times, receptions twice, and receiving yards once.
- Ranks among Vikings career leaders in rushing yards (7th), yards from scrimmage (tied for 10th), kickoff-return yards (2nd), and all-purpose yards (3rd).
- 1992 division champion.

52—ED SHAROCKMAN (DB; 1961–1972)

Career Numbers: 40 Interceptions, 804 Interception-Return Yards, 9 Fumble Recoveries, 3 TD Interceptions, 6 Touchdowns.

Notable Achievements

- Recorded at least five interceptions five times.
- Amassed more than 100 interception-return yards three times.
- Recorded three interceptions vs. Boston Patriots on December 13, 1970.
- Led NFL with 88 fumble-return yards in 1962.
- Finished second in NFL with three non-offensive TDs in 1970.
- Finished third in NFL with six interceptions in 1965.
- Led Vikings in interceptions four times.
- Ranks among Vikings career leaders in interceptions (3rd), interception-return yards (2nd), and touchdown interceptions (tied for 2nd).
- Four-time division champion (1968, 1969, 1970, and 1971).
- 1969 NFL champion.

53—TED BROWN (RB; 1979–1986)

Courtesy of George A. Kitrinos

Career Numbers: 4,546 Yards Rushing, 339 Receptions, 2,850 Receiving Yards, 7,396 Yards from Scrimmage, 7,607 All-Purpose Yards, 40 Rushing TDs, 13 TD Receptions, 53 Touchdowns, 4.1 Rushing Average.

Notable Achievements

- Rushed for more than 1,000 yards once.
- Surpassed 60 receptions and 600 receiving yards twice each.
- Amassed more than 1,500 yards from scrimmage twice.
- Scored at least 10 touchdowns three times.
- Finished third in NFL with 83 receptions in 1981.
- Led Vikings in rushing three times and receptions twice.
- Ranks among Vikings career leaders in rushing yards (5th), rushing touchdowns (4th), touchdowns (7th), yards from scrimmage (8th), and all-purpose yards (9th).
- 1980 division champion.

54—KYLE RUDOLPH (TE; 2011–2020)

Courtesy of Keith Allison

Career Numbers: 453 Receptions, 4,488 Receiving Yards, 48 Touchdown Receptions.

Notable Achievements

- Has surpassed 50 receptions four times, topping 80 catches once.
- Made nine touchdown receptions in 2012.
- Ranks among Vikings career leaders in receptions (5th), receiving yards (10th), and touchdown receptions (5th).
- Two-time division champion (2015 and 2017).
- Member of 2011 NFL All-Rookie Team.
- Two-time Pro Bowl selection (2012 and 2017).

55—TOMMY MASON (RB, KR, PR; 1961–1966)

Vikings Numbers: 3,252 Yards Rushing, 151 Receptions, 1,689 Receiving Yards, 4,941 Yards from Scrimmage, 483 Punt-Return Yards, 1,067 Kickoff-Return Yards, 6,491 All-Purpose Yards, 28 Rushing Touchdowns, 11 Touchdown Receptions, 39 Touchdowns, 4.3 Rushing Average.

Notable Achievements

- Rushed for more than 700 yards twice.
- Surpassed 40 receptions and 600 receiving yards once each.
- Amassed more than 1,000 yards from scrimmage twice.
- Amassed more than 1,000 all-purpose yards five times, topping 1,500 yards once.
- Scored 11 touchdowns in 1965.
- Finished third in NFL in rushing touchdowns twice.
- Led Vikings in rushing twice and receiving yards once.
- Ranks among Vikings career leaders in rushing yards (9th), rushing touchdowns (9th), touchdowns (10th), and punt-return yards (8th).
- Three-time Pro Bowl selection (1962, 1963, and 1964).
- 1963 First-Team All-Pro selection.

56—FRED MCNEILL (LB; 1974–1985)

Career Numbers: 1,068 Tackles, 7 Interceptions, 27 Interception-Return Yards, 16 Fumble Recoveries, 1 Touchdown.

Notable Achievements

- Finished second in NFL with six fumble recoveries in 1978.
- Ranks among Vikings career leaders in tackles (7th) and fumble recoveries (tied for 6th).
- Six-time division champion (1974, 1975, 1976, 1977, 1978, and 1980).
- Two-time NFC champion (1974 and 1976).

57—TIM IRWIN (OT; 1981–1993)

Notable Achievements

- Started 181 consecutive games from 1982 to 1993.
- Two-time division champion (1989 and 1992).

58—EVERSON GRIFFEN (DE; 2010–2019)

Courtesy of Joe Bielawa

Vikings Numbers: 74½ Sacks, 355 Tackles, 9 Forced Fumbles, 6 Fumble Recoveries, 2 Interceptions, 3 Touchdowns.

Notable Achievements

- Finished in double digits in sacks three times.
- Finished fourth in NFL with 13 sacks in 2017.
- Led Vikings in sacks three times.
- Ranks seventh in franchise history in sacks.
- Two-time division champion (2015 and 2017).
- Two-time NFC Defensive Player of the Week.
- Two-time NFC Defensive Player of the Month.
- Three-time Pro Bowl selection (2015, 2016, and 2017).
- 2017 Second-Team All-Pro selection.

59—DALVIN COOK (RB: 2017–2020)

Courtesy of All-Pro Reels

Career Numbers: 3,661 Yards Rushing, 148 Receptions, 1,275 Receiving Yards, 4,936 Yards from Scrimmage, 33 Rushing TDs, 3 TD Receptions, 36 Touchdowns, 4.8 Rushing Average.

Notable Achievements

- Has rushed for more than 1,000 yards twice, topping 1,500 yards once.
- Has surpassed 50 receptions and 500 receiving yards once each.
- Has amassed more than 1,500 yards from scrimmage twice.
- Has scored more than 10 touchdowns twice.
- Averaged 5.0 yards per carry in 2020.
- Finished second in NFL with 1,557 yards rushing, 1,918 yards from scrimmage, and 16 rushing touchdowns in 2020.
- Finished third in NFL with 17 touchdowns in 2020.
- Has led Vikings in rushing three times.
- Ranks among Vikings career leaders in rushing yards (8th) and rushing touchdowns (5th).
- 2017 division champion.
- Four-time NFC Offensive Player of the Week.
- November 2020 NFC Offensive Player of the Month.
- Two-time Pro Bowl selection (2019 and 2020).
- 2019 First-Team All-NFC selection.

60—LONNIE WARWICK (LB; 1965–1972)

Vikings Numbers: 12 Interceptions, 145 Interception-Return Yards, 6 Fumble Recoveries, 1 Touchdown.

Notable Achievements

- Recorded four interceptions in 1969.
- Led Vikings in tackles four times.
- Four-time division champion (1968, 1969, 1970, and 1971).
- 1969 NFL champion.

61—ANTOINE WINFIELD (DB; 2004–2012)

Courtesy of Beth Hoole

Vikings Numbers: 21 Interceptions, 227 Interception-Return Yards, 729 Tackles, 6½ Sacks, 11 Forced Fumbles, 9 Fumble Recoveries, 5 TDs.

Notable Achievements

- Recorded more than 90 tackles five times, topping 100 tackles once.
- Led Vikings in interceptions four times and tackles once.
- Ranks among Vikings career leaders in interceptions (10th) and forced fumbles (tied for 9th).
- Two-time division champion (2008 and 2009).
- Two-time NFC Defensive Player of the Week.
- Three-time Pro Bowl selection (2008, 2009, and 2010).
- 2008 Second-Team All-Pro selection.

62—PAT WILLIAMS (DT; 2005–2010)

Courtesy of Michi Moore via Flickr

Vikings Numbers: 7½ Sacks, 290 Tackles, 5 Forced Fumbles, 4 Fumble Recoveries.

Notable Achievements

- Led Vikings' defensive linemen in tackles twice.
- Two-time division champion (2008 and 2009).
- Three-time Pro Bowl selection (2006, 2007, and 2008).
- 2007 Second-Team All-Pro selection.
- Pro Football Reference All-2000s Second Team.

63—WARREN MOON (QB; 1994–1996)

Courtesy of MearsOnlineAuctions.com

Vikings Numbers: 10,102 Yards Passing, 58 Touchdown Passes, 42 Interceptions, 60.7 Completion Percentage, 82.8 Passer Rating.

Notable Achievements

- Passed for more than 4,000 yards twice.
- Completed more than 60 percent of passes twice.
- Posted touchdown-to-interception ratio of better than 2–1 once.
- Posted passer rating above 90.0 once.
- Led NFL with 377 pass completions in 1995.
- Finished second in NFL with 33 touchdown passes in 1995.
- Finished third in NFL in pass completions once and passing yards twice.
- Ranks among Vikings career leaders in passing yards (8th) and touchdown passes (8th).
- 1994 division champion.
- Two-time NFC Offensive Player of the Week.
- November 1995 NFC Offensive Player of the Month.
- Two-time Pro Bowl selection (1994 and 1995).

64—DARREN SHARPER (DB; 2005–2008)

Courtesy of SportsMemorabilia.com

Vikings Numbers: 18 Interceptions, 359 Interception-Return Yards, 250 Tackles, 1 Sack, 2 Forced Fumbles, 3 Fumble Recoveries, 3 TDs.

Notable Achievements

- Led NFL with 276 interception-return yards and two touchdown interceptions in 2005.
- Finished third in NFL with nine interceptions in 2005.
- Led Vikings in interceptions three times.
- Ranks among Vikings career leaders in interceptions (12th), interception-return yards (6th), and touchdown interceptions (tied-2nd).
- 2008 division champion.
- 2005 Week 10 NFC Defensive Player of the Week.
- November 2005 NFC Defensive Player of the Month.
- Two-time Pro Bowl selection (2005 and 2007).
- Two-time Second-Team All-Pro selection (2005 and 2007).
- Pro Football Reference All-2000s First Team.
- NFL 2000s All-Decade Second Team.

65—CORDARRELLE PATTERSON
(WR/KR; 2013–2016)

Courtesy of Matthew Deery via Wikimedia Commons

Vikings Numbers: 132 Receptions, 1,316 Receiving Yards, 7 Touchdown Receptions, 333 Rushing Yards, 4 Rushing Touchdowns, 4,075 Kickoff-Return Yards, 5,733 All-Purpose Yards, 5 Kickoff-Return Touchdowns, 16 Touchdowns.

Notable Achievements

- Surpassed 50 receptions once.
- Amassed more than 1,000 all-purpose yards four times, topping 2,000 yards once.
- Averaged more than 30 yards per kickoff return three times.
- Led NFL in kickoff-return touchdowns and kickoff-return average three times each.
- Finished second in NFL in all-purpose yards once, kickoff-return yards twice, and kickoff- and punt-return yards once.
- Finished third in NFL in kickoff-return yards once.
- Holds Vikings career records for most kickoff-return yards and most kickoff-return touchdowns.
- 2015 division champion.

- 2013 Week 8 NFC Special Teams Player of the Week.
- September 2013 NFC Special Teams Player of the Month.
- Member of 2013 NFL All-Rookie Team.
- Two-time Pro Bowl selection (2013 and 2016).
- Two-time First-Team All-Pro selection (2013 and 2016).
- 2015 Second-Team All-Pro selection.
- NFL 2010s All-Decade Team.

66—DAVE OSBORN (RB; 1965–1975)

Vikings Numbers: 4,320 Yards Rushing, 173 Receptions, 1,412 Receiving Yards, 5,732 Yards from Scrimmage, 6,228 All-Purpose Yards, 29 Rushing TDs, 7 TD Receptions, 36 Touchdowns, 3.7 Rushing Average.

Notable Achievements

- Finished second in NFL with 972 yards rushing in 1967.
- Finished fifth in NFL with 1,244 yards from scrimmage in 1967.
- Led Vikings in rushing three times.
- Ranks among Vikings career leaders in rushing yards (6th) and rushing touchdowns (tied for 7th).

- Seven-time division champion (1968, 1969, 1970, 1971, 1973, 1974, and 1975).
- 1969 NFL champion.
- Two-time NFC champion (1973 and 1974).
- 1970 Pro Bowl selection.

67—DANIELLE HUNTER (DE; 2015–2020)

Courtesy of Jeffrey Beall

Career Numbers: 54½ Sacks, 276 Tackles, 6 Forced Fumbles, 4 Fumble Recoveries, 2 TDs.

Notable Achievements

- Has finished in double digits in sacks three times.
- Finished second in NFL with 21 tackles for loss in 2018.
- Finished third in NFL with 12½ sacks in 2016.
- Finished fourth in NFL in sacks twice.
- Has led Vikings in sacks three times.
- Has led Vikings' defensive linemen in tackles twice.
- Ranks 11th in franchise history in sacks.
- Two-time division champion (2015 and 2017).
- Member of 2015 NFL All-Rookie Team.

- 2018 Week 9 NFC Defensive Player of the Week.
- Two-time Pro Bowl selection (2018 and 2019).
- 2018 Second-Team All-Pro selection.

68—ROBERT GRIFFITH (DB; 1994–2001)

Courtesy of MearsonlineAuctions.com

Vikings Numbers: 17 Interceptions, 168 Interception-Return Yards, 634 Tackles, 7½ Sacks, 7 Forced Fumbles, 2 Fumble Recoveries.

Notable Achievements

- Recorded more than 100 tackles three times.
- Led Vikings in interceptions once and tackles twice.
- Three-time division champion (1994, 1998, and 2000).
- 2000 Pro Bowl selection.
- Two-time Second-Team All-Pro selection (1998 and 1999).

69—ERIC KENDRICKS (LB; 2015–2020)

Courtesy of Jeffrey Beall

Career Numbers: 639 Tackles, 9 Sacks, 7 Interceptions, 111 Interception-Return Yards, 4 Forced Fumbles, 4 Fumble Recoveries, 2 TDs.

Notable Achievements

- Has recorded more than 100 tackles five times.
- Has led Vikings in tackles five times.
- Two-time division champion (2015 and 2017).
- Member of 2015 NFL All-Rookie Team.
- October 2015 NFL Defensive Rookie of the Month.
- 2016 Week 1 NFC Defensive Player of the Week.
- 2019 Pro Bowl selection.
- 2019 First-Team All-Pro selection.

70—NATE WRIGHT (DB; 1971–1980)

Courtesy of MearsOnlineAuctions.com

Vikings Numbers: 31 Interceptions, 272 Interception-Return Yards, 4 Fumble Recoveries, 1 TD.

Notable Achievements

- Recorded at least five interceptions three times.
- Led Vikings in interceptions three times.
- Ranks fifth in franchise history in interceptions.
- Eight-time division champion (1971, 1973, 1974, 1975, 1976, 1977, 1978, and 1980).
- Three-time NFC champion (1973, 1974, and 1976).
- 1974 First-Team All-NFC selection.
- 1976 Second-Team All-NFC selection.

71—MILT SUNDE (G; 1964–1974)

Notable Achievements

- Missed just seven games in 11 seasons, at one point appearing in 84 consecutive contests.
- Six-time division champion (1968, 1969, 1970, 1971, 1973, and 1974).
- 1969 NFL champion.
- Two-time NFC champion (1973 and 1974).
- 1966 Pro Bowl selection.

72—RANDALL CUNNINGHAM (QB; 1997–1999)

Courtesy of SportsMemorabilia.com

Vikings Numbers: 5,680 Yards Passing, 48 Touchdown Passes, 23 Interceptions, 59.9 Completion Percentage, 94.2 Passer Rating.

Notable Achievements

- Passed for 3,704 yards in 1998.
- Completed more than 60 percent of passes twice.
- Posted touchdown-to-interception ratio of better than 3–1 once.
- Led NFL with passer rating of 106.0 in 1998.
- Finished second in NFL with 34 touchdown passes in 1998.
- Ranks eighth in franchise history in touchdown passes.
- 1998 division champion.
- Three-time NFC Offensive Player of the Week.
- October 1998 NFC Offensive Player of the Month.
- 1998 Newspaper Enterprise Association (NEA) NFL MVP.
- 1998 Bert Bell Award winner as NFL Player of the Year.
- 1998 Pro Bowl selection.
- 1998 First-Team All-Pro selection.
- 1998 First-Team All-NFC selection.

73—KARL KASSULKE (DB; 1963–1972)

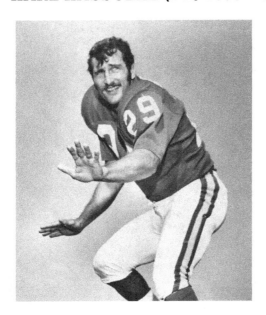

Career Numbers: 19 Interceptions, 187 Interception-Return Yards, 9 Fumble Recoveries.

Notable Achievements

- Ranks 11th in franchise history in interceptions.
- Four-time division champion (1968, 1969, 1970, and 1971).
- 1969 NFL champion.
- 1970 Pro Bowl selection.

74—KIRK COUSINS (QB; 2018–2020)

Courtesy of All-Pro Reels

Vikings Numbers: 12,166 Yards Passing, 91 Touchdown Passes, 29 Interceptions, 69.0 Completion Percentage, 103.6 Passer Rating.

Notable Achievements

- Has passed for more than 4,000 yards twice.
- Has thrown at least 30 touchdown passes twice.
- Has completed more than 70 percent of passes once.
- Has posted a passer rating above 100.0 twice.
- Has posted touchdown-to-interception ratio of better than 3–1 twice.
- Finished second in NFL with pass-completion percentage of 70.1 in 2018.
- Finished fourth in NFL with passer rating of 107.4 in 2019.
- Holds Vikings career record for highest passer rating.
- Ranks among Vikings career leaders in passing yards (4th) and touchdown passes (4th).
- Two-time NFC Offensive Player of the Week.
- October 2019 NFC Offensive Player of the Month.
- 2019 Pro Bowl selection.

75—CHRIS KLUWE (P; 2005–2012)

Courtesy of Joe Bielawa

Career Numbers: 27,683 Yards Punting, Average of 44.4 Yards Per Punt.

Notable Achievements

- Averaged more than 45 yards per punt twice.
- Holds Vikings career record for highest punting average (minimum 100 kicks).
- Ranks second in franchise history in total punt yardage.
- Two-time division champion (2008 and 2009).
- 2010 Week 9 NFC Special Teams Player of the Week.
- September 2005 NFC Special Teams Player of the Month.
- Member of 2005 NFL All-Rookie Team.

76—LINVAL JOSEPH (DT; 2014–2019)

Courtesy of Jeffrey Beall

Vikings Numbers: 15 Sacks, 350 Tackles, 6 Forced Fumbles, 2 Fumble Recoveries, 1 TD.

Notable Achievements

- Led Vikings' defensive linemen in tackles three times.
- Two-time division champion (2015 and 2017).
- 2015 Week 9 NFC Defensive Player of the Week.
- Two-time Pro Bowl selection (2016 and 2017).

77—PERCY HARVIN (WR/KR; 2009–2012)

Courtesy of Mike Morbeck

Vikings Numbers: 280 Receptions, 3,302 Receiving Yards, 20 Touchdown Receptions, 683 Rushing Yards, 4 Rushing Touchdowns, 3,183 Kickoff-Return Yards, 7,168 All-Purpose Yards, 5 Kickoff-Return Touchdowns, 29 Touchdowns.

Notable Achievements

- Surpassed 60 receptions four times, topping 80 catches once.
- Surpassed 800 receiving yards twice.
- Amassed more than 1,000 yards from scrimmage once.
- Amassed more than 1,000 all-purpose yards four times, topping 2,000 yards once.
- Averaged more than 30 yards per kickoff return twice.
- Finished third in NFL in kickoff-return average once.
- Holds share of Vikings career record for most kickoff-return touchdowns.
- Ranks among Vikings career leaders in kickoff-return yards (5th) and all-purpose yards (10th).
- 2009 division champion.

- Two-time NFC Special Teams Player of the Week.
- September 2012 NFC Special Teams Player of the Month.
- Member of 2009 NFL All-Rookie Team.
- 2009 NFL Offensive Rookie of the Year.
- 2009 Pro Bowl selection.

78—BRETT FAVRE (QB; 2009–2010)

Courtesy of Mike Morbeck

Vikings Numbers: 6,711 Yards Passing, 44 Touchdown Passes, 26 Interceptions, 65.2 Completion Percentage, 92.2 Passer Rating.

Notable Achievements

- Passed for 4,202 yards in 2009.
- Finished second in NFL with 33 touchdown passes and passer rating of 107.2 in 2009.
- Finished third in NFL with pass-completion percentage of 68.4 in 2009.
- Posted touchdown-to-interception ratio of better than 4–1 once.
- Ranks among Vikings career leaders in passing yards (8th) and touchdown passes (9th).

- 2009 division champion.
- Three-time NFC Offensive Player of the Week.
- November 2009 NFC Offensive Player of the Month.
- 2009 Pro Bowl selection.

79—E. J. HENDERSON (LB; 2003–2011)

Courtesy of Rick Burtzel

Career Numbers: 761 Tackles, 5 Interceptions, 58 Interception-Return Yards, 13 Forced Fumbles, 9 Fumble Recoveries, 1 Touchdown.

Notable Achievements

- Recorded more than 100 tackles four times.
- Led Vikings in tackles twice.
- Ranks among Vikings career leaders in forced fumbles (tied for 7th).
- Two-time division champion (2008 and 2009).
- 2010 Pro Bowl selection.

80—JOE KAPP (QB; 1967–1969)

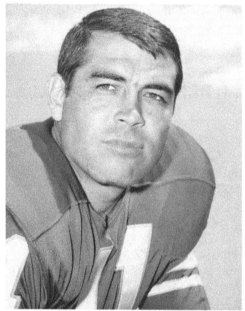

Courtesy of RMYAuctions.com

Vikings Numbers: 4,807 Yards Passing, 37 Touchdown Passes, 47 Interceptions, 50.2 Completion Percentage, 62.2 Passer Rating, 540 Yards Rushing, 5 Rushing Touchdowns.

Notable Achievements

- Two-time division champion (1968 and 1969).
- 1969 NFL champion.
- Three-time NFL Offensive Player of the Week.
- 1969 Pro Bowl selection.

GLOSSARY

C. Center.

COMP %. Completion percentage. The number of successfully completed passes divided by the number of passes attempted.

DB. Defensive back.

DE. Defensive end.

DT. Defensive tackle.

FS. Free safety.

G. Guard.

INTS. Interceptions. Passes thrown by the quarterback that are caught by a member of the opposing team's defense.

KR. Kickoff returner.

LB. Linebacker.

LCB. Left cornerback.

LE. Left end.

LG. Left guard.

LOLB. Left-outside linebacker.

LT. Left tackle.

MLB. Middle linebacker.

OT. Offensive tackle.

P. Punter.

PK. Placekicker.

PR. Punt returner.

QB. Quarterback.

QBR. Quarterback rating.

RB. Running back.

RCB. Right cornerback.

RE. Right end.

RECS. Receptions.

REC YDS. Reception yards.

RG. Right guard.

ROLB. Right-outside linebacker.

RT. Right tackle.

SS. Strong safety.

TD PASSES. Touchdown passes.

TD RECS. Touchdown receptions.

TDS. Touchdowns.

TE. Tight end.

WR. Wide receiver.

YDS FROM SCRIMMAGE. Yards from scrimmage.

YDS PASSING. Yards passing.

YDS RUSHING. Yards rushing.

BIBLIOGRAPHY

Books

Bruton, Jim. *Vikings 50: All-Time Greatest Players in Franchise History.* Chicago: Triumph Books, 2012.

Craig, Mark. *100 Things Vikings Fans Should Know & Do Before They Die.* Chicago: Triumph Books, 2016.

Jones, Danny. *More Distant Memories: Pro Football's Best Ever Players of the 50s, 60s, and 70s.* Bloomington, IN: AuthorHouse, 2006.

Silverman, Steve. *The Good, the Bad, & the Ugly: Heart-Pounding, Jaw-Dropping, and Gut-Wrenching Moments in Minnesota Vikings History.* Chicago: Triumph Books, 2007.

Tuaolo, Esera. *Alone in the Trenches: My Life as a Gay Man in the NFL.* Naperville, IL: Sourcebooks, 2007.

Williamson, Bill. *Tales from the Vikings Locker Room.* Champaign, IL: Sports Publishing, 2003.

Videos

Greatest Ever: NFL Dream Team. Polygram Video, 1996.

Websites

Biographies from Answers.com
(www.answers.com)

Biographies from Jockbio.com
(www.jockbio.com)

CBSNews.com
(www.cbsnews.com)

ESPN.com
(http://sports.espn.go.com)

Hall of Famers, online at profootballhof.com
(www.profootballhof.com/hof/member)

Inductees from LASportsHall.com
(www.lasportshall.com)

LATimes.com
(http://articles.latimes.com)

Newsday.com
(www.newsday.com)

NYDailyNews.com
(www.nydailynews.com/new-york)

NYTimes.com
(www.nytimes.com)

The Players, online at Profootballreference.com
(www.pro-football-reference.com/players)

Pro Football Talk from nbcsports.com
(http://profootballtalk.nbcsports.com)

SpTimes.com
(www.sptimes.com)

StarLedger.com
(www.starledger.com)

SunSentinel.com
(http://articles.sun-sentinel.com)

Vikings.com
(www.vikings.com)